MCAT® 528

Advanced Prep for Advanced Students

Edited By Deeangelee Pooran-Kublall, MD/MPH

KAPLAN

PUBLISHING

New York

Published by Kaplan Publishing, a division of Kaplan, Inc.
395 Hudson Street
New York, NY 10014

10 9 8 7 6 5 4 3 2 1

ISBN: 978-1-61865-631-5

Kaplan Publishing books are available at special quantity discounts to use for sales promotions, employee premiums, or educational purposes. For more information or to purchase books, please call the Simon & Schuster special sales department at 866-506-1949.

The *Kaplan MCAT 528* Team

Deeangelee Pooran-Kublall, MD/MPH
Editor-in-Chief

Christopher Durland
Kaplan MCAT Faculty, Editor

Matthew Dominick Eggert
Kaplan MCAT Faculty, Author

Samer T. Ismail
Kaplan MCAT Faculty, Author/Editor

Thomas C. C. Sargent, II
Kaplan MCAT Faculty, Author

Laura Ambler
Kaplan MCAT Faculty, Author

MCAT faculty writers/contributers:

Marilyn Engel, Jason Pflieger, Uneeb Qureshi, Neha Rao, Charles Richards, Noah Silva

Countless thanks to Kim Bowers; Eric Chiu; Samantha Fallon; Owen Farcy; Dan Frey; Robin Garmise; Rita Garhaffner; Joanna Graham; Adam Grey; Allison Harm; Alex Macnow, MD; Aaron Lemon-Strauss; Keith Lubeley; Petros Minasi; John Polstein; Rochelle Rothstein, MD; Larry Rudman; Sylvia Tidwell Scheuring; Carly Schnur; Lee Weiss; and many others who made this project possible.

About the MCAT

The structure of the four sections of the MCAT is shown below.

Biological and Biochemical Foundations of Living Systems	
Time	95 minutes
Format	• 59 questions • Score range: 118 and 132 • Most questions are passage-based, but some are discrete (standalone) questions
What It Tests	• Biochemistry: 25% • Biology: 65% • General Chemistry: 5% • Organic Chemistry: 5%
Chemical and Physical Foundations of Biological Systems	
Time	95 minutes
Format	• 59 questions • Score range: 118 and 132 • Most questions are passage-based, but some are discrete (standalone) questions
What It Tests	• Biochemistry: 25% • Biology: 5% • General Chemistry: 30% • Organic Chemistry: 15% • Physics: 25%
Psychological, Social, and Biological Foundations of Behavior	
Time	95 minutes
Format	• 59 questions • Score range: 118 and 132 • Most questions are passage-based, but some are discrete (standalone) questions
What It Tests	• Biology: 5% • Psychology: 65% • Sociology: 30%
Critical Analysis and Reasoning Skills (CARS)	
Time	90 minutes
Format	• 53 questions • Score range: 118 and 132 • All questions are passage-based. There are no discrete (standalone) questions.
What It Tests	Disciplines: • Humanities: 50% • Social Sciences: 50% Skills: • Foundations of Comprehension: 30% • Reasoning Within the Text: 30% • Reasoning Beyond the Text: 40%
Total	
Testing Time	375 minutes (6 hours, 15 minutes)
Questions	230
Score Range	472 to 528

KAPLAN

The MCAT also tests four *Scientific Inquiry and Reasoning Skills* (SIRS):

1. Knowledge of Scientific Concepts and Principles
2. Scientific Reasoning and Problem-Solving
3. Reasoning about the Design and Execution of Research
4. Data-Based and Statistical Reasoning

The MCAT is a computer-based test (CBT) and is offered at Prometric centers during almost every month of the year. There are optional breaks between each section, and a lunch break between the second and third sections of the exam.

Register online for the MCAT at **www.aamc.org/mcat**.

For further questions, contact the MCAT team at the Association of American Medical Colleges:

MCAT Resource Center
Association of American Medical Colleges

(202) 828-0690
www.aamc.org/mcat
mcat@aamc.org

How This Book Was Created

The *Kaplan MCAT 528* book was created to give advanced MCAT students an edge on the MCAT exam. This book highlights the content areas on the MCAT whose mastery will help students achieve their highest possible MCAT score on Test Day. To that end, we had learning science experts poll all of our expert MCAT faculty and trainers to discern the most high-yield and high-difficulty topics for students. Based on the results of that study, we were able to identify the content topics that even the most advanced students might need an extra. Then, we had our most qualified item writers create challenging test-like passages to provide that extra practice. Additionally, the Kaplan MCAT 528 book contains strategic callouts derived from Kaplan's experience in test-taking. In fact, skills are provided to help students work through the tough passages and get the academic boon that will allow them to get the highest score possible (528) on the 2015 MCAT.

A team of highly dedicated writers worked very long hours to create this resource. However, this book was submitted for publication in April 2014. For any updates after this date, please visit **www.kaplanmcat.com**.

If you have any questions about the content presented here, email **KaplanMCATfeedback@kaplan.com**. For other questions not related to content, email **booksupport@kaplan.com**.

This book has seen at least five rounds of review. To that end, the information presented it is true and accurate to the best of our knowledge. Still, your feedback helps us improve our prep materials. Please notify us of any inaccuracies or errors in the books by sending an email to **KaplanMCATfeedback@kaplan.com**.

KAPLAN

Using This Book

Kaplan's MCAT 528 brings the best of Kaplan's classroom experience to you—right in your home, at your convenience. This book offers the same Kaplan strategies and practice that make Kaplan the #1 choice for MCAT prep. After all, twice as many doctors prepared with Kaplan for the MCAT than with any other course.

This book is designed to help you approach the most challenging topics covered on the MCAT in a strategic way. It represents just one of the practice resources available to you from Kaplan. Additional resources are available in your Online Center, including more practice questions, video science review, and full-length practice exams. Register for your Online Center at **kaptest.com/booksonline**.

No matter how confident you are in the content for the MCAT, please understand that content review—no matter how thorough—is not sufficient preparation for the MCAT! The MCAT tests not only your science knowledge, but also your critical reading, reasoning, and problem-solving skills. Do not assume that simply memorizing the content will earn you high scores on Test Day; to maximize your score, you must also improve your reading and test-taking skills through MCAT-style questions and practice tests.

That is precisely what this book strives to offer: challenging, MCAT-style worked examples and practice targeting the most high-yield and difficult topics on the exam.

STRATEGIC OVERVIEWS

This book simplifies the skills tested by the AAMC *and* Kaplan's Methods for applying those skills in the different content areas by answering three main questions:

1) What are the skills/strategies/content you need to know?
2) How are the skills/strategies/content presented on the exam?
3) How can you get the edge in that particular skill/strategy/content area?

MCAT Practice

In this book, MCAT Practice is provided in two forms:

1) The first type of practice is in the form of worked examples. These passages and question sets were designed for the students to be able to try on their own AND/OR see how an expert would work through them using Kaplan's methods, thereby giving you the tools you need to succeed on Test Day.
2) The second type of practice is in the form of practice passages/sections (in the book and online) that help you apply the strategies and tips that were demonstrated in the worked examples so that you gain mastery and can use them seamlessly on Test Day.

SIDEBARS

The following is a legend of the four types of sidebars you'll find in *Kaplan's MCAT 528*:

- **Key Concept**: These sidebars draw attention to the most important takeaways in a given topic, and sometimes offer synopses or overviews of complex information. If you understand nothing else, make sure you get the Key Concepts for any given subject.
- **MCAT Expertise**: These sidebars point out how information may be tested on the MCAT, or offer key strategy points and test-taking tips that you should apply on Test Day.
- **Things to Watch Out For**: These sidebars will warn you of common traps students fall into when answering a specific question type.
- **Takeaways**: These sidebars will help you understand the point of a question so you won't just walk away from it bogged down with details.

To this end, this is your book, so write in the margins, draw diagrams, highlight the key points—do whatever is necessary to help you get that higher score. We look forward to working with you as you achieve your dreams and become the doctor you deserve to be!

Contents

Related MCAT Titles

Available in Print and Digital Editions

Kaplan MCAT Behavioral Sciences Review*
Kaplan MCAT Biology Review
Kaplan MCAT Biochemistry Review*
Kaplan MCAT General Chemistry Review
Kaplan MCAT Organic Chemistry Review
Kaplan MCAT Physics and Math Review
Kaplan MCAT Critical Analysis and Reasoning Skills Review*

*includes online practice

Available in Print with Bonus App Included
Kaplan MCAT Flashcards + App

Available in Print
Getting Into Medical School

MCAT Basics and Test Strategy

CHAPTER ONE

About the MCAT

At the beginning of this book, you saw an outline of the MCAT and a percentage of the general topics tested. In this chapter, we will take a closer look at the overall meaning behind those statistics. Additionally, units two through four of this book will breakdown the content areas and skills specifically tested on the exam.

1.1 The Four Sections of the MCAT

Three of the four sections on the MCAT test your basic science content knowledge by requiring you to critically use the information rather than just provide individual scientific facts. Therefore, students should know how to integrate and analyze information in different contexts using various skills and content databases.

The last section, Critical Analysis and Reasoning Skills, is a unique part of the exam in that it is a pure test of critical thinking. Passages on topics within the social sciences and humanities are presented and then a series of questions asks you to reason about the material presented–just as you would be expected to do in medical school and in your medical careers.

BIOLOGICAL AND BIOCHEMICAL FOUNDATIONS OF LIVING SYSTEMS

In this section of the MCAT, you will have to demonstrate an understanding of the basic process that foster life, such as growing, reproducing, acquiring energy, etc. Equally important in the study of medicine is your knowledge of how cells and organ systems within an organism act both independently and in concert to accomplish these processes.

CHEMICAL AND PHYSICAL FOUNDATIONS OF BIOLOGICAL SYSTEMS

In this section, you will be required to combine your knowledge of the basic physical sciences with that of the biological sciences. Therefore, an understanding of the basic chemical and physical principles that underlie the mechanisms operating in the human body, and your ability to apply an understanding of these general principles to living systems, will be essential.

PSYCHOLOGICAL, SOCIAL, AND BIOLOGICAL FOUNDATIONS OF BEHAVIOR

This section is an essential addition to the MCAT since it assesses your ability to implement research and statistical principles within the realm of behavioral and sociocultural determinants of health and health outcomes. Basically, you are required to integrate psychological, sociological, and biological bases of behaviors and relationships.

CRITICAL ANALYSIS AND REASONING SKILLS

This unique section asks you to analyze scenarios rooted in the social sciences and humanities disciplines. It is important to note that unlike the other sections, specific knowledge is *not* required for this section, as all of the information is presented in the passages. Some of the subject areas from which content is drawn include ethics and philosophy, cultural studies, and population health.

1.2 Five Common Misconceptions about the MCAT

#1 The MCAT is a Content Test, Summing Up the Courses I Took in Undergrad

Yes, the MCAT does contain a lot of content—two semesters each of physics, general chemistry, organic chemistry, and biology plus, a semester each of biochemistry, psychology, and sociology. But while you do need to know about the Doppler effect, the Henderson–Hasselbalch equation for buffers, acyl substitution reactions, and the hormones that govern the menstrual cycle (sometimes called the HPO, or hypothalamic-pituitary-ovarian axis), content alone is *not* sufficient for excellent MCAT performance.

Rather, **critical thinking**—the ability to reason, to integrate, to look at a problem in a creative way and find efficient methods to solve it—**is the primary driver of a high score.**

Why is this? Well, schools can get a sense of your content knowledge by looking at your undergraduate or post-baccalaureate grades. But the thinking process and ability to *use* these sciences is not tested evenly across schools; thus, the MCAT acts as a great equalizer, testing your ability to *think*—and not just *memorize*. And perhaps most importantly, critical thinking underlies your ability to succeed as a physician.

Consider the patient coming into the emergency department with acute abdominal pain of four hours' duration. Sure, you could memorize all of the possible diagnoses, work-ups, and treatments for every condition that causes abdominal pain ... or could you? The differential diagnosis (list of likely causes) is extensive; but considering the age of the patient, the patient's gender, comorbidities (other illnesses he or she has), and the description of the pain, you can reason what questions would be best to ask to decide on the diagnosis.

#2 The MCAT likes to Test the Exceptions, the Unusual Examples, the Esoteric Content

This is a common misconception about the MCAT, which leads many premedical students to take additional coursework that is not necessary for success on Test Day. While advanced organic synthesis, anatomy and physiology, and modern physics can show up in an MCAT passage, the outside knowledge required by the AAMC still adheres to the eight-semester sequence previously mentioned.

It's certainly not a bad idea to take more advanced science courses if your schedule permits—an understanding of anatomy and physiology before you get to medical school will undoubtedly make cadaver dissection a bit easier—but recognize that these courses should not be taken specifically for the MCAT. All the information necessary to answer the questions will be in the passages, or in outside knowledge as listed by the AAMC's content outlines.

#3 Passages are Included on the MCAT to Slow Me Down

Students sometimes assume that passages are included as background information for those unfamiliar with the content covered in a given set of questions. Therefore, they misinterpret the passages as merely introducing a time crunch, rather than being a critical part of the test.

The change to passage-based questions in 1992 came from a far more sophisticated drive than timing: they require you to integrate new information with the corpus of knowledge you already have, and see how they jive together. MCAT passages will frequently challenge common assumptions about a given scientific process, or introduce an experiment testing the validity of a scientific idea. Only by reading the passage and actually seeing what happens can you be prepared for the accompanying questions.

Medicine is a field requiring continuous learning. Our advancements in technology belie our advancements in understanding the human body. Much like how you will have to integrate new information with what you already know while reading MCAT passages, you will have to stay abreast of the newest studies in medicine through academic journals, conferences, and trainings. Admissions committees (and your future patients!) are very interested in your ability to adjust to new data, to manipulate it, and to absorb it into your schemata of how the world works.

#4 I'll Never Use this Information Again—Especially as a Doctor!

The concepts and critical thinking that underlie the MCAT are *both* important to decisions you'll make as a doctor. We've discussed the critical thinking, but why are these concepts important? There's probably no better way to prove it than with a few examples.

When a patient breaks a bone, the translational forces and torques still acting on the bone can be used to predict what structures might be damaged if the fracture is angulated or displaced (moved from its starting position). We also must understand these forces and torques if we are to reset the bone correctly.

Acid and base chemistry dictates the blood disturbances we see in everything from chronic obstructive pulmonary disease (COPD), to altitude sickness, to acute kidney failure. We further use the principles of acid–base chemistry and the semipermeable membrane to increase the excretion of toxins; a patient with an overdose of aspirin (acetylsalicylic acid) can excrete more of the toxin when it is *deprotonated,* since it takes on a negative charge and thus cannot cross the cell membrane to reenter the body from the renal tubules. Urinary alkalization (when titrated correctly) can therefore help avoid a toxic overdose.

The continuity equation and Bernoulli principle explain the pathophysiology of a number of valvular and vascular disorders in the body. In fact, one of the diagnostic findings in valvular stenosis (the narrowing of a heart valve) is an increased velocity of blood flow. Physicians know from the continuity equation that as cross-sectional area decreases, velocity increases (assuming a constant flow rate/cardiac output).

Isomerism is a critical consideration in drug design. Consider the proton-pump inhibitor omeprazole (used for gastroesophageal reflux disease, peptic ulcers, and other acid-excess states). When this medication was going to come off patent, a new drug was developed: esomeprazole. Take a look at the names there. Omeprazole is a racemic mixture; esomeprazole is only the *S*-enantiomer of the same drug. Yet the receptor here is achiral! Thus, for a huge difference in cost, the patient sees very little difference when taking one drug versus the other. Yet a patient will be thankful when the therapy you prescribe doesn't break the bank!

There are hundreds of additional examples. But, to be clear, drawing out these connections between science and medicine, and making them more explicit, is a critical component of the MCAT.

#5 The MCAT is not Particularly Predictive of My Success in Medical School

While it may have been a bit harder to draw a correlation between your SAT score and success in undergrad, the MCAT has been demonstrated multiple times to be highly predictive of first- and second-year grades in medical school and success on the United States Medical Licensing Examination, Step 1 (USMLE, or the "Boards"). A landmark study by Ellen Julian in 2005 found that the MCAT was 59 percent correlated with first- and second-year grades, 46 percent correlated with clerkship (third-year) grades, and 70 percent correlated with Step 1 scores. This was significantly higher than undergraduate GPA alone, at 54 percent, 36 percent, and 49 percent, respectively. The brief takeaway: dominating the MCAT bodes well for your success in medical school.

1.3 What the MCAT Will Look Like

PASSAGES

Passages on the MCAT are written to test science concepts *in the context of living systems*. In other words, you will not see a passage describing a roller coaster car descending a track at an angle θ, with a given height h and coefficient of kinetic friction μ_k that is accompanied by questions asking for plug-and-chug application of these principles. Rather, solution chemistry could be tested as an underlying theme in our understanding of urolithiasis (the formation of kidney and bladder stones); organic oxidation and reduction mechanisms as a component of the metabolism of toxins like ethanol; and atomic absorption and emission spectrometry as it relates to bioluminescence.

The recommendations, as made by the AAMC, include two semesters each of physics, general chemistry, organic chemistry, and biology; one semester each of psychology, sociology, and biochemistry; and an understanding of statistics and research design. Note that, while it is not given its own section, biochemistry will make up a full 25 percent of the Biological and Biochemical Foundations of Living Systems *and* of the Chemical and Physical Foundations of Biological Systems sections of the exam.

QUESTIONS AND SKILLS

A full-length MCAT 2015 will contain questions divided into four Scientific Inquiry and Reasoning Skills (SIRS). While these skills are further explained in Unit II, it is worthwhile to note here that there will be a greatly increased number of questions focusing on research design and bias (Skill 3), as well as data interpretation and statistical analysis (Skill 4). These previously made a minimal appearance on the MCAT, but will now constitute a significant proportion of the questions—perhaps about 20 percent, combined between the two skills.

Content Updates

BIOCHEMISTRY

In an AAMC survey of medical school faculty, biochemistry was rated the most important science for students to master for the medical school curricula of the future (average score 3.34 on a five-point Likert scale, with 5 being the highest). Six of the top-ten rated topics in the survey belonged to the related field of cell and molecular biology. So it's clear that biochemistry is considered important for the medical student of the future.

PSYCHOLOGY AND SOCIOLOGY

Given the expanding diversity in American society, our interconnectedness during the digital age, and the aging of the patient population, there has been an increasing focus in medical schools on cultural sensitivity. Further, many of the top causes of morbidity and mortality in the United States are caused by behavioral and environmental determinants of health: smoking and drug use, diet and exercise, and inequities in care due to socioeconomic status.

Three main themes were identified for why this material should be included in the MCAT. First, the diverse theoretical frameworks used in the behavioral and social sciences underscore the importance of thinking through "complex (and often chaotic) systems"—like the biopsychosocial model—to understand the patient. Second, the strong connections to research methods and data analysis in these fields align well with the testmaker's goal of increasing questions on these topics and the need for medical students to design and critically analyze research, as part of evidence-based medicine. Finally, the content of psychology and sociology is a welcome addition to a medical student's fund of knowledge.

BIOLOGICALLY BASED PASSAGES

How often have you wondered to yourself—while cramming for that organic chemistry or physics final—"Why do I need to know this as a doctor?" Many premedical students question the relevance of some of the material on the MCAT.

The presentation of this content is changing as an answer to this question of relevance. Rather than testing thermodynamics through a gas-piston system, which fails to demonstrate why a doctor would actually need to understand these principles, why not present it in a passage on the proper treatment of frostbite (slow rewarming through a convection current in a rotating water bath at 40–42°C)?

Some schools are better than others at establishing these connections for students; integrated and clinically based courses are extremely helpful with this goal. But by making this application of hard science in a biological context a top priority, MCAT 2015 can increase this exposure among students even *before* they arrive for their white-coat ceremony.

A LONG (AND MORE POWERED) EXAM

The greatly increased length of MCAT actually reflects its use in admissions decisions. Historically, the total score was the most important for admissions committees; section subscores in Physical Sciences, Verbal Reasoning, and Biological Sciences merely showed the breakdown in this score so schools could pick up on students who were highly lateralized toward one section.

Thus, the increased number of questions on the new MCAT represents a number large enough to give reliable, valid data for both section scores and an overall score—while still being manageable for a test taken in only one day.

CHAPTER TWO

Reading the Kaplan Way

MCAT reading is unlike any other reading that you have done in the past. In the same way that one reads a novel differently than a textbook, MCAT reading requires its own unique approach. Reading the Kaplan way involves noting keywords, proper passage outlining, and anticipating questions while reading. In passages, keywords are vital clues that point out the relationships between major themes, highlight the author's opinion, and elucidate the reasoning in a text. Passage outlining is essentially doing the writing process in reverse. You will learn how to extract an outline from each passage, which will serve as road map to assist in handling detail-oriented questions as well as focus your reading on the most testable passage content. And finally, anticipating questions is all about understanding passage structure and how this is predictive of question types.

2.1 How to Read Strategically Using Keywords

The MCAT sections are packed with dense academic prose. There are several distinct levels in which the text should be evaluated: **content**, **organization**, **perspective**, and **reasoning**. Addressing all four modes of reading is essential for Test Day success.

Read for Content—extract the information from the text, discovering precisely *what* is being said.

Read for Organization—consider how the different ideas presented in the passage relate to one another. If the informational content is the *what* of the text, then the organization is the *how*.

Read for Perspective—pay attention to the different perspectives contained in the passage. Many authors of passages, especially in the CARS section, do not state their intentions overtly. In these cases, it is key to attend to the rhetorical aspects of the text, especially goal, tone, and voice.

Key Concepts

Any passage can be understood in four different ways, which we call the modes of reading. Each mode answers at least one vital question:

- Content–*What does the text say?*
- Organization–*How do sentences connect? How do ideas relate?*
- Perspective–*Why does the author write? How does the author feel? Who else has a voice?*
- Reasoning–*How are claims supported? How are claims challenged?*

Read for Reasoning–examine the structure of the reasoning presented in a passage. In other words, it is important to determine how the author structures his or her argument.

RELATION KEYWORDS

When tackling a passage, it is essential to be able to understand how what you're reading now fits into the whole. While there are many ways in which ideas might be related to one another, the vast majority of **Relation keywords** will fall into one of two subcategories: **Similarity** or **Difference**.

Similarity keywords indicate that more of the same idea is coming in the text.

Difference keywords signify a change in the author's focus, or a direct contrast between two things.

More Complex Relationships
- **Opposition keywords** indicate an outright conflict between ideas.
- **Sequence keywords** suggest a series of events advancing in time.
- **Comparison keywords** are used to evaluate ideas and rank them relative to others.

Table 2.1 lists examples of Relation keywords in each category. Note that some words can fit into more than one category; for example, *not* reveals a difference, and can also create a direct opposition.

Similarity	Difference	Opposition
and	but	not/never/none
also	yet	either … or
moreover	however	as opposed to
furthermore	although	on the contrary
like	(even) though	versus
same/similar	rather (than)	on one hand … on the other hand
that is	in contrast	otherwise
in other words	on the other hand	**Sequence**
for example	otherwise	before/after
take the case of	nevertheless	earlier/later
for instance	whereas	previous/next
including	while	initially/subsequently/finally
such as	different	first/second/third/last
in addition	unlike	historically/traditionally/used to
plus	notwithstanding	now/currently/modern
at the same time	another	**Comparison**
as well as	instead	better/best
equally	still	worse/worst
this/that/these/those	despite	less/least
: [colon]	alternatively	more/most
; [semicolon]	unless	−er/−est
— [em dash]	not	primarily
( ) [parentheses]	conversely	especially
" " [quotes]	contrarily	above all

Table 2.1 Common Relation keywords

AUTHOR KEYWORDS

Author keywords are verbs, nouns, adjectives, and adverbs that hint at the author's opinions. Author keywords have a connotation of either approval or disapproval. Authors may use characteristic words and short phrases to make their claims more extreme, as well as others that moderate their claims.

Positive *vs.* Negative

- **Positive keywords**–include nouns such as *masterpiece*, *genius*, and *triumph*; verbs such as *excel*, *succeed*, and *know*; adjectives such as *compelling*, *impressive*, and *elegant*; and adverbs such as *correctly*, *reasonably*, and *fortunately*
- **Negative keywords**–include nouns like *disaster*, *farce*, and *limitation*; verbs like *miss*, *fail*, and *confuse*; adjectives like *problematic*, *so-called*, and *deceptive*; and adverbs like *questionably*, *merely*, and *purportedly*

Note that in addition to positive, negative, or neutral, an author can also be **ambivalent**. Ambivalence literally means "feeling both ways," and it is different from **impartiality**.

EXTREME

Extreme keywords are words that enhance the charge of what the author is saying, forcing the author into one or the other extreme.

MODERATING

Moderating keywords are words that set limits to claims in order to make them easier to support, because a stronger statement is always more difficult to prove than a weaker one.

Table 2.2 lists examples of Author keywords in each category.

Positive	Negative	Extreme	Moderating
masterpiece	disaster	must	can/could
genius	farce	need/necessary	may/might
triumph	limitation	always	possibly
excel	miss	every	probably
succeed	fail	any	sometimes
know	confuse	only	on occasion
compelling	problematic	should/ought	often
impressive	so-called	indeed	tends to
elegant	deceptive	very	here
correctly	questionably	especially	now
reasonably	merely	obviously	in this case
fortunately	purportedly	above all	in some sense

Table 2.2 Common Author keywords

MCAT Expertise

Most passages on the MCAT contain strong, but not extreme, opinions. Rarely will an author be completely neutral, because there is little reasoning to test if the author does not express at least a moderately positive or negative opinion.

Key Concept

While they are both overall neutral, these two attitudes are very different:
- Ambivalent = having both a positive and negative opinion.
- Impartial = having neither a positive nor negative opinion.

LOGIC KEYWORDS

The final level of reading (for reasoning) is perhaps the most difficult, because the special one-way relationship between a conclusion and its evidence is among the most complex you'll encounter on Test Day. **Logic keywords** tend to be relatively rare, occurring less frequently than either Relation or Author keywords in most passages.

Evidence and Conclusion

A **conclusion** is a claim that the author is trying to convince the audience to believe, while pieces of **evidence** are the reasons that are given for believing it.

Refutation

Refutation keywords are the opposite of evidence–countervailing reasons for rejecting a conclusion.

Table 2.3 lists examples of Logic keywords in each category.

Evidence	Conclusion	Refutation
because (of)	therefore	despite
since	thus	notwithstanding
if	then	challenge
for	so	undermined by
why	consequently	object
the reason is	leading to	counter(argument)
as a result of	resulting in	critique/criticize
due to	argue	conflict
as evident in	conclude	doubt
justified by	imply	problem
assuming	infer	weakness
after all	suggest	called into question by

Table 2.3 Common Logic keywords

2.2 How to Critically Analyze Passages

THE KAPLAN METHOD FOR PASSAGES

The Kaplan Method for critically reading passages consists of four steps: **Scan**, **Read**, **Label** and **Reflect**.

- **Scan**–Scan for words that stand out because of capitalization, italics, quotation marks, parentheses, or any other distinctive textual features to decide which passages to do first. Always start with passages that you're most comfortable with.
- **Read**–Use keywords and the four modes of reading to read strategically.
  - ○ Identify **Relation keywords** (to connect different ideas in the text), **Logic keywords** (to reveal the passage's arguments), and **Author keywords** (to offer glimpses of the writer's intentions).
  - ○ Don't reread text excessively.
  - ○ Evaluate the role that each paragraph plays in the larger whole of the passage.
- **Label**–Write down the purpose of each paragraph of the passage.
  - ○ Label paragraphs right after you read them.
  - ○ Use symbols, abbreviations, and other shorthand.
- **Reflect**–Articulate the author's overall goal for writing the passage.
  - ○ Begin the statement with an infinitive verb (the form of a verb starting with *to*).
  - ○ Occasionally, authors may have multiple purposes (use multiple verbs).

There are several important differences between CARS passages and the science passages. CARS passages are longer and much more variable, both in their vast range of topics and their endless diversity of writing styles. They are usually written by authors who take sides and express their opinions, although not always in a straightforward manner.

REVERSE-ENGINEERING THE AUTHOR'S OUTLINE

In this section, we discuss how to optimize your scratch paper usage, what to include in your outline, and which portions of the passage are worth highlighting on the screen.

Scratch Paper Strategy

During the Scan step, begin to construct your outline. Each paragraph should be numbered using brief notation like *P4*. Be sure to include a spot at the end for the author's goal, which will always start with an infinitive verb, so you can write the word *to* as a reminder. For instance, you could set up your scratch paper for a six-paragraph passage as follows:

P1.

P2.

P3.

P4.

P5.

P6.

Goal:

Note that writing the goal is critical for CARS passages because most questions will require an overall understanding of the passage's goal.

Label each paragraph appropriately as you read through a passage. Be sure to keeps labels concise. Generally, five to seven words are ideal, but ten to twelve words are acceptable for more complex passages.

What to Label

The four modes of reading discussed earlier in this chapter serve as *guidelines* for the kind of material to include in each Label.

- **Content**–Write down the key ideas of each paragraph.
- **Organization**–Write down how each paragraph functions within the larger whole of the passage.
- **Perspectives**–Note in your map where the author or other prominent voices offer an opinion. Use '+' or '−' to designate positive and negative tone, respectively.
- **Reasoning**–Identify whether each paragraph bolsters or objects to an argument.

HOW TO HIGHLIGHT

Highlighting is never an adequate substitute for Outlining, but it is an extremely effective complement to the Kaplan Method for CARS Passages when used sparingly. One should *never* rely on highlighting as the primary strategy for reading a passage because highlighting will actually disappear if you leave a passage and return to it later. Remember that highlighting works through contrast: if you highlight most of the text, the unmarked portions would actually stand out more. Consequently, strive to adhere to the following guidelines when using this feature.

- Double-Click *vs.* Click-and-Drag
  - Highlight an entire word by double-clicking on any part of it.
  - When highlighting a phrase, do not obsess over highlighting it completely.
  - Never highlight more than one line of text.
- Find the First Occurrence
  - Highlight terms introduced by an author, especially when the author provides an overt definition or offers essential background information.
- Proper Nouns and Numbers
  - Names and proper nouns, as well as dates and other numbers, have a tendency to show up in question stems.
- Keywords
  - Do not highlight keywords.

2.3 How to Attack Different Passage Types

Science Passages

The science sections on the MCAT generally presents content in two types of passages. The first type is best described as information passages, where you will need to pay attention to definitions and relationships. The second, and most common type, are experimental passages. For these passages, your job is to pay attention to why the experiment was done and what the overall findings are. It is important to note that any figures or tables are also worth labeling for the science passages since they will also contain testable information.

VARIETIES OF CARS PASSAGES

The AAMC lists ten different fields in the humanities and a dozen different social sciences, as shown in Table 2.4. On the other hand, most CARS passages fit into one of just a few basic types. Quickly identifying the form of a passage during the Scan step of the Kaplan Method can help shape your expectations about what the passage will include and what the accompanying questions will test.

MCAT Expertise

According to the AAMC, approximately 50 percent of questions in the *Critical Analysis and Reasoning Skills* section will be from the humanities and 50 percent will be from the social sciences.

Humanities	Social Sciences
Architecture	Anthropology
Art	Archaeology
Dance	Cultural Studies
Ethics	Economics
Literature	Education
Music	Geography
Philosophy	History
Popular Culture	Linguistics
Religion	Political Science
Theater	Population Health
	Psychology
	Sociology

Table 2.4 Humanities and social sciences disciplines in the CARS section

HUMANITIES

Passages in the humanities tend to fall into two broad categories. The first category, which includes most of the passages from architecture, art, dance, literature, music, popular culture, and theater, could be considered **Arts passages**. The second category, **Philosophical passages**, includes ethics, philosophy, and many religion passages.

- **Arts passages** often use quotations from both artists and critics, include strong opinions, and use descriptive language to illustrate artistic examples.
- **Philosophical passages** tend to be abstract and heavy on logic as well as focus on concepts and the relations between them.

Keep in mind that there will be plenty of humanities passages that mix characteristics of Arts and Philosophical passages.

SOCIAL SCIENCES

When it comes to the social sciences, some passages take what might be called a **Scientific** form, such as passages in anthropology, education, linguistics, population health, psychology, and sociology. The counterpart to Scientific would be **Historical passages**, which include many instances from archaeology, cultural studies, economics, geography, history, and political science.

- **Scientific passages** include heavy references to empirical studies. Usually the author's opinion is more subtle.
- **Historical passages** tend to draw on historical events and quotations from sources alive at the time of the events they discuss. Sometimes empirical studies are referenced.

SUPPORT IN PASSAGES

Because a majority of questions in the CARS section will have some connection to logical support, it's essential to understand the different kinds of support that can be found in CARS passages.

Categories of Support

- **Unsupported Claims**–Not every assertion in a passage is backed up with evidence. Unsupported claims lack logical connections to other parts of the passage.
- **Empirical Evidence**–Whenever the author appeals to experience, particularly in the context of scientific studies, he or she is using empirical evidence.
  - Historical accounts and case studies draw upon experience, but are limited in value because they only represent single cases.
  - Surveys, statistical analyses, and controlled experiments are more solid evidence since variables can be isolated and evidence can be gathered by examining a wide swath of experience.
- **Logical Appeals** refer to the usage of logic, claims, or evidence to argue for a point.
  - **Analogical reasoning**–Two things known to be alike are declared to be alike in a different respect for which there may not be direct evidence.
  - **Reduction to absurdity** is supporting a position by elimination of alternative possibilities.
- **Appealing to Authority** is drawing upon another person or test to support a claim.
  - The level of support depends on the credibility of the authority.
    - **Primary sources** provide the most support, whereas **secondary sources** are dubious in value and vary based on the expertise of the authority being cited.
- **Appeals to the Reader**–In this case, the author uses the reader to help ground an argument. Sometimes the author will begin an argument with points that the reader is likely to agree with. Another possibility is that the author uses charged language and colorful descriptions to evoke particular responses from the reader.
- **Faulty Support** involves backing up a controversial claim with another claim that is similarly controversial. This kind of assertion is extremely weak at best.

ANTICIPATING QUESTIONS

While reading CARS passages, it is essential to anticipate the questions. Certain passage characteristics lend themselves to specific question types. The following are a few examples of passage types and what types of questions typically accompany each:

- **Heavily opinionated** passages lend themselves to questions that require understanding what the author would agree or disagree with.
- Passages that are **abundant in detail** are likely to have questions that necessitate combing through the passage searching for particular bits from the text.
- Passages **lacking in support** will probably have questions that incorporate new information.
- Passages that **use numerous Logic keywords** will tend to have questions that ask about the author's argumentative structure.
- When the author introduces **new terminology or concepts**, it is likely that the questions will test for understanding of the novel information.
- When passages **offer two opposing viewpoints**, then expect questions that ask you to compare and contrast the viewpoints.

CHAPTER THREE

Kaplan's Question and Answer Strategy

In this chapter, we shift our strategic focus away from the passages to consider the treatment of question stems and answer choices. We begin by outlining the Kaplan Method for MCAT Questions. Subsequently, we will look at the recurring traps that the testmakers set for the unwary student, which we call Wrong Answer Pathologies. In the final portion of the chapter, we'll consider the counterpart to pathologies: patterns common in correct answers.

3.1 Kaplan Method for Questions

In the previous chapter, we saw how the general Kaplan Method for tackling MCAT passages could be refined to the needs of the CARS section. In this section, we'll do the same with our question method, which takes the basic form shown in Figure 3.1.

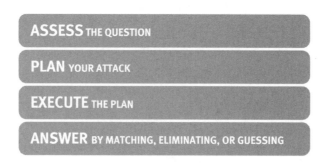

Figure 3.1 Kaplan Question Method.

This same four-step approach should be used on all questions on the MCAT—in both the Critical Analysis and Reasoning Skills section and the science sections. The CARS-specific version is shown in Figure 3.2.

ASSESS THE QUESTION

- Read the question, **NOT** the answers
- Identify the question type and difficulty
- Decide to attack *now* or *later*

PLAN YOUR ATTACK

- Establish the task set by the question type
- Find clues in the stem on where to research
- Navigate the passage using your outline

EXECUTE THE PLAN

- Predict what you can about the answer
- Set expectations for wrong choices
- Be flexible if your first Plan flops

ANSWER BY MATCHING, ELIMINATING, OR GUESSING

- Find a match for your prediction, or
- Eliminate the three wrong options, or
- Make an educated guess

Figure 3.2 Detailed Steps of the Kaplan Question Method.

It is important to note that the worked-out practice passages in Unit III of this book all focus on how to effectively implement the four steps of this question strategy.

STEP ONE: ASSESS

You might notice that the first step of the question method is in many ways similar to the Scan step of the Kaplan Method for Passages. This is not a coincidence, but is a consequence of the timing constraints posed by the section. Because every question is worth the same number of points, there's no reason to get derailed by any one of them. Be honest with yourself: at least a few questions in each section are so difficult that you're likely to get them wrong, no matter how many minutes you spend on them. Wouldn't it be better to recognize which questions those are right away, so you can instead use that precious time where it will actually pay off?

Toward that end, your first task with any question will be to read the stem, and only the stem, for the sake of making the decision to either work on it *now*, or to triage (to use an apt medical metaphor) and save it for *later*. Assessing the difficulty will be made easier if you can identify the **question type**. Through extensive research of all released MCAT material, we've discovered that almost all of the CARS section's *Foundations of Comprehension* questions fall into one of four types, and its *Reasoning Within the Text* and *Reasoning Beyond the Text* categories can each be split into two predominant types with assorted Others making rare appearances. Determining the question type will make devising and executing a plan much easier, which is why we devote the next three chapters to the different types of questions and their unique strategic concerns.

Why avoid looking at the answer choices in the CARS section? The primary reason is that most of them are wrong. If you glance at just one of them, for instance, it's three times more likely to be incorrect than correct, and could seriously mislead you about the question. Inexperienced test-takers immediately jump to the answers, and the AAMC punishes them for it by wording wrong options seductively. Selecting the first answer that looks good without really formulating a plan is just a recipe for failure. Thus, until you get in the habit of ignoring the answers entirely until the Answer step, use your hand or a sticky note to cover them up whenever you start to work on a question.

On the other hand, you can afford a glance at the answer choices for the science questions. While you should not read the choices, just look to see what form the answer choice is in so that you will know what form the prediction should take.

MCAT Expertise

To avoid getting seduced by wrong answer choices, only scroll down far enough to read the question stem, and leave the answer choices off-screen until you're reading for the Answer step. This will save you significant time and effort, so that you avoid putting active consideration towards (and possibly being misled by!) the three wrong answer choices.

STEP TWO: PLAN

Once you've decided to attack a question, it's time to plan your attack. First, be clear about what it is that the question requires of you—what we call the **task**. Simpler question types like Main Idea and Definition-in-Context always involve one specific task (recognizing the big picture, and explaining the meaning of part of the text as used in the passage, respectively), and even the more complex ones only have a small number of common objectives, such as Apply questions, almost all of which will fall into one of three tasks: gauging the author's response, predicting a likely outcome, or finding a good example.

In the journey to a correct answer, the task is your destination. To reach where you're headed, you need to know where you're starting from, your point of departure. Thus, the other major aspect of the Plan step is to determine where you'll find the information that you need to answer the question. Note that there are only four viable **sources** of information on Test Day: the *question stem*, the *passage*, your *outline*, and your *memory*.

It's rare, but occasionally you'll find that the stem gives you everything you need to answer the question. In other cases, the relevant information might be fresh in your mind, although human memory is notoriously faulty, and it doesn't hurt to check another source. This is one reason why it's so valuable to create an outline as you read, to serve as a memory aid, capturing important aspects of the text that could slip your mind. In fact, sometimes the outline is the only place you'll need to check, saving you the trouble of researching the passage. For instance, with Main Idea questions, the author's Goal in your outline is usually all you'll need to examine. Not every question on the CARS section requires rereading the text: if a simple plan yields immediate success, accept it and don't second-guess yourself.

Whenever you're facing less straightforward tasks, though, it's advisable to you reread at least part of the passage. Stems almost always contain clues hinting at where to research, taking one of three forms:

- Paragraph or sentence references
- Direct quotations
- Paraphrases

MCAT Expertise

If you ever find yourself scanning the passage to find an answer choice, you're doing it wrong! The information you need for the answer is often in your outline; even if not, using your outline to determine where in the passage to look for the answer means that you'll usually scan—at most—one paragraph of text.

Sometimes paragraph numbers will be listed in parentheses, or you'll see a phrase like *the final sentence of the passage*, which makes location a breeze. The other clues may be harder to work with. Keep in mind that not all quotations taken from the passage will be surrounded by quote marks, particularly if only a single word or short phrase is mentioned—these brief terms are sometimes italicized but may appear without any embellishment at all. Keep in mind that shorter quotations could actually appear in multiple paragraphs. Although mercifully rare, paraphrases of passage claims without additional clues can be especially tricky: always remember that stems can use synonyms instead of the author's original language. A good outline will help you find the paragraph that contains the information for a less direct clue.

Once you've figured out where to go in the passage, you'll want to make sure you cast a large enough net to find what you need. While the necessary information is often found directly in the portion of the passage that the stem points to, not infrequently you will find that the answer is in the surrounding text, in sentences immediately before or after. As a general rule of thumb, plan to start rereading one sentence before the reference and to stop one sentence after it.

What should your Plan be if you can't locate the clues, or with vague questions that lack them entirely? Typically, such questions are best to try later, at the very end of a passage set, after you've researched the other questions and already reread much of the text. You may find that by the time you return to it, the efforts you put into others ended up revealing an unhelpful question stem's correct answer. When you do attempt these questions, the process of elimination will usually end up being the best Plan.

On a similar note, the Plan step for the science questions is where you will decide where you will have to go to predict the answer; the passage, your background knowledge, or both.

STEP THREE: EXECUTE

Every question has exactly one correct answer but typically will have more than one way to reach it. Indeed, the only difference between discovering the one correct answer and ruling out the three wrong ones is that the latter approach usually takes more time; the result is identical. Consequently, you want to strive for the quickest approach, but be flexible, so that if Plan A fails, you have Plans B and C to fall back on.

In the Plan step for most questions, you'll identify where you need to reread (in your outline or in the passage itself). Keep in mind the task of the particular question type as you now Execute the Plan and look over your outline or the text again. Here, unlike with your first strategic reading of the passage, it's okay to reread the crucial sentences a few times if you need to, because points are now on the line. In most cases, Plan A is to use the text to predict everything that you can about the correct answer, while Plan B is to set analogous expectations about what would rule out choices. The more specific these dual expectations, the easier it will be to isolate the answer.

Where you look for information, as well as the way in which you approach rereading (including which keywords you pay attention to) will vary depending on the task.

STEP FOUR: ANSWER

All that remains now is selecting to select the correct Answer. Scan the choices, and if you see an item that closely resembles what you expected, reread every word of that answer choice carefully to make sure it says precisely what you think it does. Then, select it and move on to the next question. At that point, *reading the other choices will not be worth your time*—be confident that you've answered the question correctly when you find a near perfect match. When a good match is not available, elimination is always an option.

That said, don't feel that you immediately need to resort to the process of elimination if you read one answer choice and discover that the correct answer is going to take a completely different form than you first predicted. Part of being flexible is being able to revise your initial plan, to set new expectations if the *answer choices* point you in that direction. The answer choices could technically be considered a fifth *source* of information, but keep in mind that they include a lot of misinformation and should be treated with caution.

For example, a question stem may ask for a claim that undermines the author's thesis, a classic Strengthen–Weaken (Within the Passage) task. For such a question, you may go into the answer choices expecting that the answer is an objection mentioned in the passage. As soon as you read choice (A), though, you discover it's something entirely new, never even hinted at by the author. Such questions fall into the related Strengthen–Weaken (Beyond the Passage) type instead. Before moving on to read choice (B), you should think about whether choice (A) answers the question in a way you didn't anticipate. If not, use it to help you alter your expectations. Avoid the temptation to abandon the critical thinking you performed during the Execute step by reading the remaining three answer choices. Instead, formulate a new prediction and find a match among the three remaining answer choices.

Sometimes the question stem just doesn't give you very much to work with, and on other occasions you'll search through the answers but find no likely match. In these cases, you will have to use the process of elimination, which may require multiple returns to the text as you research each choice individually. If you were able to set expectations during the Execute step for wrong choices, however, less additional research will be required. When evaluating choices, remember that the answer choices will sometimes vary from the language used in the passage. Don't rule out a choice just because the wording is not quite what you anticipated; conceptual consistency matters more than terminological exactness. Keep in mind that an answer only requires one major flaw for elimination, so the Wrong Answer Pathologies described below can greatly expedite the process.

MCAT Expertise

If you read a question stem and it doesn't give you very much to work with, don't just say *I don't know* and jump straight to the answer choices. Use your outline to remember the main themes of the passage, and then use those themes to help with the process of elimination. This will help you avoid being distracted by answer choices that are seductive but which do not fit into the passage.

MCAT Expertise

Should I compare answer choices?

Your default assumption should be that only one answer choice is correct and that the others contain at least one flaw each, sufficient for ruling them out. However, you may occasionally find questions containing superlatives (*strongest challenge, most supported, best example,* and so on) in which you need to compare two or more answers that have the same effect but to different degrees. When making such comparisons, don't assume that an extreme answer is necessarily wrong, especially if the question stem includes the words *if true* or similar language. A stronger answer that nevertheless produces the desired outcome would actually be the correct choice.

When all else fails, you can fall back on educated guessing. Eliminate whatever you can and then go with your gut among the remaining options. Never make a blind guess unless you're completely out of time and need to fill in an answer choice. Even crossing off just one wrong answer will increase your chances of randomly choosing the correct one by 33 percent. Crossing off two wrong answers will double your chances. If possible, work on any unanswered questions for the passage, and see if that allows you to return to rule out additional wrong options.

KAPLAN

3.2 Wrong Answer Pathologies

The American Association of Medical Colleges (AAMC), the maker of the MCAT, has designed sections of the exam to be fair tests of critical thinking skills. The need for fairness is great news, because it means that the questions won't play tricks on you! There will never be a question with two correct answer choices or one in which all of the options are wrong. Each question you encounter on Test Day will have one and only one right answer and three that are incorrect for at least one reason. Even better, there can only be so many of these reasons: in fact, a few of them are found so frequently that you can treat them like recurring signs and symptoms of answer choice illness. Naturally, we call them **Wrong Answer Pathologies**.

A choice only needs one fatal flaw to be worth eliminating, but often wrong answer options have many issues, so don't necessarily be alarmed if you ruled out a wrong answer for a different reason than the one mentioned in a practice question's explanation. In addition to having some occasional overlap, the following list of pathologies is not meant to be exhaustive, but only includes the four patterns we've identified as the most common through researching all of the released MCAT material. In the Kaplan Method for Questions just detailed, pathologies function as recurring expectations for wrong answers, which you can assume fit for most of the questions you encounter (with a few significant departures noted below).

FAULTY USE OF DETAIL (FUD)

The testmakers will often include accurate reflections of passage details in wrong answers, primarily to appeal to those students who jump at the familiar language. What makes the use of a detail "faulty" is that it simply doesn't answer the question posed. It may be too specific for a question that requires a general answer, or it may be that the detail comes from the wrong part of the passage. Even if a choice comes from the right paragraph, the detail cited might not be relevant to the question posed, often the case in Strengthen–Weaken (Within the Passage) questions. A thorough prediction makes catching these FUDs much easier.

OUT OF SCOPE (OS)

With the noteworthy exception of *Reasoning Beyond the Text* questions (for which this pathology does not apply), an answer choice that is outside the scope of the passage will inevitably be wrong. Typically, such answers will be on-topic but will bring in some element that the text does not discuss. For instance, if an author never makes comparisons when discussing different ideas, an Out of Scope answer choice might involve the author ranking two or more of them. Another common OS pattern is the suggestion that a view was the first of its kind or the most influential, when the author entirely avoids discussing its historical origins or relative popularity. Keep in mind that information can be unstated by the passage but not count as out of scope, as will be the case with the correct answers to many *Reasoning Within the Text* questions, so don't be too quick to reject a choice as OS just because the author does not explicitly say it.

OPPOSITE

Whenever an answer choice contains information that directly conflicts with the passage, we call it an Opposite. Often the difference is due simply to the presence (or absence) of a single word like *not* or *except*, a prefix like *un–* or *a–*, or even a suffix like *–less* or *–free*. Be especially careful when stems or choices involve double- (or triple-) negatives; they're much less difficult to assess if you reword them with fewer negations. Moreover, don't assume that just because two answer choices contradict, that one of them has to be correct. For example, suppose an author argues that it is impossible to prove whether or not a divine being exists, a variant of the religious view known as agnosticism. If a question accompanying the passage was to ask for a claim the author agreed with, *God exists* and *There is no God* would both be Opposites of the correct answer.

DISTORTION

Extreme answers and others that "twist" the ideas in the passage further than the author would prefer are what we call Distortions. Although they do not automatically make a choice incorrect, the following are common signals of distorted claims:

- Strong words like *all*, *always*, *none*, *never*, *impossible*, or *only*
- A prefix like *any–* or *every–*
- A suffix like *–est* or *–less*

MCAT authors typically do not take radical positions on issues, so it's worth noting whenever they do. In those rare cases, extreme choices would not actually be Distortions of the author's view, and would actually be more likely to be correct. The other major case in which extreme answer choices should not be immediately ruled out is when the question stem tells you that you can treat the answer choices as true, and your task is only to gauge which would have the greatest impact on a particular argument. This is often the case with Strengthen–Weaken (Beyond the Passage) questions.

This chapter continues on the next page ▶ ▶ ▶

3.3 Signs of a Healthy Answer

If you're like most students prepping for the MCAT. you've had a dispute with at least one question explanation. *Hey, what about what the author says in the first paragraph?* you may have wondered, or perhaps you've said to yourself (or aloud!) *But couldn't you think of it like **this** instead?* While you may be in the habit of arguing for points with college professors, it does you no good to try to argue with the MCAT. The testmakers are extremely deliberate about how they word correct answers, always taking care to include exactly one per question.

Correct answer choices can vary widely in appearance, but there are patterns in how they are written as well. If the traps that can lead you astray on Test Day are appropriately called Wrong Answer Pathologies, then these corresponding traits can be thought of as indications of good health. While the following signs are not enough by themselves to make an answer right, you can treat them as general expectations for the correct choices in most types of questions.

APPROPRIATE SCOPE

You might say correct answers follow the "Goldilocks principle" when it comes to scope: not too broad, not too specific, but just right. The scope defines the limits of the discussion, or the particular aspects of the larger topic that the author really cares about. In your outline, the Goal that you jotted down should give you an idea of the scope of the passage overall. As a general rule (with one important exception), correct answers to MCAT questions will remain within the scope of the passage, but you can formulate a more precise expectation of what scope the correct answer needs to have by identifying the question's type and task.

Main Idea questions will always have correct answers that match the scope of the entire passage. They will typically include at least one wrong answer choice that is too focused (Faulty Use of Detail) and at least one that goes outside the passage entirely (Out of Scope). In contrast, Detail and Definition-in-Context questions usually require more refined scopes for their correct answer choices. If a clue directs to a particular portion of the passage, then the correct answer more often than not will have the same scope as the referenced text (or what immediately surrounds it).

The important exception to the rule that answers must remain within the scope of the author's discussion applies to the category of *Reasoning Beyond the Text* questions, addressed in Chapter 11 of *MCAT Critical Analysis and Reasoning Skills Review*. Like their name suggests, these broaden the scope to new contexts, sometimes appearing to have no connection to the passage whatsoever. Note, however, that some

MCAT Expertise

The scope of a text refers to the particular aspects of a topic that the author addresses. Every paragraph in a CARS passage has its own scope, and together you can think of them as constituting the scope of the whole passage. Similarly, each answer choice will have its own scope, which could mimic any part of the author's discussion or depart from the passage entirely. It is essential to note that having the same scope doesn't necessarily mean having identical content. For instance, unstated assumptions in an argument are definitely within the scope of the passage, even though the information they contain is left unsaid by the author.

Reasoning Beyond the Text questions will present new information in the stem but have answers that stick to the scope of the passage anyway. So be savvy with the answer choices in *Reasoning Beyond the Text* questions: while the correct answer choice tends to move slightly outside the scope of the passage, don't automatically rule out an answer choice just because it happens to be in scope.

AUTHOR AGREEMENT

Unless a question stem explicitly asks about an alternative viewpoint or a challenge to the information presented in the passage, a correct answer choice will be one that is consistent with what the author says. This is one reason why considerations of *tone* and *voice* (most clearly reflected by Author keywords) are usually important enough to be worth including in your passage outline. Generally, a correct answer should not contradict anything that the author says elsewhere in the passage, with the possible exception of sentences that speak in a different voice than the author's (such as quotes or references to others' opinions). In short, if it doesn't sound like something the author would say, you'll most likely want to rule it out.

WEAKER IS USUALLY BETTER

One final consideration is a consequence of the fact that the AAMC tends to select passages in which the authors do not take extreme views. You may find one or two passages on Test Day with more radical writers; for them, a stronger claim in the answer choices may actually be a good sign. However, for most of the passages you'll encounter, authors tend to use numerous Moderating keywords to limit the strength of their claims. Because a stronger claim has a higher burden of proof (that is, stronger evidence must be provided to support the claim), most authors avoid them to make what they write more plausible. Thus, you should generally give preference to answer choices that use weaker language such as *can, could, may, might, is possible, sometimes, often, likely, probably,* and *in some sense*. Exceptions to this tendency were addressed previously in the discussion of Distortions.

3.4 Getting the Edge Using the Question Strategy

This chapter is only an introduction to the question method; the worked examples that follow in Unit III are a necessary supplement for seeing how the method functions in practice. Specific strategy suggestions and worked examples are included for each of the most common question tasks, together constituting a large proportion of what you'll encounter on Test Day. The explanations accompanying these sample questions will also identify their Wrong Answer Pathologies, giving you some concrete examples to go with the explanations provided here.

3.5 Concept and Strategy Summary

KAPLAN METHOD FOR CARS QUESTIONS

- Assess
  - Read the question, **NOT** the answers
  - Identify the question type and difficulty
  - Decide to attack *now* or *later*
- Plan
  - Establish the task set by the question type
  - Find clues in the stem on where to research
  - Navigate the passage using your outline
- Execute
  - Predict what you can about the answer
  - Set expectations for wrong choices
  - Be flexible if your first plan flops
- Answer
  - Find a match for your prediction, or
  - Eliminate the three wrong options, or
  - Make an educated guess

WRONG ANSWER PATHOLOGIES

- **Faulty Use of Detail (FUD)** answer choices may be accurate statements, but fail to answer the question posed.
  - The answer choice may be too specific for a question that requires a general answer.
  - The answer choice may use a detail from the wrong part of the passage.
  - The answer choice may be from the right paragraph, but still not be relevant to the question posed.
- **Out of Scope (OS)** answer choices usually bring in some element that the passage does not discuss (and which cannot be inferred from the passage).
  - The answer choice may make connections or comparisons that the author did not discuss.
  - The answer choice may make a statement about the significance of the history of an idea that the author did not.
  - The answer choice may otherwise bring in information that does not adhere to the constraints of the passage.
- **Opposite** answer choices contain information that directly conflicts with the passage.
  - The answer choice may contain (or omit) a single word like *not* or *except*.
  - The answer choice may contain a prefix like *un–* or *a–* or a suffix like *–less* or *–free*.
  - The answer choice may say that a given claim is true, when the author is ambivalent.
- **Distortion** answer choices are extreme or twist the ideas in the passage further than the author would prefer.
  - The answer choice may use a strong word like *all, always, none, never, impossible,* or *only.*
  - The answer choice may contain a prefix like *any–* or *every–* or a suffix like *–est* or *–less.*
  - The answer choice is usually more radical than the author because radical positions are rare in MCAT passages.

SIGNS OF A HEALTHY ANSWER

- Correct answers tend to have the right scope—not too broad, not too specific, but just right.
- Correct answers tend to be consistent with what the author said.
- Correct answers tend to use Moderating keywords, such as *can, could, may, might, is possible, sometimes, often, likely, probably,* and *in some sense.*

Strategic Inquiry and Reasoning Skills

CHAPTER FOUR

Skills 1 and 2

There is no question that a high score on the MCAT requires extensive content knowledge in biology, biochemistry, general chemistry, organic chemistry, physics, psychology, and sociology. However, the MCAT is not a content test. One of the most common mistakes that test-takers make when studying for the MCAT is treating it like a content test and studying for it like an undergraduate course. The MCAT is actually a critical thinking test, designed to test your ability to apply your knowledge to new situations. In addition, questions on the MCAT have been expanded to include additional skills, such as evaluation of experimental design and execution as well as interpretation of data and statistical reasoning. The AAMC has separated these categories into four skills, appropriately called Skills 1, 2, 3, and 4. In this chapter, we will discuss how the MCAT will test Skills 1 and 2.

4.1 What Are Skills 1 and 2?

Unlike many tests administered to undergraduates, the questions are carefully crafted and tested to ensure that the MCAT tests the specific skills and content areas that the AAMC believes is most essential for success in medical school. To do this, the AAMC creates questions reflecting four different skills. Skills 1 and 2 are designed to evaluate your scientific knowledge and reasoning ability.

SKILL 1

Skill 1 is the simplest of the skills, testing knowledge of scientific concepts and principles. These questions will be fairly straightforward, asking you to identify relationships between related concepts. Essentially, Skill 1 questions test your content knowledge in a very specific manner. Skill 1 questions are designed to test:

- Knowledge and recognition of scientific principles
- Ability to identify relationships between related concepts
- Identification of relationships between graphical, symbolic, and verbal representations of information
- Identification of observations that illustrate specific scientific principles
- The application of mathematical principles to solve problems

SKILL 2

Skill 2 is more complex than Skill 1 in that Skill 2 tests your scientific reasoning and problem-solving skills. Essentially, Skill 1 tests your content knowledge, while Skill 2 tests your ability to apply that knowledge. You will be asked to reason about scientific principles, models, and theories as well as to evaluate and analyze predictions and explanations related to scientific concepts.

Overall, Skill 2 questions are going to test your critical thinking skills. But what are "critical thinking skills?" Critical thinking is a method of processing and using information. It has been defined as "the process of actively and skillfully conceptualizing, applying, analyzing, synthesizing, and evaluating information to reach an answer or conclusion." Critical thinking is not just memorizing information; it is using this information through higher order processing. However, critical thinking requires some level of knowledge about a topic, beyond basic memorization.

One of the ways that we can tackle critical thinking is by changing how we learn information. Many students use memorization as a primary method of learning, and are successful in passing undergraduate level science courses. But medical school is very different from undergraduate science courses. The volume of information is astounding, often covering the same volume of information in an entire semester of an undergraduate science course in two weeks or less. Medical students are expected to learn this information and be able to systematically apply this information to patient care. But, without the gift of superhuman photographic memory, getting through medical school by brute force memorization is just not realistic. But, more relevant to the MCAT, higher test scores result from the ability to think, analyze, and apply information you already know to situations and concepts that you may not know. This particular skill is essential for medicine, as you will have to apply the information you know about the human body to a patient about whom you may know little.

So, how can you improve your ability to learn and apply information? By focusing on your learning behavior.

One of the tools used in educational psychology for assessing learning is known as Bloom's taxonomy (See Figure 4.1). In this taxonomy, there are six levels of intellectual behavior that are important for learning. These are:

- Remembering–can you recall the information?
- Understanding–can you explain the information to a classmate?
- Applying–can you apply the information to a new situation?
- Analyzing–can you compare and contrast difference parts of the concept? Can you differentiate between the details within the concept?
- Evaluating–can you use the information to support a judgment based on the information?
- Creating–can you incorporate the information to create another structure/document/theory?

In each content area on the MCAT, it is Bloom's taxonomy that is being tested, regardless of the skill. When evaluating your knowledge of a particular subject, you can use Bloom's taxonomy to determine your level of learning and to increase your level of learning. Try this step-by-step method for deepening your learning of a concept:

- Do you think you remember and understand a particular concept? Then, explain it to a friend or classmate.
- If you can do that, then try to find situations that are different but to which the same concept applies.
- Then, compare and contrast the concept to a similar theory or concept.
- Once you can see the differences and the similarities, work through a passage and questions, explaining why each answer choice is correct or incorrect.
- Finally, can you write something about a concept? Try to write a passage similar to one seen on the MCAT.

While it is unrealistic to do this for every topic on the MCAT, as it would be highly inefficient, the levels of Bloom's taxonomy represent the different levels of learning the MCAT requires. It also explains why so many students spend thousands of hours studying for the MCAT, but are not successful on Test Day. Many focus only on the "remembering" part of learning, and only a little bit on the "understanding" part.

The secret to MCAT success on Test Day is not just in remembering the content, it is having a higher level of understanding of the content. If you can complete all levels of Bloom's taxonomy with a concept, then not only do you really know that topic, but you are also far more likely to recall that topic on Test Day. Memorized information does not have nearly the same level of recall as information that is deeply understood and able to be synthesized and actively used to solve problems. In other words, you are not going to remember everything you study for Test Day. In fact, it is unlikely that you will be comfortable with every single topic on Test Day. However, if you build your knowledge to such a degree that you focus on a deeper level of learning, you will be able to use logic to go from what you DO know to determine answers to questions you may not specifically "know" the answer to.

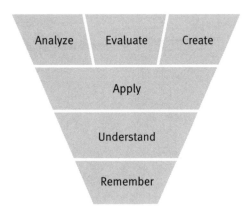

Figure 4.1 Bloom's taxonomy

Skill 2 questions specifically test the skills mentioned in Bloom's taxonomy. Skill 2 questions are designed to test:

- Ability to reason about scientific models, principles, and theories
- Evaluation and analysis of scientific predictions and explanations
- Interpretation and evaluation of arguments regarding causes and consequences
- Unification of observations, theories, and evidence to come to conclusions
- Recognition of scientific findings that pose a challenge or invalidate a scientific theory or model
- Identification and use of scientific formulas to solve problems

Skill 1 *vs.* Skill 2

	Skill 1	Skill 2
This skill tests:	Basic scientific knowledge	Scientific reasoning skills
Questions will require:	Identification of the task Selection of the correct answer	Identification of the task Planning of an attack that will involve a multistep process to determine an answer Selection of the correct answer

4.2 How Will Skills 1 and 2 Be Tested?

The differences between Skills 1 and 2 require a different approach in order to assess whether you have acquired the reasoning skills that will help you to be successful in medical school and as a physician. In this section, we will explore how the skills will be tested on each of the four question types, as well as how these questions are going to appear on Test Day.

SKILL 1

Skill 1 questions will be fairly simple. These are often easy points on Test Day, as long as you have conducted a thorough and effective content review prior to Test Day. However, getting Skill 1 questions correct on Test Day is only a small piece of earning a high score; you will have to be proficient in all four skills.

Discrete questions
- Straightforward, direct questions, either addressing relationships between concepts or identification of a single detail or characteristics regarding a concept.

Questions that stand alone from the passage
- Very similar to discrete questions, often thematically related to the passage.
- Will require identification of a single concept or relationship without a multistep reasoning process.

Questions that require data from the passage
- Will require minimal analysis of data from the passage, often connection of information from the passage to scientific concepts
- Identification of a scientific concept with a graph or table may be required.
- A mathematical equation may be presented and you may be requested to use this equation to solve a problem.

Questions that require the goal of the passage
- Skill 1 questions are unlikely to require this level of analysis. When they do, the questions will be simple and require identification of a relationship between a scientific concept and a fundamental piece of information in the passage.

SKILL 2

Skill 2 questions will be extremely common on Test Day. In fact, this was an extremely common question type on previous versions of the MCAT.

Discrete questions
- Will require you to understand a particular concept, and then link that concept with the task of the question.
- No passage will be associated, thus the scope of the answer will be limited to the scope of the question.

Questions that stand alone from the passage
- Much like discrete questions, but often thematically related to the passage.
- May require application of knowledge related to the passage, but not specifically mentioned in it.

Questions that require data from the passage
- Likely to require calculations, evaluation of data and connection of the data with scientific principles, and use of scientific data and knowledge to draw conclusions related to information presented in the passage.
- May require interpretation or analysis of graphs, tables, or diagrams.
- You may have to apply information obtained from the passage to a new situation not presented in the passage.
- You may be asked to analyze the relationship between two variables, in terms of causation and correlation.

Questions that require the goal of the passage
- Will require you to interpret the passage as a whole, and connect the passage with your knowledge about scientific principles or your knowledge about natural or social phenomenon.
- May require you to identify arguments about cause and effect as supported by the passage or new evidence provided in the question stem.
- Information may be presented in the question stem that either strengthens or weakens the argument made in the passage. You will be asked to identify how this new information is related to the passage as a whole.
- You may be expected to draw conclusions from the information presented in the passage, or evaluate the validity of a conclusion based on evidence from the passage.

4.3 Getting the Edge with Skills 1 and 2

Content knowledge is required for the MCAT, especially for Skill 1 questions. However, content knowledge is not enough for success on Test Day. The MCAT uses science as a vehicle to test critical thinking skills, especially on Skill 2 questions. In order to get the edge on Skills 1 and 2, a thorough and efficient content review must be coupled with a significant number of practice questions. A common mistake made by students when studying for the MCAT is focusing too heavily on content review and not enough on practice questions and passages. The only way to be successful on Test Day is to integrate content review with practice questions and passages. Success on Skill 2 questions requires that you acquire a deeper level of learning than what is required in undergraduate science courses. In order to do this, ensure that you review content and then immediately apply content to practice passage and questions.

Every question that you answer incorrectly on a practice passage or question is an opportunity to review how you approached the question. Systematically reviewing questions to determine weaknesses in your critical thinking skills will help you to identify and address those weaknesses. If you find that you are stuck at a score plateau on practice tests, it is essential to take an honest look at your critical thinking skills to break through that plateau.

When the AAMC released the specifications for the 2015 MCAT, it established the expected distribution to be **35% Skill 1** and **45% Skill 2** questions for each of the science sections.

CHAPTER FIVE

Skill 3

Modern medicine requires the practical application of research in the practice of evidence-based medicine. As a physician, you will constantly be seeking answers in research to determine prognoses, assess the appropriateness of a treatment modality for a given patient, and answer patients' questions. Evaluation of research is critical to the progress of all fields of medicine and will be a key component of your life as a physician.

In order to practice medicine in this way, certain basic skills are required, such as the ability to reason about the design and execution of research, otherwise known as Skill 3. In this section, we will discuss the specific characteristics of Skill 3 as well as how Skill 3 will be tested on the MCAT.

5.1 What Is Skill 3?

Skill 3 is divided into two main components: concepts behind scientific research and reasoning about ethical issues in research. This means that you must understand how studies are designed using the scientific method as a guiding principle, as well as the ethical issues present in research, especially in the use of human subjects.

SKILL 3 QUESTIONS TEST:

- Identification of the roles of past findings, theory, and observations in scientific inquiry
- Identification of testable hypotheses and research questions
- Ability to distinguish between samples and populations, and the identification of results that support generalizations about populations
- Identification of independent and independent variables
- Ability to reason about the features of research studies that suggest relationships among variables, including causality
- Ability to draw conclusions from results produced by research studies
- Identification of how results from research may apply to real-world situations
- Reasoning skills with respect to ethical issues in scientific research

5.2 Fundamental Concepts of Skill 3

Skill 3 questions will ask you to apply scientific concepts to your understanding of research in both the life sciences and behavioral sciences. However, this information is rarely, if ever, covered in your undergraduate science classes. The scientific method is usually mentioned, but it is unlikely that it is covered in the level of detail that you will need on Test Day. In this section, we will discuss the basic concepts that you need to be successful on Skill 3 questions on Test Day.

THE SCIENTIFIC METHOD

The scientific method is the basic paradigm of all scientific inquiry. It is the established protocol for transitioning from a question to a new body of knowledge. The steps in the scientific method are:

Generate a testable question
- Occurs after observing something anomalous in another scientific inquiry or in daily life

Gather data and resources
- Phase of journal and database searches and information compilation
- Look at all information, not just those consistent with the opinion of the investigator

Form a hypothesis
- Often in the form of an if-then statement, which will be tested in subsequent steps

Collect new data
- Collect data by experimentation (manipulation and control of variables of interest) or by observation (usually involves no changes in the subject's environment)

Analyze the data
- Look for trends
- Perform mathematical manipulations to solidify the relationship(s) between the variables

Interpret the data and existing hypothesis
- Consider whether the data analysis is consistent with the original hypothesis
- If data is inconsistent, consider alternate hypotheses

Publish
- Provide an opportunity for peer review
- Summarize what was done during the previous steps in the publication

Verify results
- Repeat the experiment to verify results under new conditions

BASIC CONCEPTS IN SCIENTIFIC RESEARCH

Basic science research—the kind conducted in a laboratory, and not on people—is generally the easiest to design because the experimenter has the most control. Often a causal relationship is being examined because the hypothesis generally states a condition and an outcome. In order to make generalizations about our experiments, the outcome of interest must not be obscured. In addition, there must also be a method by which causality may be demonstrated, which is relatively simple in basic science research, but less so in other research areas. This requires the use of a control, or standard, and an identified set of variables.

Controls

In basic science research, conditions are applied to multiple trials of the same experiment that are as near to identical as possible.

- A control or standard is a method of verifying results.
- Controls can also be used to separate experimental conditions altogether.
- Positive and negative controls are used as points of comparison or a group of controls that can be used to create a curve of known values.
  - Positive controls are those that ensure a change in the dependent variable when it is expected. For example, if a new assay is developed for the detection of HIV infection, a number of blood samples known to contain HIV virus can act as a positive control.
  - Negative controls ensure no change in the dependent variable when no change is expected. For example, the same new HIV assay would be used to test samples known to be normal. In pharmaceutical trials, a negative control could be used to assess the placebo effect. An observed or reported change when an individual is given an inactive substance such as a sugar pill is an example of the placebo effect.

Causality

By manipulating all of the relevant experimental conditions, basic science researchers can often establish causality. Causality is an if-then relationship, and is often the hypothesis being tested.

- Independent variable–the variable that is manipulated or changed.
- Dependent variable–the variable that is measured or observed.
- If a change in the independent variable always causes a change in the dependent variable, and the change in the dependent variable does not change without change in the independent variable, then a relationship is said to be causal.

Error Sources

In basic science research, experimental bias is usually minimal. The most likely way for an experimenter's personal opinions to be incorporated is through the generation of a faulty hypothesis from incomplete early data and resource collection. Other sources of error include manipulation of results by eliminating trials without appropriate background, or by failing to publish works that contradict the experimenter's own hypothesis.

The low levels of bias introduced by the experimenter do not eliminate all error from basic science research. Measurements are especially important in the laboratory sciences, and the instruments may give faulty readings. Instrument error may affect accuracy, precision, or both. Accuracy, also called validity, is the ability of an instrument to measure a true value. Precision, also called reliability, is the ability of the instrument to read consistently, or within a narrow range. Since bias is a systematic error in data, only an inaccurate tool will introduce bias, but an imprecise tool will still introduce error.

HUMAN SUBJECTS RESEARCH

Research using human subjects is considerably more complex, and the level of experimental control is invariably lower than basic science research. In human subjects research, there are both experimental and observational studies.

EXPERIMENTAL APPROACH

Experimental research, similar to basic science research, attempts to establish causality. An independent variable is manipulated and changes in a dependent variable are identified and quantified (if possible). Since subjects are in less-controlled conditions, the data analysis phase is more complicated than in laboratory studies. Two of the most fundamental concepts of the experimental approach are randomization and blinding.

Randomization

- Method used to control for differences between subject groups in biomedical research.
- Uses an algorithm to place each subject into either a control group that receives no treatment or a sham treatment, or one or more treatment groups.
- Results are measured in all groups.
- Ideally, each group is perfectly matched on conditions such as age and gender.

Blinding

- Many measures in biomedical research are subjective. Perception of the subject and the investigator may be biased by knowing the group to which the subject has been assigned.
- When a study is blinded, the subject and/or the investigator are not aware of the group in which the subject has been placed.
- Single-blind experiments–only the patient or the assessor is blinded
- Double-blind experiments–neither the subject nor the assessor (or even the investigator) are aware of the group into which the subject has been placed
- Lack of blinding results in diminished placebo effect in the control group, but the presence of the placebo effect in the treatment group

In biomedical research, data analysis must account for variables outside the independent and dependent variables. Most often, these include gender and age; lifestyle variables such as smoking; body mass index; and other factors that may affect the measured outcomes. Confounding variables, or variables that are not controlled or measured, may also affect the outcome.

KAPLAN

OBSERVATIONAL APPROACH

The observational approach is often adopted to study certain causal relationships for which an experiment is either impractical or unethical. Observational studies in medicine fit into three different categories:

Cohort studies

- Subjects are sorted into two groups based on differences in risk factors (exposures), and then assessed at various intervals to determine how many subjects in each group had a certain outcome.

Cross-sectional studies

- Patients are categorized into different groups at a single point in time based on the presence or absence of a characteristic, such as a disease.

Case-control studies

- Subjects are separated into two groups based on the presence or absence of some outcome.
- The study looks backwards to assess how many subjects in each group had exposure to a particular risk factor.

Identifying causality isn't necessarily simple. Hill's criteria describe the components of an observed relationship that increase the likelihood of causality in that relationship. While only the first criterion is necessary for the relationship to be causal, it is not sufficient. Increased likelihood of causality is signified by an increased number of met criteria. Hill's criteria do not provide an absolute guideline on causality of a relationship. Thus, for any observational study, the relationship should be described as correlation.

Hill's Criteria	
Criterion	**Description**
Temporality	Exposure (independent variable) must occur before the outcome (dependent variable)
Strength	Greater changes in the independent variable will cause a similar change in the dependent variable if the relationship is causal
Dose-response Relationship	As the independent variable increases, there is a proportional increase in the response (dependent variable)
Consistency	The relationship is found in multiple settings
Plausibility	The presence of a reasonable mechanism for the relationship between the variables as supported by existing literature
Consideration of Alternate Explanations	If all other plausible explanations have been eliminated, the remaining explanation is more likely
Experiment	An experiment can confirm causality
Specificity	Change in the outcome (dependent) variable is only produced by an associated change in the independent variable
Coherence	New data and hypotheses are consistent with the current state of scientific knowledge

ERROR SOURCES

In addition to the measurement error found in basic science research, we must be aware of bias and error introduced by using human subjects as part of an experimental or observational model. As mentioned earlier, bias is a systematic error. As such, it generally does not impact the precision of the data, but rather skews the data in one direction or the other. Bias is a result of flaws in the data collection phase of an experimental or observational study. Confounding is an error during analysis.

Selection Bias

- Most prevalent type of bias
- Occurs when subjects used for the study are not representative of the target population
- May also apply in cases where one gender is more prevalent than another, or when there are differences in the age profile of the experiment group and the population
- Measurement and assessment of selection bias occurs before any intervention

Detection Bias

- Results from educated professionals applying knowledge in an inconsistent manner
- Often occurs when prior studies have indicated that there is a correlation between two variables; when the researcher finds one of the variables, then he or she is more likely to search for the second, possibly related variable. That makes the second variable more likely to be found, since the investigator is looking for it.

Observation Bias

- Also known as the Hawthorne effect
- Occurs when the behavior of study participants is altered when the participants are aware that they are being studied
- Systematic and occurs prior to data analysis

Confounding

- Data analysis error
- Data may or may not be flawed, but an incorrect relationship is characterized
- Variables that are not controlled or measured, but present

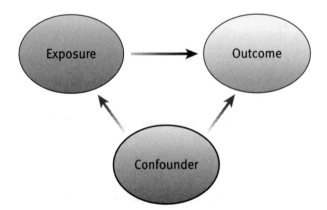

KAPLAN

ETHICAL ISSUES IN RESEARCH

In medicine, there are four core ethical tenets: beneficence, nonmaleficence, autonomy, and justice.

- Beneficence: the obligation to act in the patient's best interest
- Nonmaleficence: the obligation to avoid treatments or interventions in which the potential for harm outweighs the potential for benefit
- Patient autonomy: the responsibility to respect patients' decisions and choices about their own healthcare
- Justice: the responsibility to treat similar patients with similar care, and to distribute healthcare resources fairly

In research, these principles are replaced by a slightly modified set as defined by the Belmont Report, a landmark document published by the National Commission for the Protection of Human Subjects in Biomedical and Behavioral Research. According to the Belmont Report, the three necessary pillars of research include respect for persons, justice, and a slightly more inclusive version of beneficence.

Respect for persons
- Includes the need for honesty between the subjects and the researcher and generally, but not always, prohibits deception.
- Also includes the process of informed consent, in which a patient must be adequately counseled on the procedures, risks, benefits, and goals of a study to make a knowledgeable decision about whether or not to participate. Consent may be withdrawn at any time.
- Prohibits a coercive influence over the subjects.
- Institutional review boards are in place to provide systematic protections against unethical studies.
- Vulnerable persons, including children, pregnant women, and prisoners, require special protections above and beyond those taken with the general population.
- Confidentiality is generally considered to be part of respect for persons during research.

Justice

- Applies to both the selection of a research topic and the execution of the research.
- Morally relevant differences are defined as those differences between individuals that are considered an appropriate reason to treat them differently. These differences include age and population size. Race, ethnicity, sexual orientation, and financial status are NOT considered morally relevant differences. However, religion is a special case in that certain interventions are prohibited by a given religion. Thus, avoidance of that treatment in individuals of that religion is consistent with patient autonomy.
- Risks inherent in the study must be distributed fairly so as not to impose undue harm on a particular group. However, when there is a population that is likely to receive a greater benefit from a study, this group may necessarily bear a greater proportion of the risk. Thus, likelihood of benefit may be a morally relevant difference between individuals in certain situations.

Beneficence

- It must be the intent of a study to cause a net positive change for both the study population and the general population, and it must be done in such a way as to minimize any potential harm.
- Research should be conducted in the least invasive, painful, or traumatic way possible. When choosing between two methods of measurement, the least painful and invasive method should be employed.

5.3 How Will Skill 3 Be Tested?

Skill 3 questions will require a considerable amount of background information, as study design and execution are generally not coverable in a single question stem. Thus, the more complex and nuanced Skill 3 questions are likely to either require data from the passage or the goal of the passage. These Skill 3 questions are likely to also require the scientific reasoning skills tested in Skill 2. It is important to note that while the four skills have been separated neatly into categories by the AAMC, the separations may not be quite so distinct on Test Day, as most questions will still require some level of scientific reasoning.

Discrete questions
- Questions that are NOT associated with a descriptive passage
- Likely to focus on basic research concepts, including identification of variables; and concepts of measurement, including accuracy and precision

Questions that stand alone from the passage
- Similar to discrete questions
- Likely to focus on more basic concepts of study design and execution

Questions that require data from the passage
- Be prepared for questions that require you to use data from the passage to identify variables and relationships between variables and test your the ability to distinguish between causation and correlation

Questions that require the goal of the passage
- These questions will require an understanding of the passage as a whole and identification of the goal of the passage
- May ask for alternative explanations for the phenomena described in the passage as well as examination of evidence presented in the passage
- Questions may require you to draw conclusions from evidence presented in the passage, as well as identify conclusions that are not supported by the passage
- Expect to evaluate study design in light of results and conclusions drawn from the information
- Identification of independent and dependent variables as well as confounding variables and types of bias

5.4 Getting the Edge in Skill 3 Questions

Much of what is tested in Skill 3 is not necessarily presented in introductory level courses. Some test-takers will have taken courses with more emphasis in research, while others may have little to no experience in this area. You can maximize your score by developing a thorough understanding of the topics discussed in this chapter. The MCAT will assume a certain level of knowledge in the area of research, and it is essential that you develop that knowledge by reading research articles and becoming comfortable with the general format and discussion present in all research studies, including background, literature review, procedure, results, and discussion. As you read more research studies, you will gain increasing comfort with research as a part of scientific inquiry. Be sure to read research in all subject areas tested on the MCAT, including biology, biochemistry, general chemistry, organic chemistry, physics, psychology, and sociology. Most students are comfortable with lab research, but are less comfortable with research involving human subjects. Focus your review of study design in the areas that are more likely to involve human subjects, including biology, psychology, and sociology.

When the AAMC released the specifications for the 2015 MCAT, it established the expected distribution to be **10% Skill 3** for each of the science sections.

CHAPTER SIX

Skill 4

By now, you have no doubt realized that the MCAT places a high level of importance on your ability to understand the process by which new scientific and medical knowledge is acquired by research. As discussed previously, Skill 3 questions will test your ability to reason about the design and execution of research in the life sciences and behavioral sciences. However, it is Skill 4 questions that will test your ability to understand and draw conclusions using the data collected by research.

6.1 What Is Skill 4?

Academic papers are extremely predictable. A research paper generally starts with an abstract—a few short paragraphs reflecting the major points of the rest of the paper. The authors then provide an expanded introduction, materials and methods, data, and discussion. The key to a high-quality research paper is making this discussion unnecessary–any scientists, when given the prior sections, should be led to the same conclusions as those given by the author. The testmakers are keenly aware of this fact. On Test Day, you may be presented with research in the form of an experiment-based passage, and part of your task will be inferring the important conclusions that can be supported by the findings of the study.

Skill 4 questions will test your ability to draw conclusions using both raw data and graphical representations of data. Skill 4 can be divided into two main components: interpretation of patterns in tables, figures, and graphs; and drawing conclusions from the data presented. However, you will be expected to use statistical reasoning skills in order to draw conclusions. While identification of patterns is important, you must also be able to determine if these patterns are statistically significant.

SKILL 4 QUESTIONS TEST:

- Use, analysis, and interpretation of data in tables, graphs, and figures
- Determination of the most effective way to represent data for specific scientific observations and data sets
- Use of central tendency (mean, median, and mode) and dispersion measures (range, interquartile range, and standard deviation) to describe data
- Identification and reasoning regarding random and systematic error
- Determination of the statistical significance and uncertainty of a data set using statistical significance levels and confidence intervals
- Identification of relationships and explanations of those relationships using data
- Prediction of outcomes using data
- Ability to draw conclusions and answer research questions using data

6.2 Fundamental Concepts of Skill 4

Many students take biostatistics or some other statistics class in preparation for a major in biology or the life sciences. However, many students who take the MCAT have not taken a statistics course. Thus, the basic information required to answer these questions is briefly covered in this section.

MEASURES OF CENTRAL TENDENCY

Measures of central tendency describe a central value around which the other values in the data set are clustered. However, this central value can be described in multiple ways, including the mean, median, and mode.

Mean

The mean or average of a set of data is calculated by adding up the individual values within the data set and dividing the result by the number of values. Mean values are a good indicator of central tendency when all of the values tend to be fairly close to one another. Having an outlier, or an extremely large or extremely small value compared to the other data values, can shift the mean toward one end or the other.

Median

The median value for a set of data is its midpoint, where half of the data points are greater than the value and half are smaller. In data sets with an odd number of values, the median will actually be one of the data points. In data sets with an even number of values, the median will be the mean of the two central data points. To calculate the median, a data set must first be listed in increasing order. The median position can be calculated as shown in Equation 6.1:

$$\text{median position} = \frac{(n + 1)}{2}$$

Equation 6.1

where n is the number of data values. In a data set with an even number of data points, this equation will solve for a number such as 9.5. This means that the median lies between the ninth and tenth value of the data set, and is the average of the ninth and tenth values.

The median tends to be the least susceptible to outliers, but may not be useful for data sets with very large ranges (the distance between the largest and smallest data points) or multiple modes.

If the mean and median are far from each other, this implies the presence of outliers or a skewed distribution, as discussed later in this chapter. If the mean and the median are very close, this implies a symmetrical distribution.

Mode

The mode, quite simply, is the number that appears most often in a data set. There may be multiple modes in a data set, or—if all numbers appear equally—there can even be no mode for a data set. When we examine distributions, the peaks represent modes. The mode is not typically used as a measure of central tendency for a data set, but the number of modes, and the distance between the modes, is often informative. If a data set has two modes with a small number of values between the modes, it may be useful to analyze these portions separately or to look for confounding variables that may be responsible for dividing the distribution into two parts.

DISTRIBUTIONS

Often a single statistic for a data set is insufficient for a detailed or relevant analysis. In this case, it is useful to look at the overall shape of the distribution as well as specifics about how that shape impacts our interpretation of data. The shape of a distribution will impact all of the measures of central tendency, as well as some measures of distribution.

Normal Distributions

In statistics, normal distributions are the most common. Even when we know that this is not quite the case, we can use special techniques so that our data will approximate a normal distribution. This is very important because the normal distribution has been "solved" in the sense that we can transform any normal distribution to a standard distribution with a mean of zero and a standard deviation of one, and then use the newly generated curve to get information about probability or percentages of populations. The normal distribution is also the basis for the bell curve seen in many scenarios and in Figure 6.1 below, including exam scores on the MCAT.

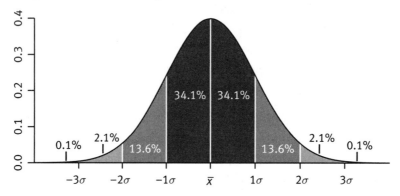

Figure 6.1 The normal distribution
The mean, median, and mode are at the center of the distribution.
Approximately 68% of the distribution is within one standard deviation
of the mean, 95% within two, and 99% within three.

Skewed Distributions

Distributions are not always symmetrical. A skewed distribution is one that contains a tail on one side or the other of the data set (see Figure 6.2). On the MCAT, skewed distributions are most often tested by identification of the type of skewed distribution. This is often an area of confusion for students because the visual shift in the data appears opposite the direction of the skew. A negatively skewed distribution has a tail on the left (or negative) side, whereas a positively skewed distribution has a tail on the right (or positive side). In summary, use the tail (not the peak) to determine the direction of the skew.

Because the mean is more susceptible to outliers than the median, the mean of a negatively skewed distribution is generally lower than the median, while the mean of a positively skewed distribution is generally higher than the median.

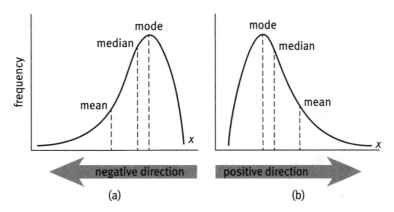

Figure 6.2 Skewed distributions
(a) Negatively skewed distribution, with mean lower than median;
(b) Positively skewed distribution, with mean higher than median.

Bimodal Distributions

Some distributions have two or more peaks. A distribution containing two peaks with a valley in between is called bimodal (see Figure 6.3). It is important to note that a bimodal distribution might have only one mode if one peak is slightly higher than the other. The presence of two peaks of different sizes does not discount a distribution from being considered bimodal. If there is sufficient separation of the two peaks, or a sufficiently small amount of data within the valley region, bimodal distributions can often be analyzed as two separate distributions.

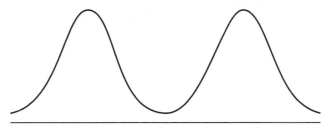

Figure 6.3 Bimodal distribution

MEASURES OF DISTRIBUTION

Distributions can also be characterized by distance between the highest and lowest values, as well as distance from the mean value.

Range

Range is an absolute measure of the spread of a data set. The range of a data set is the difference between the highest and lowest values. Range does not consider the number of items in the data set, nor does it consider the placement of any measures of central tendency. Therefore, range is heavily affected by the presence of data outliers. In cases where it is not possible to calculate the standard deviation for a normal distribution because the entire data set is not provided, it is possible to approximate the standard deviation as one-fourth of the range.

Standard Deviation

Standard deviation is the most informative measure of distribution, but it is also the most mathematically laborious. It is calculated relative to the mean of the data. On Test Day, you may be asked to calculate a standard deviation. However, it is more likely that you will have to apply the concept of the standard deviation to identifying an outlier. In addition, standard deviation can also be used to describe the distance from the mean of a particular value.

- Sixty-eight percent of the data points fall within one standard deviation of the mean.
- Ninety-five percent of the data points fall within two standard deviations of the mean.
- Ninety-nine percent of the data points fall within three standard deviations of the mean.
- Values that are more than four standard deviations from the mean care considered outliers.

Outliers

Outliers typically result from one of three causes:

- A true statistical anomaly
- A measurement error
- A distribution that is not approximated by the normal distribution

When an outlier is found, it should trigger an automatic investigation to determine which of the three causes applies. It is likely that you will be asked to determine the most likely cause of an outlier on Test Day. If there is a measurement error, the data point should be excluded from analysis. However, the other two situations are less clear.

If an outlier is the result of a true measurement, but it is not representative of the population, it may be weighted to reflect its rarity, including normally, or excluded from the analysis depending on the purpose of the study and preselected protocols. The decision should be made before a study begins—not once an outlier has been found. When outliers are an indication that a data set may not approximate the normal distribution, repeated samples or larger samples will generally demonstrate if this is true.

STATISTICAL TESTING

Hypothesis testing and confidence intervals allow us to draw conclusions about populations based on our sample data. Both are interpreted in the context of probabilities and what we deem an acceptable risk of error.

Hypothesis Testing

Hypothesis testing begins with an idea about what may be different between two populations. We have a null hypothesis, which is always a hypothesis of equivalence. In other words, the null hypothesis says that two populations are equal, or that a single population can be described by a parameter equal to a given value. The alternative hypothesis may be nondirectional (saying that the populations are not equal) or directional.

The most common hypothesis tests are z- or t-tests, which rely on the standard distribution or the closely related t-distribution. From the data collected, a test statistic is calculated and compared to a table to determine the likelihood that the statistic was obtained by random chance (under the assumption that our null hypothesis is true). This is our p-value. We then compare our p-value to a significance level (α); 0.05 is commonly used. For a directional test, if the p-value is greater than α, then we fail to reject the null hypothesis, which means that there is not a statistically significant difference between the two populations. If the p-value is less than α, then we reject the null hypothesis and state that there is a difference between the two groups. If the alternative hypothesis is not directional, we compare p-value to $\frac{\alpha}{2}$ instead. Again, when the null hypothesis is rejected, we state that our results are statistically significant.

The value of α is a level of risk that we are willing to accept for incorrectly rejecting the null hypothesis. This is also called a type I error. In other words, a type I error is the likelihood that we report a difference between two populations when one does not actually exist. A type II error occurs when we incorrectly fail to reject the null hypothesis. In other words, a type II error is the likelihood that we report no difference between two populations when one actually exists. The probability of a type II error is sometimes symbolized by β. The probability of correctly rejecting a false null hypothesis (reporting a difference between two populations when one actually exists) is referred to as power, and is equal to $1-\beta$. Finally, the probability of correctly failing to reject a true null hypothesis (reporting no difference between two populations when one does not exist) is referred to as confidence. Table 6.1 summarizes all of these scenarios for your review.

		Truth About the Population	
		H_0 true (no difference)	H_a true (difference exists)
Conclusion Based on Sample	Reject H_0	Type I error (α)	Power ($1 - \beta$)
	Fail to reject H_0	Confidence	Type II error (β)

Table 6.1 Results of hypothesis testing

Confidence Intervals

Confidence intervals are essentially the reverse of hypothesis testing. With a confidence interval, we determine a range of values from the sample mean and standard deviation. Rather than finding a p-value, we begin with a desired confidence level (95 percent is standard) and use a table to find its corresponding z- or t-score. When we multiply the z- or t-score by the standard deviation, and then add or subtract this number from the mean, we create a range of values. For example, consider a population for which we wish to know the mean age. We draw a sample from that population and find that the mean age of the sample is 30, with a standard deviation of 3. If we wish to have 95 percent confidence, the corresponding z-score (which would be provided on Test Day) is 1.96. Thus, the range is $30 - (3)(1.96) = 24.12$ to 35.88. We can then report that we are 95 percent confident that the true mean age of the population from which this sample is drawn is between 24.12 and 35.88.

APPLYING DATA

In an academic paper, the discussion portion is where the data gathered and interpreted is applied to the original problem. We can then begin drawing conclusions and creating new questions based on our results.

Correlation and Causation

Correlation refers to a connection—direct relationship, inverse relationship, or otherwise—between data. Correlation does not necessarily imply causation; we must avoid this assumption when there is insufficient evidence to draw such a conclusion. If an experiment cannot be performed, we must rely on Hill's criteria. Remember, the only one of Hill's criteria that is universally required for causation is temporality.

In the Context of Scientific Knowledge

When interpreting data, it is important that we not only state the apparent relationship between data, but also begin to draw connections to other concepts in science and to our background knowledge. At a minimum, the impact of the new data would be integrated into all future investigations on the topic. Additionally, we must develop a plausible rationale for the results. Finally, we must make decisions about our data's impact on the real world, and determine whether or not our evidence is substantial and impactful enough to necessitate changes in understanding or policy.

6.3 How Will Skill 4 Be Tested?

Skill 4 questions are likely to appear in a variety of scenarios on Test Day. This skill lends itself easily to a variety of scenarios and levels of information.

- **Discrete questions**
  - Questions NOT associated with a descriptive passage.
  - Likely to ask fairly simple questions related to Skill 4.
  - Calculations of a mean, median, mode, or range are likely to appear.
  - May also be related to fundamental concepts, including types of error or bias.

- **Questions that stand alone from the passage**
  - Very similar to discrete questions.
  - Likely to be fairly simple and not require a large amount of analysis.

- **Questions that require data from the passage**
  - May require analysis or interpretation of a chart, graph, or table.
  - Calculations may be required.
  - Comparisons between variables may be required.

- **Questions that require the goal of the passage**
  - These questions are the most in-depth of all the Skill 4 question types.
  - Likely to require you to evaluate data to determine if the data support the conclusion presented in the passage.
  - May also ask you to draw conclusions from the data and information presented in the passage, requiring integration of the passage, data, and statistical analysis.
  - Expect that some Skill 4 questions in this category will require you to identify relationships between variables or evaluate the study for error or bias based on your statistical analysis.

6.4 Getting the Edge in Skill 4

Skill 4 requires an understanding of how research data is evaluated. The best way to identify your strengths and weaknesses in this area is to actually read academic papers. However, just reading the academic paper is not enough. You have to go through each calculation that they have performed and interpret the paper in light of your own statistical analysis. Think of yourself like a teacher grading a research paper. Read critically, and identify any flaws in their analysis of data, including miscalculations. Finally, after reading the paper, summarize the value of the information. If you had a patient whose disease or treatment course could be affected by the information in the paper, do you believe that the information in the paper is reliable? Is it statistically significant? Did the discussion in the paper actually address the questions set forth at the beginning of the paper? As you read more papers, these questions will become easier to answer.

In addition to reading papers, it is essential that you do a considerable number of practice questions in this area. Often, passages that are steeped in research will also present a number of Skill 3 questions. While we present these skills separately here, both are essential to understanding academic research papers. By seeking out practice passages and question sets that utilize both of these skills, these question types will become easier, and you will be able to maximize your score on Test Day.

When the AAMC released the specifications for the 2015 MCAT, it established the expected distribution to be 10% Skill 4 questions for each of the science sections.

Science Subject Review

CHAPTER SEVEN

Science Unit Overview

Now that you are more comfortable with the MCAT and the Kaplan Methods for the exam, it is time for us to dive into practice mode. The following chapters summarize the most salient takeaways of the testmaker's, or the AAMC's, content outlines with special emphasis on how you can use the information to succeed on Test Day.

7.1 Topic Overview

For your convenience, each science discipline covered on the exam is presented for your review before the practice. The content review for each subject includes:

- What is unique about that topic on the exam
- How you should expect to see the content on the exam
- How you can get the edge by using the Kaplan Methods
- A detailed, annotated outline of the topics and subtopics covered

7.2 Passages as Worked Examples

After the overview, you will have the opportunity to see exactly how the Kaplan Method can help tackle a challenge passage with passages as worked examples. You not only have the opportunity to try the passage on your own, but you also can see the Kaplan Method for questions demonstrated for each of the worked passages

7.3 Passages as Practice Problems

Following the science overview and worked examples, you will then have the opportunity to practice the Kaplan Methods on your own with practice problems (in the book and online).

In order to get the most out of your practice, be sure to note Question Types, Wrong Answer Pathologies, and Clues to the Correct Answer.

CHAPTER EIGHT

Behavioral Sciences

A significant factor influencing a patient's ability to heal from an injury or manage a chronic disease is that person's psychiatric and socioeconomic status. In considering treatment options for a patient, a physician must take into account the patient's ability to understand and adhere to a treatment plan. Patients with a psychiatric disorder or who are unable to afford their prescriptions are not likely to take medications as prescribed, unless the treatment regimen is simple and affordable. In an effort to emphasize the psychological and social aspects of medicine, the AAMC has added a section to the MCAT known as the Psychological, Social, and Biological Foundations of Behavior section. This section will be approximately 65 percent psychology, 30 percent sociology, and 5 percent biology. In addition, 5 percent of the psychology questions will cover biologically relevant topics.

8.1 Reading the Passage

Like the other sections, there will be two main passage types: information and experiment. However, the distinction is not as clear as in the other sections. Behavioral science passages will almost always discuss an experiment or study, even if the passage seems to be more informational. Many of these passages will be designed to test your ability to analyze experimental data and evaluate experimental design. The informational aspects of the passage will provide background or discuss a fundamental concept, and the attached experiment or study will be related to the passage topic. As such, you will be expected to use the same critical reading skills you have been using all along, but in a much more integrated way.

PASSAGE TYPES

Almost all of the passages will contain an experiment. However, the experiment itself will often be in the form of a large study. The data from the large study is most likely to be presented in the form of a chart or graph indicating the probability of some outcome or the likelihood of some characteristic among the study population.

However, the early parts of the passage will read like an information passage, much like the background portion of a peer-reviewed paper within the scientific disciplines. The passage will then often change course to present the hypothesis, variables, and procedure of the study. Finally, the results will be presented. Thus, the early parts of the passage containing information should be treated like an information passage, with reading aimed at getting the gist of the paragraph(s), without spending time analyzing the details. When discussion of the study begins, switch to a more experiment-based reading strategy, seeking out the hypothesis, procedure, and results. Finally, the chart, graph, or table will require analysis, but this analysis need not be done until a question requires it.

What to Expect: Behavioral Sciences

- Almost all passages will contain an experiment, especially psychology passages.
- Any passages that do not contain an experiment are more likely to be sociology passages. These passages will focus primarily on sociological theory.
- Many passages will blend subject matter and you will be expected to understand the connections between biology, psychology, and sociology.

The Sciences *vs.* Behavioral Sciences		
	The Core Sciences	**Behavioral Sciences**
Topics	Biology, Biochemistry, General Chemistry, Organic Chemistry, Physics	Biology, Psychology, Sociology
Passage Types	Information and experiment	Passages will mainly consist of information and experiment portions, but many passages will not fall neatly into either category
Questions	Will require a variety of skills from basic recall of information, application of information to a new situation, analysis of data, and evaluation of experiment design	Will require a variety of skills, but data analysis and evaluation of experiment design will be emphasized

OUTLINING THE PASSAGE

Regardless of how the passages in this section differ from those found in the other sections, the same Kaplan strategy should be applied. Read the passage quickly and efficiently, and create an outline to help you locate information when you start answering questions.

Scan for Structure

- Note the structure of the passage, noting the location of the paragraphs and any figures such as charts, graphs, tables, or diagrams.
- Determine the topic and degree of difficulty.
- Identify whether this passage will require a large time investment.
- Decide whether this passage is one to do now or later.

Read Strategically

- While reading the passage, decide whether the paragraph you are reading is presenting information or discussing an experiment.
- If the paragraph is presenting information, read it like an information passage by getting the gist of the paragraph and identifying the location of details.
- If the paragraph is describing an experiment, read it like an experiment passage by paying special attention to the hypothesis, procedure, and results.
- Identify the location of the data, but do not begin your analysis until a question requires it.

Label Each Component

- For information paragraphs, note the purpose or main idea of the paragraph.
- If there is list of details, note how the details are related to the main idea of the paragraph, and move on.
- If an experiment is discussed, note the hypothesis, procedure, and results.
- Note the relationship between any paragraphs and any charts, graphs, or tables.
- For each figure, write down what the figure is discussing.

Reflect on Your Outline

- At the end of the passage, determine the goal of the passage. Why was this passage written? What was the author trying to do? Another thing to consider is what the testmaker is trying to achieve with presenting this passage. Remember, passages in the behavioral sciences section are designed to test your ability to analyze and apply concepts in a logical fashion.

8.2 Answering the Questions

Behavioral sciences questions will seek to integrate concepts, especially with regard to data analysis and experimental design. However, the same basic four questions will be present.

- Discrete questions
  - Questions that are not connected to a passage.
  - Will be preceded by a warning such as "Questions 12–15 are NOT based on a descriptive passage."
  - Often will require you to recall or apply a basic concept, such as a theory or process.
  - Not likely to evaluate experimental design or data analysis.
- Questions that stand alone from the passage
  - Questions that accompany a passage but do not require information or data from the passage to identify the correct answer.
  - More likely to require application of a basic concept, theory, or process to a situation presented in the question stem.
- Questions that require data from the passage
  - Questions that require a piece of data or information from the passage, but do not require the goal of the passage.
  - These questions are likely to focus on data analysis or evaluation of experimental procedure.
  - May also focus on the information section of the passage, and require you to identify a detail presented.
- Questions that require the goal of the passage
  - Questions that require the goal of the passage, or a fundamental grasp of the passage as a whole.
  - These questions are likely to focus on the results and discussion of the results of an experiment.
  - May also assess your ability to analyze data or evaluate an experimental design but from a broader perspective, such as a change that could be made in the procedure that would affect the results in a particular way.
  - May also require you to evaluate the results of an experiment and apply those results to the information presented earlier in the passage.
  - Likely to require application of basic concepts and theories to understanding the passage as a whole.

DETERMINING THE PURPOSE OF THE QUESTION

Even though the behavioral sciences passages and questions are somewhat different from those seen in the sciences, the questions are still designed to test the same basic analytical skills. Thus, the same Kaplan question strategy applies. In addition, having a basic strategy that you go to for each and every question combats any nervousness you may experience, especially as you encounter topics with which you are not as comfortable. The Kaplan question strategy provides a framework that aids in the identification of the correct answer, prevents hasty selection of incorrect answers, and combats test anxiety.

1. Assess the Question

- Read the question, but avoid reading the answer choices.
- Assess the topic and degree of difficulty.
- Identify the level of time involvement: is this question likely to take a tremendous amount of time to identify the answer?
- Make a decision–is this question one to do now or later?
- Good questions to do now in the behavioral sciences are those that stand alone from the passage, as these are generally quick and easy points.

2. Plan Your Attack

- If you decide to do the question now, determine a plan.
- Identify the task of the question. What are you being asked to do?
- Does the question require information from the passage? How much information and where can that information be found?
- Does this question focus on theory presented in the passage or analysis of data and/or experimental procedure?

3. Execute Your Plan

- Carry out the plan as determined in the previous step.
- Analyze the data, evaluate the experimental design, locate the information required, and connect the information, data, and experimental design with the information you already know.

4. Answer the Question by Matching, Eliminating, or Guessing

- Match your answer with the correct answer choice.
- If there is no clear match, proceed to elimination of incorrect answers. Incorrect answers in this section will resemble those in the sciences and those in CARS. Some of the answer choices may be extreme with words such as never, always, and only. Other incorrect answer choices will not make sense, running counter to your knowledge base.
- If you cannot come to a clear answer, get down to two probable answer choices. Make an educated guess by at least having a reason for choosing an answer choice. Your reason need not be concrete or irrefutable, just a reason why that one seems more correct.
- Mark your answer and move on to the next question.

8.3 Getting the Edge in Behavioral Sciences

Earning a high score on Test Day in behavioral sciences requires the ability to reason and apply what you already know to new situations. This requires a level of learning that is often different from that required by undergraduate courses. Not only do you need to understand the definitions and theories, but you also need to know the real world applications of those theories. Getting the edge in behavioral sciences requires practice by working through a significant number of questions in the topic in order to grasp the level of thinking required for this topic.

In addition, some level of flexibility in approaching the passages will be required. In the sciences, the passages will fall neatly into two categories: experiment and information. In the behavioral sciences, this distinction is no longer possible on many passages. The first half of many passages will read like an information passage, and the second half will present an experiment related to the information presented earlier in the passage. This forces you, as the test-taker, to handle both aspects within one passage. In your outline, note if the paragraph is related to information or experiment—this will help you find the information you need in a timely manner.

Identification of the task of the question will ensure that you look for information in the correct place in the passage. Some questions will require data analysis and evaluation of experimental procedure, meaning that the experiment portion of the passage will be required. More theoretical questions are likely to require the information portion. However, this may vary depending on the task of the question. The task of the question will guide you to the correct location in the passage.

8.4 Step-by-Step Guide to Behavioral Sciences Passages

OUTLINING THE PASSAGE

- Scan for structure
  - ○ Determine whether to do this passage now or later.
  - ○ Identify the structure of the passage, including charts, graphs, tables, or diagrams.

- Read strategically
  - ○ Identify the portions of the passage that are more related to information, and those that describe an experiment.
  - ○ Identify the topic area of the passage: sociology or psychology.
  - ○ Pay special attention to the relationships between concepts.
  - ○ Determine the hypothesis, procedure, and results of the experiment.
  - ○ Identify which information is presented in each table, graph, or chart.

- Label each component
  - ○ Write down the purpose of each paragraph and figure.
  - ○ Note which portions of the passage are information and which are related to an experiment or study.
  - ○ Identify any connections between concepts within the passage.

- Reflect on your outline
  - ○ Determine the goal of the passage and write it down.
  - ○ Identify the concepts within the passage in an effort to anticipate questions.
  - ○ Anticipate the type of analysis that may be required.

ANSWERING THE QUESTIONS

1. Assess the question
- Determine whether this question should be done now or later.
- Identify the topic and the degree of difficulty.
- Good questions to do now in behavioral sciences are those that do not require the passage or do not require extensive analysis.

2. Plan your attack
- Determine what you already know, and what information you need.
- Identify the task of the question.
- Identify where to find the required information: the passage, the question, your outline, or your own knowledge.
- If you have to go back to the passage, determine where to find the required information by using your outline.
- If data analysis is required, identify the correct data set, as there may be multiple data representations.

3. Execute your plan
- Analyze the data, go back to the passage, and carry out your plan.
- If you get stuck analyzing data, remember that the trend of the data is often enough to yield a correct answer choice.

4. Answer the question by matching, eliminating, or guessing
- Match your answer to the answer choices.
- If there is not match, eliminate incorrect answer choices. Some of the answer choices may not make sense; eliminate those first.
- If elimination does not provide a clear answer, guess between two probable answers.

KAPLAN

8.5 Preparing for the MCAT: Psychology

These are the psychology topics you are likely to see on Test Day.

SENSORY PROCESSING

- Familiarity with the fundamentals of sensation, including thresholds, Weber's law, signal detection theory, and sensory adaptation, and psychophysics
- Knowing how sensory information is received via sensory receptors, including sensory pathways and types of sensory receptors

VISION

- Recognizing the structure and function of the eye
- Processing of visual information, including visual pathways in the brain, parallel processing, and feature detection

HEARING

- Recognizing the structure and function of the ear
- Processing of auditory information, including auditory pathways in the brain
- Understanding the role of hair cells in sensory reception

OTHER SENSES

- Perception of the body (somatosensation) and pain perception
- Taste, including taste buds as chemoreceptors that detect specific chemicals
- Smell, including the olfactory cells/chemoreceptors that detect specific chemicals, pheromones, and olfactory pathways in the brain
- Determining how the brain senses the location of the body in space, including kinesthetic sense and vestibular sense

PERCEPTION

- Processing of information, including bottom-up and top-down processing
- Organization of perception, including depth, form, motion, and constancy
- Explaining Gestalt principles

ATTENTION

- Recalling the definitions of attention, including selective attention and divided attention

COGNITION

- Recalling the definition and characteristics of the information-processing model
- Knowing fundamental concepts of cognitive development, including Piaget's stages of cognitive development, cognitive changes in late adulthood, role of culture in cognitive development, and the influence of heredity and environment on cognitive development
- Identifying biological factors that affect cognition
- Models of problem-solving and decision-making, including types of problem-solving, barriers to effective problem-solving, and approaches to problem-solving
- Fundamental concepts of problem-solving including heuristics and biases, biases, including overconfidence and belief perseverance
- Fundamental concepts of intellectual functioning, including multiple theories of intelligence, influence of heredity and environment on intelligence, and variations in intellectual ability

CONSCIOUSNESS

- Identification of various states of consciousness, including alertness, sleep, hypnosis, and meditation
- Fundamental concepts of sleep, including stages of sleep, sleep cycles and changes to sleep cycles, sleep and circadian rhythms, dreaming, and sleep-wake disorders
- Definition of a consciousness-altering drug as well as the types of consciousness-altering drugs and their effects on the nervous system and behavior, and the drug addiction and reward pathway in the brain

MEMORY

- Memory creation; the process of encoding information and processes that aid in encoding information
- Memory storage; types of memory storage, including sensory, working, and long-term memory; semantic networks and spreading activation
- Memory retrieval; recall, recognition, and relearning; retrieval clues; and the processes that aid retrieval and the role of emotion
- Memory loss, aging and memory, dysfunctions of memory (such as Alzheimer's disease and Korsakoff's syndrome), decay, interference, memory construction, and source monitoring
- Definition of neural plasticity as a change in synaptic connections that aid in memory and learning; long-term potentiation

LANGUAGE

- Language acquisition theories, including learning, Nativist, and Interactionist
- The influence of language on cognitive processes
- Identification that language and speech are controlled by different brain areas

EMOTION

- Identification of cognitive, psychological, and behavioral
- Emotions that are universal to all humans, including fear, anger, happiness, surprise, joy, disgust, and sadness
- Role of emotion as an adaptive strategy
- Fundamental theory of emotions, including the James–Lange theory, Cannon–Bard theory, and Schachter–Singer theory
- The role of biological processes in perception of emotion
- Brain regions involved in the generation and experience of emotions
- Identification of the role played by the limbic system in emotion
- The nature of emotional experience as stored memories that may be recalled by similar experiences
- The interaction between emotion and the autonomic nervous system
- Identification of the relationship between physiology and emotion, including the physiological markers of emotion (signatures of emotion)

STRESS

- Identification of the nature of stress, including appraisal, different types of stressors (including cataclysmic and personal events) and the effects of stress on psychological function
- Physiological, emotional, and behavioral outcomes and responses to stress
- Strategies for managing stress, including exercise, relaxation techniques, and spirituality

BIOLOGICAL BASES OF BEHAVIOR

- General structure and function of the nervous system, including neurons, the reflex arc and neurotransmitters
- Structures and function of the peripheral nervous system
- Structure and functions of the central nervous system including the forebrain, midbrain, hindbrain, and spinal cord
- Lateralization of cortical functions to specific hemispheres
- Methods used to study the brain
- The interaction and influence of neurons on behavior
- Influence of neurotransmitters on behavior
- The relationship between the endocrine system and the nervous system, including components of the endocrine system and the effects of the endocrine system on behavior
- Fundamental concepts of behavioral genetics, including genes, temperament, heredity, adaptive value of traits and behaviors, and the interaction between heredity and environmental influences
- The influence of genetics and environmental factors on the development of behaviors, including experience and behavior, and genetically based behavioral variation in natural populations
- Processes of human physiological development, including prenatal development, motor development, and developmental changes in adolescence

PERSONALITY

- Fundamental theories of personality, including psychoanalytic, humanistic, trait, social cognitive, biological, and behaviorist
- Situational approach to explaining behavior

PSYCHOLOGICAL DISORDERS

- Identification of approaches to psychological disorders, including biomedical and biopsychosocial approaches
- Classification and rates of psychological disorders
- Identification of the major psychological disorders including anxiety disorders, obsessive-compulsive disorder, traumatic and stress-related disorders, mood, schizophrenia, dissociative and personality disorders
- Identification of the role of biology in nervous system disorders, including schizophrenia, depression Alzheimer's disease and Parkinson's disease

MOTIVATION

- Factors that influence motivation, including instinct, arousal, drives, and needs
- Identification of the role of negative feedback systems in managing drives
- Theories about the role of motivation in human behavior, including drive reduction theory, incentive theory, and other cognitive and need-based theories
- The application of theories as a way to understand behaviors such as sociocultural eating, sex, and drug and alcohol use, including biological factors in regulation of motivational processes and sociocultural factors in regulation of these motivational processes

ATTITUDES

- Cognitive, affective, and behavioral components of attitudes
- The interaction between attitudes and behavior, including the processes by which behavior influences attitudes (foot-in-the-door phenomenon, role-playing effects), the processes by which attitudes behavior influence behavior, and cognitive dissonance theory

HOW THE PRESENCE OF OTHERS AFFECTS INDIVIDUAL BEHAVIOR

- Definition and significance of social facilitation
- Definition and significance of deindividuation
- Definition and outcome of the bystander effect
- Definition of social loafing
- Definition of social control
- Definition and impact of peer pressure
- Definition and impact of conformity
- Definition of obedience

GROUP DECISION-MAKING PROCESSES

- Definitions and significance of group polarization

NORMATIVE AND NONNORMATIVE BEHAVIOR

- Description of social norms

SOCIALIZATION

- Identification of the agents of socialization such as family, mass media, peers, and the workplace

HABITUATION AND DISHABITUATION

- Fundamental concepts of habituation and dishabituation

ASSOCIATIVE LEARNING

- Fundamental concepts of classical conditioning, including neutral, conditioned, and unconditioned stimuli; conditioned and unconditioned responses; processes of conditioning, including acquisition, extinction, spontaneous recovery, generalization, and discrimination
- Fundamental concepts of operant conditioning, including processes of shaping and extinction; types of reinforcement, including positive, negative, primary, and conditional; reinforcement schedules, including fixed-ratio, variable-ratio, fixed-interval, and variable-interval; punishment; and escape and avoidance learning
- Impact and identity of cognitive processes that affect associative learning
- Impact and identity of biological factors that affect associative learning, including instinctive drift and biological predispositions

OBSERVATIONAL LEARNING

- Modeling as mode of learning
- Impact of biological processes on learning, including mirror neurons and the role of the brain in experiencing vicarious emotions
- Explanation of individual behavior by application of observational learning principles

THEORIES OF ATTITUDE AND BEHAVIOR CHANGE

- Concept of the elaboration likelihood model, including information processing routes to persuasion (central and peripheral route processing)
- Fundamental concepts of social cognitive theory
- Factors that contribute to a change in attitude, including changing behavior, characteristics of the message and target, and social factors

SELF-CONCEPT AND IDENTITY

- Fundamental factors in self-concept and self-identity, including the role of self-esteem, self-efficacy, and locus of control
- Recognizing the different types of identity with respect to race/ethnicity, gender, age, sexual orientation, and class

FORMATION OF IDENTITY

- The process and stages of identity development, including theories of identity development (such as gender, moral, psychosexual, and social development)
- Recognizing the influence of social factors on identity formation, specifically the influence of individuals and groups, respectively
- Understanding the influence of culture and socialization on identity formation

ATTRIBUTING BEHAVIOR TO PERSONS OR SITUATIONS

- Concepts of attribution theory, including fundamental attribution error and how culture affects attributions
- Identification of how self-perceptions affect the perceptions of others
- Identification of how perceptions of the environment shape our perceptions of others

PREJUDICE AND BIAS

- Delineation of processes that contribute to prejudice, such as the role of emotion and cognition
- Definition of stereotypes and stigma,

PROCESSES RELATED TO STEREOTYPES

- Definition and impact of self-fulfilling prophecy
- Definition of stereotype threat

SELF-PRESENTATION

- Expression and detection of emotion, including the roles of gender and culture on the expression of emotion
- Presentation of self, including impression management and the dramaturgical approach
- Fundamental concepts of verbal and nonverbal communication
- Identification of how animals signal and communicate

SOCIAL BEHAVIOR

- Fundamental concepts of attraction, aggression, attachment, altruism, and social support
- The role of biology in the social behaviors of animals, including foraging behavior, mating behavior and mating choice, and altruism

8.6 Preparing for the MCAT: Sociology

While some of the sociological topics described previously are integrated with their psychological counterparts, these are the sociology topics you are likely to see on Test Day in isolation as well:

HOW THE PRESENCE OF OTHERS AFFECTS INDIVIDUAL BEHAVIOR

- The roles played by social control, peer pressure, conformity, and obedience

GROUP DECISION-MAKING PROCESSES

- The role played by groupthink

NORMATIVE AND NON-NORMATIVE BEHAVIOR

- The role of social norms, including sanctions, folkways, mores, taboos, and anomie
- The role of deviance, including perspectives on deviance, such as differential association, labeling theory, and strain theory
- The aspects of collective behavior, such as fads, riots, and mass hysteria

SOCIALIZATION

- The agents of socialization, including families, mass media, peers, and workplaces

SOCIAL BEHAVIOR

- The role of social support in social behavior

DISCRIMINATION

- Comparison of individual *vs.* institutional discrimination
- Relationship between prejudice and discrimination
- The effect of power, prestige, and class on facilitating discrimination

SELF-CONCEPT AND IDENTITY

- Definitions of self-concept, identity, and social identity
- Identification of the different types of identities, including race/ethnicity, gender, age, sexual orientation, and class

FORMATION OF IDENTITY

- Theories of identity development, including gender, moral, psychosexual, and social development
- The role of social factors on identity formation, including the influences of individuals (imitation, role-taking) and the influences of groups (reference group)
- The role of culture and socialization on identity formation

PREJUDICE AND BIAS

- Definition of prejudice
- Identification of the processes that contribute to prejudice, including power, prestige, and class
- Definition and identification of stereotypes and stigmas
- Definition and role of ethnocentrism in prejudice and bias, including in-group/out-group; ethnocentrism *vs.* cultural relativism

ELEMENTS OF SOCIAL INTERACTION

- The types of status, such as achieved and ascribed status
- The effects of roles, including role conflict, role strain, and role exit
- The effects of groups, including primary and secondary groups, in-groups *vs.* out-groups, and group size (including dyads and triads)
- The effects of networks
- The effects of organizations, including formal organization
- The concept of bureaucracies, including characteristics of an ideal bureaucracy and perspectives on bureaucracy (such as the iron law of oligarchy and McDonaldization)

SELF-PRESENTATION AND INTERACTING WITH OTHERS

- Detecting and expressing emotion, including the role of gender and culture
- Management of impressions in the social context, including front stage *vs.* back stage self (dramaturgical approach)
- Verbal and nonverbal communication

THEORETICAL APPROACHES

- Fundamental characteristics of micro, and macrosociology, functionalism, conflict theory, symbolic interactionism, social constructionism, exchange-rational choice, and feminist theory

SOCIAL INSTITUTIONS

- The role of education including hidden curriculum, teacher expectancy, and educational segregation and stratification
- The role of family, including forms of kinship, diversity of family forms, marriage and divorce, violence within families, religion
- The role of religion, including the concept of religiosity, types of religious organizations (including churches, sects, and cults), and the role of religion in social change (such as modernization, secularization, and fundamentalism)
- The role of government and the economy, including power, authority, and division of labor
- Comparative economic and political systems
- The role of health and medicine, including medicalization, the "sick role" and the illness experience, delivery of health care, and social epidemiology

CULTURE

- Identification and characteristics of material culture
- Identification and characteristics of symbolic culture, including language, symbols, values, beliefs, norms, and rituals
- The impact of culture lag, culture shock, assimilation, multiculturalism, sub- and countercultures, mass media and popular culture, and the transmission and diffusion of culture

DEMOGRAPHIC STRUCTURE OF SOCIETY

- The role of aging, including aging and the life course, aging cohorts, and its social significance
- The role of gender, including the distinction between sex and gender, the social construction of gender, and gender segregation
- The role of race and ethnicity, including social construction of race, racialization, and racial formation
- The concept of push and pull factors in migration
- The concept of immigration status, including patterns of immigration and its intersections with race and ethnicity
- The role of sexual orientation

DEMOGRAPHIC SHIFTS AND SOCIAL CHANGES

- Theories of demographic change, including Malthusian theory and demographic transitions
- The concept of population growth and decline, including population projections and population pyramids
- The concepts of fertility and mortality, including rate types and patterns
- The concept of push and pull factors in migration
- The role of social movements, including relative deprivation, their organization, and movement strategies and tactics
- The role of globalization, including contributing factors such as communication technology and economic interdependence, perspectives on globalization, and social changes such as civil unrest and terrorism

SPATIAL INEQUALITY

- Identification and impact of residential segregation, including safety and violence in neighborhoods
- Impact and role of environmental justice in terms of location and exposure to health risks

SOCIAL CLASS

- Fundamental aspects of social stratification, including class, status, power, cultural and social capital, social reproduction, privilege, prestige, socioeconomic gradients in health and global inequalities
- Relationships between social stratification and race, gender, and age
- Social mobility patterns, including intergenerational and intragenerational mobility, downward and upward mobility, and meritocracy
- Definitions and impact of poverty, including relative and absolute poverty, social exclusion (segregation and isolation)

HEALTH DISPARITIES

- The impact of race, gender, and class inequalities on health

HEALTHCARE DISPARITIES

- The impact of race, gender, and class inequalities on healthcare

8.7 Behavioral Sciences Worked Examples

PASSAGE I: BIOLOGICAL BASIS OF BEHAVIOR

The classic dopamine (DA) hypothesis is the most well-studied and longest-standing of the schizophrenia hypotheses. The hypothesis is centered upon the mesolimbic pathway of the brain—specifically, D_2 receptors located in the subcortical region of the brain, which are strongly associated with the positive symptoms of schizophrenia (e.g. hallucinations and delusions). Treatment of schizophrenic patients with antipsychotic medications known to block D_2 receptors alleviates some symptoms. Furthermore, DA-enhancing drugs proved psychotogenic, thus establishing the connection between dopamine and schizophrenia.

The classic dopamine hypothesis has evolved to explain the enduring symptoms (e.g., apathy and antisocial behavior) and cognitive symptoms (e.g., memory loss and attention deficits). These functional deficits were only marginally treatable with D_2 antagonists. Hypostimulation of D_1 receptors in the prefrontal cortex (PFC) has been implicated in the negative symptoms of schizophrenia.

Research also suggests an association between the PFC and the subcortical region of the brain, including the ventral tegmental area (VTA) and the ventral striatum (VST). Mesolimbic dopaminergic (ML DA) neurons and mesocortical dopaminergic (MC DA) neurons of the ventral tegmental area (VTA) project to the ventral striatum and cortex, respectively. Glutamatergic neurons from the cortex project to the VTA and upregulate the MC DA neurons. At the same time, other glutamatergic neurons indirectly downregulate ML DA neurons through an intermediate GABAergic neuron.

Researchers conducted an imaging study to investigate the influence of glutamate on schizophrenia. Ketamine, a potential NMDA antagonist, was administered to four groups of patients: active schizophrenics, schizophrenics in remission (no psychotic episode within six months), abusers of psychostimulants, and healthy subjects. Dopamine levels were measured in the subcortical region. The results of the study are illustrated in Figure 1.

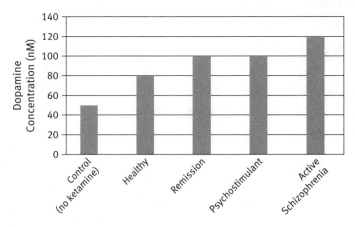

Figure 1. Dopamine measurements in various individuals treated with 0.5 mg ketamine per pound of body weight

P1.

P2.

P3.

P4.

FI.

1. Ecopipam, an antipsychotic drug, is administered to a healthy patient who, following treatment, begins hallucinating. Which of the following could correctly characterize the function of ecopipam?

    A. It increases activity of the MC DA neurons.
    B. It increases activity of the ML DA neurons. ✓
    C. It acts as a D_2 receptor antagonist.
    D. It acts as an NMDA receptor agonist.

2. Patients with the high activity allele coding for the enzyme COMT exhibit negative symptoms of schizo-phrenia. Which of the following best explains this discovery?

    A. COMT converts L-DOPA to dopamine in the PFC.
    B. COMT converts plasma dopamine to dopamine sulphate.
    C. COMT oxidizes dopamine to dopamine-melanin.
    D. COMT deactivates dopamine through methylation. ✓

3. Which of the following would lead to both positive and negative symptoms of schizophrenia?

    A. Administration of a sufficient amount of ketamine. ✓
    B. Administration of acamprosate, a GABA receptor agonist.
    C. Administration of talipexole, a D_2 receptor agonist.
    D. Administration of a benzazepine derivative, a D_1 receptor antagonist.

4. The "dopamine hypothesis" is useful for the clinical treatment of schizophrenia. However, some researchers believe the name is misleading. Why might they think this?

    A. GABA neurons act as a deactivating system to keep subcortical dopamine levels low.
    B. Glutamatergic neurons are located upstream of the dopaminergic neurons.
    C. Multiple types of dopaminergic receptors exist, making the name ambiguous. ✗
    D. Psychostimulants exacerbate the positive symptoms of schizophrenia.

5. Which of the following individuals would experience the most pronounced negative symptoms after treatment with ketamine?

    A. Active psychostimulant abusers
    B. Healthy individuals ✗
    C. Schizophrenics in remission
    D. It is impossible to determine

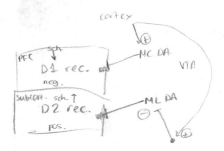

Key Concepts

Mechanism of Neurotransmitter Function

Behavioral Sciences Passage I Explanation:

USING THE KAPLAN METHODS

P1. Dopamine hypothesis of schizophrenia; hyperstimulation of subcortical D_2 receptors

P2. Prefrontal cortex; hypostimulation of D_1 receptors

P3. Link between PFC and subcortical region of brain

P4. Experimental design; ketamine administration

FI. Dopamine levels in ketamine treated patients

---

1. Ecopipam, an antipsychotic drug, is administered to a healthy patient who, following treatment, begins hallucinating. Which of the following could correctly characterize the function of ecopipam?

    A. It increases activity of the MC DA neurons.
    B. It increases activity of the ML DA neurons.
    C. It acts as a D_2 receptor antagonist.
    D. It acts as a NMDA receptor agonist.

 Assess the question

The antipsychotic properties of ecopipam are not outlined in the question stem, so it is not a good idea to speculate about its use. In other words, it would not be wise to assume that ecopipam is used to treat schizophrenia as opposed to other mental illnesses. The question stem explains that ecopipam induces hallucinations. This piece of evidence, along with information throughout the passage, will be key in answering this question.

 Plan your attack

In the first paragraph, it's implied that hyperstimulation of subcortical D_2 receptors is a possible cause of hallucinations. The correct answer will likely address this fact. It's tough to predict beyond that (and might be a waste of time), so the best way to tackle this question is through the process of elimination.

Execute the plan

Choice (A) discusses MC DA neurons. These neurons project to the cortex, which is largely filled with D_1 receptors, not D_2 receptors. Since only D_2 receptors are linked to the positive symptoms of schizophrenia, **(A)** is not correct.

Choice (B) mentions ML DA neurons, which project to the VST (part of the subcortical region). Upregulation of these neurons would increase dopamine concentration in the subcortical region, increasing the likelihood of hallucinations. Therefore, **(B)** is likely the correct answer.

Choice (C) may be tempting because it directly mentions D_2 receptors. However, it states that ecopipam is a D_2 receptor *antagonist*. Because antagonists decrease receptor activity, ecopipam would reduce hallucinations.

Choice (D) states that ecopipam is a NMDA receptor agonist. According to Figure 1, the NMDA antagonist, ketamine, increases dopamine concentration in the subcortical region. Therefore, if ecopipam were a NMDA receptor agonist, it would decrease dopamine concentration in the subcortical region. A decrease in dopamine concentration would reduce the prevalence of hallucinations, so **(D)** is also incorrect.

Answer by matching, eliminating, or guessing

The process of elimination quickly led to the selection of the correct answer, **(B)**.

Key Concepts

Reactions of Neurotransmitters

> 2. Patients with the high activity allele coding for the enzyme COMT exhibit negative symptoms of schizophrenia. Which of the following best explains this discovery?
>
> A. COMT converts L-DOPA to dopamine in the PFC.
> B. COMT converts plasma dopamine to dopamine sulphate.
> C. COMT oxidizes dopamine to dopamine-melanin.
> D. COMT deactivates dopamine through methylation.

 Assess the question

No specific information is provided about the high activity allele of COMT except that it causes the negative symptoms of schizophrenia. The answer choices all describe possible functions of COMT.

 Plan your attack

The second paragraph elaborates on the negative symptoms of schizophrenia. Specifically, it states that the negative symptoms result from hypostimulation of D_1 receptors in the prefrontal cortex. The process of elimination is the ideal approach to answering this question.

 Execute the plan

Choice (A) states that COMT will cause the conversion of L-DOPA to dopamine in the PFC, thereby increasing dopamine levels. However, negative symptoms arise from hypostimulation of D_1 receptors, NOT *hyper*stimulation, so (A) is out.

Choice (B) states that COMT converts plasma dopamine to dopamine sulphate. Plasma dopamine is in the blood, not the brain, so this conversion would not cause the negative symptoms.

Choice (C) states that COMT converts dopamine to dopamine-melanin. Melanin is the compound that determines skin color. The more melanin present, the darker the skin becomes. Since this function has nothing to do with the brain, this cannot be correct.

Finally, **choice (D)** describes a mechanism that is plausible and would result in hypostimulation of D_1 receptors. Hence, **(D)** is correct.

Answer by matching, eliminating, or guessing

Predicting that the correct answer must address the hypostimulation of D_1 receptors in the prefrontal cortex allowed for efficient elimination of answer choices that were either out of scope or opposite.

Key Concepts

Functions of Neurotransmittersr

> 3. Which of the following would lead to both positive and negative symptoms of schizophrenia?
>
>   A. Administration of a sufficient amount of ketamine.
>   B. Administration of acamprosate, a GABA receptor agonist.
>   C. Administration of talipexole, a D_2 receptor agonist.
>   D. Administration of a benzazapine derivative, a D_1 receptor antagonist.

1 Assess the question

The answer choices discuss different drugs and their functions, since knowledge of the drugs is not pertinent, focus on the function as it relates to passage information.

2 Plan your attack

The positive and negative symptoms of schizophrenia are discussed in paragraphs 1 and 2, respectively. Therefore, these are the paragraphs that must be referred to in order to make a prediction sufficient for the process of elimination.

3 Execute the plan

The positive symptoms of schizophrenia arise from hyperstimulation of D_2 receptors in the subcortical region of the brain whereas the negative symptoms of schizophrenia come about from the hypostimulation of D_1 receptors in the prefrontal cortex. The correct answer will fulfill both conditions.

4 Answer by matching, eliminating, or guessing

Choice (B) proposes a GABA receptor agonist. GABA inhibits ML DA neuronal activity. Since ML DA neurons secrete dopamine into the subcortical region, inhibiting them would result in less dopamine in this region. Less dopamine in the subcortical region will translate into less psychotic episodes because D_2 receptors will be less stimulated.

Choice (C) suggests a D_2 receptor agonist. Although this would lead to increased dopamine release in the subcortical region, it does not explain the absence of dopamine in the prefrontal cortex.

Choice (D) is wrong for the same reason that **(C)** is wrong. A D_1 receptor antagonist will decrease dopaminergic activity in the cortex. However, it does not explain the hyperstimulation of D_2 necessary for positive symptoms to occur.

Choice (A) is the only choice remaining and the correct answer. Looking closely at paragraph 3, it is possible to determine the role of NMDA receptors (and the associated neurotransmitter, glutamate) in schizophrenia. ML DA neurons project to the VST (subcortical region) and are indirectly inhibited by glutamate while the MC DA neurons project to the cortex and are upregulated by glutamate. Limiting the activity of the NMDA receptors would lead to disinhibition of the ML DA neurons (causing hyperstimulation of D_2 receptors) and inhibition of the MC DA neurons (causing hypostimulation of D_1 receptors). Therefore, ketamine administration would produce the desired result.

Key Concepts

Neurotransmitter Function

> **4.** The "dopamine hypothesis" is useful for the clinical treatment of schizophrenia. However, some researchers believe the name is misleading. Why might they think this?
>
> **A.** GABA neurons act as a deactivating system to keep subcortical dopamine levels low.
>
> **B.** Glutamatergic neurons are located upstream of the dopaminergic neurons.
>
> **C.** Multiple types of dopaminergic receptors exist making the name ambiguous.
>
> **D.** Psychostimulants exacerbate the positive symptoms of schizophrenia.

 Assess the question

The question indicates that the name "dopamine hypothesis" is misleading. It can be inferred that the dopamine hypothesis is either an oversimplification or incorrect characterization of the origin of schizophrenia.

 Plan your attack

It is necessary to determine why abnormal dopamine concentration is probably not the best explanation of schizophrenia. Paragraphs 3 and 4 investigate the other neurotransmitters involved in schizophrenia, so these are a good place to start in the search for a prediction.

3 **Execute the plan**

Taking a closer look at paragraph 3, it is clear that glutamate is a key player in schizophrenia. Its presence causes upregulation of MC DA neurons and indirectly causes downregulation of ML DA neurons. In all likelihood, the correct answer will include a reference to glutamate or the associated NMDA receptors.

4 **Answer by matching, eliminating, or guessing**

Choice (A) mentions GABAergic neurons, which downregulate ML DA neurons. This is only a small piece of the puzzle and does not explain why "dopamine hypothesis" is a misleading title.

Choice (C) states that multiple dopaminergic receptors exist. While ambiguity might be a cause for concern, "the dopamine hypothesis of schizophrenia" is fairly clear and this is not the best explanation based on the provided passage information.

Choice (D) brings up psychostimulants. This answer choice is out of scope and therefore does not answer the question.

Choice (B) matches the prediction that the correct answer would mention glutamate. In addition, it is true that glutamatergic neurons are located upstream of the dopaminergic neurons. Researchers might argue that it would almost make sense to rename the hypothesis, the "glutamate hypothesis".

Key Concepts

Biological Bases of Behavior

5. Which of the following individuals would experience the most pronounced negative symptoms after treatment with ketamine?

A. Active psychostimulant abusers
B. Healthy individuals
C. Schizophrenics in remission
D. It is impossible to determine.

1 Assess the question

The answer choices are the different groups included in Figure 1.

2 Plan your attack

The question stem is focused on the negative symptoms associated with schizophrenia. Recall that the negative symptoms are linked to hypostimulation of the D_1 receptors of the *prefrontal cortex*. Note that Figure 1 illustrates the change in dopamine concentration in the *subcortical region* after ketamine administration. There is no data provided about the relative impact of ketamine on the D_1 receptors of the PFC.

3 Execute the plan

Since there is no data available about ketamine's impact on the PFC, it is impossible to determine which group will experience the most pronounced negative symptoms.

4 Answer by matching, eliminating, or guessing

The prediction is met with a match. It is impossible to determine which group will experience the most pronounced negative symptoms, therefore, **choice (D)** is correct.

This chapter continues on the next page ▶ ▶ ▶

BEHAVIORAL SCIENCES PASSAGE II: MEMORY

Long-term memory storage is ultimately the result of strengthened synaptic connections. The process of long-term memory formation utilizes cytoplasmic polyadenylation element binding (CPEB) proteins which, remarkably, resemble prions in that they act as a template for promoting the local formation of other CPEB proteins. These proteins, once formed, stack together to form oligomers. The presence of stacked CPEB proteins in the axon terminal strengthens the synaptic connection and helps maintain memory. Regulation of these proteins, however, presents a biological problem: too much oligomerization can lead to the formation of too many memories. While this might initially seem desirable, it is important to consider that forgetting nonessential memories strengthens recall of important ones.

Searching for a mechanism of regulation, researchers studied *drosophila*. The CPEB protein in *drosophila* is Orb2, which exists in A and B isoforms. Orb2A is far less common, but shows more prion-like activity. The researchers observed that Orb2A binds with Tob, another protein that seemed to regulate Orb2A levels. They hypothesized that Tob stabilized Orb2A, which is usually labile. Tests confirmed that increasing Tob reduced Orb2A decay by a factor of two, and that neuronal stimulation was shown to increase Tob-Orb2A binding. The other Orb2 protein, Orb2B, is far more common, but requires an Orb2A "seed" to promote oligomerization. Once the seed is formed, Orb2B can continue to stack with itself. This mechanism is demonstrated in Figure 1.

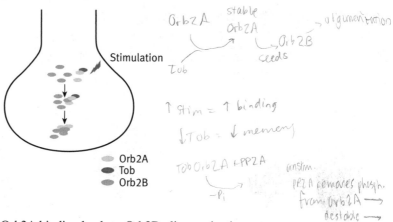

Figure 1. Tob-Orb2A binding leads to Orb2B oligomerization

To test the behavioral effects of the Tob-Orb2A complex, researchers examined courtship behavior, a well-documented application of long-term memory, in *drosophila*. Typically, a male fly will display courtship behavior towards a newly introduced female, but over time this behavior is prone to extinction if the female is unreceptive. Using RNA interference techniques, researchers suppressed Tob production and found that Tob deficient flies continued to try to mate with unreceptive females after repeated exposure.

Finding the mechanism for timing of long-term memory formation proved more difficult, but relied on the discovery that phosphatase PP2A is contained in the Orb2A-Tob complex. PP2A is an enzyme that removes phosphates from Orb2A. When dephosphorylation was chemically blocked, this had the effect of destabilizing Tob but stabilizing Orb2A, as well as causing an overall reduction in Tob-Orb2A binding. Researchers hypothesized that the primary function of PP2A is to remove phosphates from Orb2A and destabilize it when the synapse is unstimulated, thus preventing oligomerization. Stimulation promotes Tob binding, which stabilizes Orb2A and forms the seed required for the more abundant Orb2B to continue oligomerization.

P1.

P2.

Fig1.

P3.

P4.

1. The results of the study in the passage suggest that the Tob-Orb2A complex is a mechanism for which of the following?

   A. Neuroplasticity
   B. Synaptic pruning
   C. Spreading activation
   D. Potentiation ✓

2. If Orb2B stacking did not require an Orb2A seed, which of the following effects is most likely to be observed?

   A. Increased efficiency of and higher success rate for elaborative rehearsal ✓
   B. An increase in the ratio of automatic processing to effortful processing ✓
   C. An increased necessity for maintenance rehearsal in forming new pathways
   D. Stronger and more efficient semantic networks throughout the cortex

3. Hyperthymesia is a neurological condition that results in an exceptionally strong autobiographical memory; individuals with the condition are able to recall an abnormally large number of their life experiences. Which of the following describe(s) the type(s) of memory affected by this condition?

   I. Implicit
   II. Episodic ✓
   III. Declarative ✓

   A. I only
   B. II only ✓
   C. I and III only
   D. II and III only ✓

4. Based on the study cited in the passage, which of the following can most reasonably be concluded regarding courtship behavior in *drosophila*?

   A. Tob-resistant male flies are less responsive than normal flies to negative reinforcement cues from females.
   B. Without the ability to differentiate receptive from unreceptive females, courtship behavior is prone to instinctive drift. ✓
   C. Lacking Tob to regulate long-term memory formation, male flies exhibit spontaneous recovery of extinct behaviors.
   D. The Tob-Orb2A complex in male *drosophila* aids in their learning to discriminate between similar stimuli. ✓

5. Suppose that it were discovered that, during binding, Tob recruits LimK, a kinase that phosphorylates Orb2A. What effect would this have on the researcher's conclusions?

   A. They would be weakened, because phosphorylation destabilizes Tob, making it less likely for an Orb2B seed.
   B. They would be strengthened, because the finding shows how Orb2A conformation changes can cause Orb2B stacking.
   C. They would be strengthened, because the finding provides a potential mechanism by which Tob can stabilize Orb2A. ✓
   D. These findings are superfluous and would have no effect because PP2A already performs this function in the axon.

Key Concepts

Memory is a high-yield topic in the Biological Foundations of Behavior section of the MCAT. Make sure to know the basics of all four memory processes: Encoding, Short-term, Long-term and Retrieval, as well as common failures of these systems.

Behavioral Sciences Passage II Explanation:

USING THE KAPLAN METHODS

P1. CPEB protein stacking helps long-term memory formation

P2. Mechanism: after stimulation, Tob binds to Orb2A, forms a seed that promotes Orb2B stacking

Fig1. Mechanism diagram

P3. Application to behavior: Tob-deficient male flies forget female unreceptiveness

P4. Timing: PP2A removes phosphates from Orb2A causing degradation until neuron stimulated

---

1. The results of the study in the passage suggest that the Tob-Orb2A complex is a mechanism for which of the following?

    A. Neuroplasticity
    B. Synaptic pruning
    C. Spreading activation
    D. Potentiation

 Assess the question

This passage seems very technical; follow the *basic* biological processes discussed and you should be able to incorporate the new ideas with the required knowledge of memory systems. This question is testing knowledge of memory vocabulary and uses the overall topic and scope of the passage to do it. Attack this question right away.

 Plan your attack

Start with an analysis of the Tob-Orb2A complex. According to the passage, the Tob-Orb2A complex is a mechanism for long-term memory that helps strengthen the connections between synapses. Eliminate any answers that don't refer to long-term memory.

Execute the plan

Start with **choice (A)**; neuroplasticity describes the ability of the brain to mold its function to adapt to changes in general, and so is too broad to be explained by the mechanism described by the passage.

Choice (B) is the process of removing synaptic connections over time. This is nearly the opposite of the correct answer.

Choice (C), spreading activation, is the process by which nodes that are close together in a semantic network stimulate each other. This sounds relevant, but refers to a process that occurs once the memories are already formed.

Finally **choice (D)**, potentiation, is the process by which synaptic activation is strengthened through repeated stimulation, turning a short-term memory into a long-term one.

 Answer by matching, eliminating, or guessing

Executing the plan leads to the elimination of **(A), (B)**, and **(C)**, which did not agree with the assessment of the Tob-Orb2A complex. Recalling the definition of potentiation allows one to choose **(D)** with confidence.

Takeaways

Sometimes the studies described get quite technical; if so, your goal should be to focus on procedure and results. Questions will focus on the application of our psychology and sociology content knowledge to the overall structure of the experiments in the passages.

Things to Watch Out For

Memory and Learning are both subjects that contain quite a bit of vocabulary. Expect questions that test critical thinking to also require keeping terminology straight.

2. If Orb2B stacking did not require an Orb2A seed, which of the following effects is most likely to be observed?

A. Increased efficiency of and higher success rate for elaborative rehearsal

B. An increase in the ratio of automatic processing to effortful processing

C. An increased necessity for maintenance rehearsal in forming new pathways

D. Stronger and more efficient semantic networks throughout the cortex

 ## Assess the question

This is an inference question, which asks for extrapolation based on the passage. While this one could be saved for later, the 2A/2B interaction was discussed succinctly in the passage, so a little bit of passage research should be enough to answer this one quickly.

 ## Plan your attack

Paragraph 2 mentions Orb2B explicitly, and paragraph 1 describes the overall relationship between the oligomers involved and long-term memory. Research these paragraphs, and with a strong outline, thorough investigation may be avoided.

 ## Execute the plan

Paragraph 2 says that Orb2B can oligomerize with itself once it attaches to an Orb2A seed. The paragraph also mentions that Orb2B is quite common in the axon terminal. It stands to reason, then, that if Orb2B were allowed to oligomerize more freely, synaptic connections would be stronger in general, and long-term memories would be far easier to form, perhaps even pathologically so. Look for the correct answer to describe this, in other words.

Answer by matching, eliminating, or guessing

Choice (A) seems to match, after consideration of memory vocabulary. Elaboration is the kind of rehearsal that links new concepts to preexisting memories. If Orb2B is able to stack freely, this synaptic connection should be far less effortful. **(A)** matches the prediction, and is correct.

Choice (B) describes automatic and effortful processing, which are important concepts in encoding. Synaptic connection strength shouldn't affect the way in which information is obtained.

Choice (C), like **(A)**, describes rehearsal, but this time mentions maintenance. This type of rehearsal is simply a way to keep information in short-term memory and prevent it from being forgotten. Short-term memory does not rely on synaptic connection strength.

Choice (D) is tempting but extreme. The expectation is that long-term memories will form more easily, but this will not necessarily have any bearing on how those memories are organized.

Takeaways

Questions that ask for a modification of a study are relatively common. Attempt these only after obtaining points from more straightforward questions.

> **3.** Hyperthymesia is a neurological condition that results in an exception-ally strong autobiographical memory; individuals with the condition are able to recall an abnormally large number of their life experiences. Which of the following describe(s) the type(s) of memory affected by this condition?
>
> I. Implicit
> II. Episodic
> III. Declarative
>
> **A.** I only
> **B.** II only
> **C.** I and III only
> **D.** II and III only

❶ Assess the question

This is a Roman numeral question, and the third question in a row that will reward vocabulary knowledge. It's also a pseudo-discrete, and so can be done right away.

❷ Plan your attack

The stem describes hyperthymesia, so little research should be necessary. The goal should be to make a prediction based on the stem itself. As a Roman numeral strategy, eliminate until only one answer choice remains.

❸ Execute the plan

Hyperthymesia is described as causing an overload of life-experience memory. This might immediately bring to mind the concept of episodic memory, which is a choice, but keep in mind that the diagram of the different types of memory is a branching tree, so more than one answer may be correct here.

Answer by matching, eliminating, or guessing

Based on our prediction, Roman numeral II should be a part of the correct answer. Eliminate (**A**) and (**C**). Neither of the remaining choices includes Roman numeral I, so we need only to consider whether III should be included. Declarative memory is the part of long-term memory that is conscious, and that includes both episodic and semantic memory. Roman numeral III should therefore be part of our answer, so **choice (D)** is correct.

Takeaways

Predicting is a helpful tool in Roman numeral questions, but keep an open mind given that more than one statement can be correct.

Key Concepts

It's important to keep straight the different kinds of memory and the ways in which psychologists classify each.

4. Based on the study cited in the passage, which of the following can most reasonably be concluded regarding courtship behavior in *drosophila*?

A. Tob-resistant male flies are less responsive than normal flies to negative reinforcement cues from females.

B. Without the ability to differentiate receptive from unreceptive females, courtship behavior is prone to instinctive drift.

C. Lacking Tob to regulate long-term memory formation, male flies exhibit spontaneous recovery of extinct behaviors.

D. The Tob-Orb2A complex in male *drosophila* aides in their learning to discriminate between similar stimuli.

 Assess the question

This question is asking for an inference that can be drawn from the passage, and the question stem indicates exactly where to go, so approach this question immediately. If the passage was read actively, a prediction may have already been made.

 Plan your attack

The study in question is presented in paragraph 3, so review the procedure and results there. Your outline will be invaluable for a question like this because you've likely summarized the basics already.

 Execute the plan

According to the passage, male flies that lacked Tob were not able to learn which females were unreceptive, and continued to try to mate even after being rejected. The study supports the ideas presented earlier in the passage, that a lack of the Tob-Orb2A complex prevents long-term memory formation. Look for an answer that matches.

Answer by matching, eliminating, or guessing

Choice (A) mentions negative reinforcement, which refers to an increase in behavior resulting from removal of an unwanted stimulus. If anything, the female flies are signaling that they would like the males to decrease courtship behavior, so **(A)** seems unlikely.

Choice (B) mentions instinctive drift, which is another learning phenomenon in which an animal learning a complicated behavior will revert to a more natural one. There is no such complicated behavior described in the study.

Choice (C) only makes sense if the males' courtship behavior became extinct; that is, the males learned not to pursue unresponsive females in the first place. This is not supported by the study, so **(C)** can likely be eliminated.

By elimination, **choice (D)** must be correct. It discusses discrimination, which is a phenomenon by which an organism can differentiate between two similar, but distinct, stimuli. Here, the similar stimuli are the receptive and unreceptive females. Since male flies are usually able to remember the difference and only exhibit courtship behavior toward receptive females (whereas Tob-deficient males are not), it stands to reason that Tob is at least partly responsible for the difference.

Takeaways

Whenever a passage presents the results of a study without a conclusion, expect to formulate that conclusion on your own. As you create your outline for that portion of the passage, take a moment to summarize the results so that you can be ready for such a question.

Things to Watch Out For

Always beware of extreme answer choices for questions that ask you to make conclusions based on a study. Choices that mention "proof" or "causes" are likely to be incorrect.

5. Suppose that it were discovered that, during binding, Tob recruits LimK, a kinase that phosphorylates Orb2A. What effect would this have on the researcher's conclusions?

A. They would be weakened, because phosphorylation destabilizes Tob, making it less likely for an Orb2B seed.

B. They would be strengthened, because the finding shows how Orb2A conformation changes can cause Orb2B stacking.

C. They would be strengthened, because the finding provides a potential mechanism by which Tob can stabilize Orb2A.

D. These findings are superfluous and would have no effect because PP2A already performs this function in the axon.

 **Assess the question**

This question requires incorporation of new information with the passage information. Questions like these should be saved for last.

 **Plan your attack**

The question stem mentions phosphorylation, a process discussed in paragraph 4. It's likely that we'll need to understand the role of phosphorus, so start with some research.

 **Execute the plan**

According to paragraph 4, PP2A removes phosphorus from Orb2A, and that when this was blocked, Orb2A was stabilized. If during binding, Tob causes phosphorus to be added to dephosphorylated Orb2A, this provides an answer to the question of *how* binding strengthens Orb2A. Armed with this prediction, look for a match.

Takeaways

When answer choices are grouped as they are here, even a general prediction can eliminate half of the answer choices.

 **Answer by matching, eliminating, or guessing**

Choices **(A)** and **(D)** are out immediately, because the process mentioned in the question stem helps to qualify a previously unexplained portion of the hypothesis. Of the rest, **choice (C)** matches the prediction perfectly.

This chapter continues on the next page ▶ ▶ ▶

8.8 Behavioral Sciences Practice

PASSAGE III (QUESTIONS 1–6)

Throughout the day, humans experience innumerable sensory stimuli. These stimuli originate from a variety of sources, and are usually categorized based on the five traditional human senses of sight, smell, hearing, taste, and touch. Psychologists sort stimuli based on their physical constituents, which are referred to as stimulus modalities. These modalities match up fairly closely with the five senses, but are slightly more general. Some stimulus modalities are light, sound, temperature, taste, smell, and pressure. These modalities are also called the *distal stimuli*, which refers to the fact that they directly stimulate the sensory organs of the body like the eyes, nociceptors, or the bones of the inner ear.

The distal stimulus initiates neural processing. For the eye, the modality is the electromagnetic radiation (in the visible spectrum) that reflects from an object and makes its way to the retina. Through phototransduction the stimulus is turned into nerve action potentials, the *proximal stimulus*. From the neural information, the brain (re)creates an image of the object. The process is analogous for the other sensory modalities, for instance, the sound of a barking dog and the perception of a dog, or the scent of a rose and the perception thereof. The brain takes proximal stimuli and transforms them into what we detect as our world.

There are hundreds of proximal stimuli running through the brain at any given time. How can humans take all of this information and organize it into something meaningful and useful? One theory is gestaltism, which is explained as the tendency of humans to integrate pieces of information into meaningful wholes. For example, someone looking at a bookshelf would see a shelf full of books, as a whole, before noticing that there were individual books, or that the books had different titles, or that the books were made of paper, or that they were arranged in a certain way. Gestalt theorists attempt to understand how top-down processing affects perception. To account for the seemingly innate organization that occurs in the human brain, Gestalt theorist devised the principles of grouping. These principles are organized into six categories: proximity, similarity, closure, good continuation, common fate, and good form.

Another organizational principle that influences human perception is the idea of *perceptual sets*. Also shaped by top-down processing, the concept of perceptual sets implies that stimuli may be perceived in different ways depending upon the perceiver. For instance, an individual may be exceptionally sensitive to the sound of their name, especially if they are waiting for it to be called. The thinker may even shape their perceptions so that reality correlates more closely to their expectations. For instance, an individual waiting to hear their name may be more apt to mistakenly identify a similar sounding name as their own.

P1.

P2.

P3.

P4.

1. Suppose that an observer can discriminate between a 50 cd light and a 55 cd light, but not a 50 cd light and a 54 cd light. Assuming the same setup, what is the faintest intensity of light that can be discriminated from a 300 cd light?

   A. 270 cd ✓
   B. 305 cd
   C. 330 cd
   D. 355 cd

2. Which of the following statements would best support the idea of perceptive sets?

   A. A mother reserving judgment for her child's performance at a musical contest until the judges have returned their decision.
   B. A sports fan cheering for the other team when they make a skillful play, even if it results in their own team losing points.
   C. A mother advocating for her child in a competition, but reminding the child to be a good sport whether they win or lose.
   D. A sports fan perceiving the referees in a game to be against their team when the referees make any calls that hurt their team. ✓

3. Which of the following would NOT be considered a distal stimulus?

   A. Light bouncing off of a flower and into the eye
   B. Small, volatile molecules released by a flower
   C. Pollen released by a flower into the air ✓
   D. The sound waves created by a bee's wings

4. Which of the following most accurately describes the body's reaction to a bee sting?

   A. An efferent action potential arrives at a relay neuron, which sends an afferent action potential to the effector muscle after which the signal arrives and is interpreted at the brain.
   B. An afferent action potential arrives at a relay neuron, which sends an efferent action potential to the effector muscle after which the signal arrives and is interpreted at the brain. ✓
   C. An afferent action potential arrives at a relay neuron, which sends a signal to the brain which then interprets the signal and sends an efferent action potential to the effector muscle.
   D. An efferent action potential arrives at a relay neuron, which sends a signal to the brain which then interprets the signal and sends an afferent action potential to the effector muscle.

5. Phantosmia is a disorder characterized by olfactory hallucinations in the absence of any physical odors. Which of the following is most likely to cause phantosmia?

   A. An odor molecule stimulating the wrong kind of chemoreceptor
   B. Seizures occurring in a patient's occipital lobe of their brain
   C. Temporal lobe atrophy due to Alzheimer's disease ✓
   D. Parietal lobe activation caused by schizophrenia

6. Some children's games involve searching for a known character amid other similarly dressed characters and similarly colored objects. The thought process involved in this type of game could best be considered:

   A. top-down processing with multimodal stimuli.
   B. bottom-up processing with unimodal stimuli.
   C. top-down processing with unimodal stimuli. ✓
   D. bottom-up processing with multimodal stimuli.

Behavioral Sciences Practice Passage Explanations

P1. Stimulus modalities, distal stimuli

P2. Processing of distal stimuli into proximal stimuli

P3. Gestalt theory, top-down processing

P4. Perceptual sets affect our thinking

1. (A)

The just-noticeable difference for the discrimination of light (in this particular setup) can be determined from the question stem. According to Weber's law, the just-noticeable difference is calculated as a ratio. From the given information the JND is: $\frac{5}{50}$ or $\frac{1}{10}$ of the intensity of the light. Using this information, it can be predicted that the observer would be able to differentiate between a 300 cd light and another light as long as their intensities vary by 10 percent. The question asks for the *faintest*, which matches **(A)**. A 270 cd light could be differentiated from a (270 x 1.1) 297 cd light, so the observer would be able to differentiate between the two.

2. (D)

Perceptive sets are the expectations that affect one's perception. It may result in the organization and processing of information so that perceptions match one's expectations or motivations. This is the essential attribute that must be found in the correct answer. In **choice (A)**, **choice (B),** and **choice (C)** the perception isn't being modified in this way. **Choice (D)**, however, has the sports fan's perceptions being changed because of their commitment to their own team and is the correct response.

3. (C)

Distal stimuli are the physical stimuli that directly stimulate the sensory organs. This question asks which answer is NOT a distal stimulus, so the correct answer will be unlike the others. **Choice (A)** was discussed in the passage as an example of distal stimuli, so it is out. **Choice (B)** could be a little confusing, but these criteria all point towards an odorant and an example of a distal stimulus. **Choice (D)** is stimulus that will travel to the sensory system and be converted into an action potential, and thus could be a distal stimulus. This leaves **choice (C)**; since pollen molecules are large and are not processed by the olfactory system, but rather create an immune response, they are not a distal stimulus.

4. (B)

When the body experiences a stimulus that elicits a reflex arc, there is a specific order for how the signal travels through the system. The afferent neuron takes the signal from the sensory organ to the central nervous system. In reflex loops, this signal is taken in by a relay neuron and then sent directly back out through an efferent neuron to the effector muscle to try and move the body away from the painful stimulus. It isn't until after this signal and reflex has happened that the brain realizes the stimulus or the action at all, or **choice (B).**

5. (C)

Looking at the answers, three have to do with different parts of the brain while the other looks at a mix-up at the chemoreceptor. **Choice (A)** can be eliminated since the question stem states that there is an absence of odor, thus no mix-up could occur since there is no odor molecule to stimulate the chemoreceptor. From there this question is a matter of remembering which area of the brain is responsible for interpreting scent. The answer to that question is the temporal lobe and phantosmia can be caused by Alzheimer's disease when it atrophies the temporal lobe, or **choice (C).**

6. (C)

Taking a look at the answer choices reveals that this question is looking for the modality of the sensory stimulus and how the children's game is being processed. The question states that the child will be looking for something amid a field of other objects. This means the child already has an idea of what he is looking for and is parsing a larger image looking for a specific thing. This means that the child is using top-down processing, which eliminates **choices (B)** and **(D)**. The modality of the stimulus has to do with what senses are being used. In this case, light is collected and vision is being used exclusively–implying a unimodal stimulus and **choice (C).**

CHAPTER NINE

Biochemistry

The MCAT will now test introductory biochemistry as a portion of both the Chemical and Physical Foundations of Biological Systems and the Biological and Biochemical Foundations of Living systems. Each of these sections will be approximately 25 percent biochemistry. The information tested is material likely to be covered in an introductory biochemistry course for those studying the life sciences. Therefore, it is important that you take your preparation for biochemistry very seriously, as a significant portion of your score will depend on biochemistry. That being said, the biochemistry tested in each of these sections is likely to be in different contexts. In this chapter, we will explore how the MCAT will be testing your knowledge of biochemistry in both the Chemical and Physical Foundations of Biological Systems and the Biological and Biochemical Foundations of Living Systems sections.

9.1 Reading the Passage

When glancing at a biochemistry passage for the first time, it is likely that you will notice images, data, and/or chemical equations. The images may represent a cellular structure, a biochemical experiment, or a graph representing experimental data. The images present in these passages are likely to be very different from those encountered in physics. In fact, these passages will be different in both scope and structure compared with those seen in physics. Thus, the way that biochemistry passages must be read is different from reading passages in physics.

PASSAGE TYPES

Much like the physics passages, biochemistry passages can be either experiment or information passages. However, the experiment passages in biochemistry are much different from those found in the other sciences. In biochemistry, experiment passages may be related to a biological process, and data may be represented visually as a change in structure of a cell or tissue or as a graph, rather than raw numerical data points. Questions on these passages are likely to assess your ability to analyze visual evidence. Experiment passages will require the test-taker to put together all of the information in order to answer questions. While the passage presentations will be similar in both sections, the scope of the information tested will be different.

Chemical and Physical Foundations of Biological Systems

Passages in the Chemical and Physical Foundations of Biological Systems section will likely be accompanied by chemical equations. In addition, those biochemistry passages are likely to fall more within the context of chemistry, both organic and inorganic (general) chemistry. Success on biochemistry passages in this section will rely on your ability to connect the concepts in biochemistry, organic chemistry, and general chemistry and to apply these connections to biological situations. Biochemistry passages in this section are more likely to reflect changes that occur at the molecular and tissue level.

- Experiment passages in this section may include organic synthesis pathways and molecular structures.
  - Experimental results will likely be summarized in the form of a graph, chart, or other visual representation of data.
  - Experiment passages will require integration of biochemistry concepts at the molecular level.
- Like information passages in physics, information passages in biochemistry will also present information, but understanding this information will require a fundamental understanding of biology, even though this is not in the Biological and Biochemical Foundations of Living Systems section.
  - These passages will integrate multiple subject areas.
  - Connections between topics in the passage may be present but not explicitly stated. The test-taker will have to make these connections in order to fully understand the passage.

Overall, biochemistry passages in this section are a perfect opportunity for the testmaker to present questions and passages that require a thorough understanding in the areas of general chemistry, organic chemistry, biochemistry, and biology. The divisions between these sciences will be blurred on the MCAT, such that a single passage with questions is likely to test multiple areas, with individual questions requiring knowledge in multiple subjects.

Biological and Biochemical Foundations of Living Systems

Biochemistry passages in this section are likely to focus strongly on biology, and less on the details of organic and general chemistry. While knowledge of the fundamentals of chemistry will be required, the biochemistry passages in this section are more likely to explore how the biochemistry of an organism will affect the organism and its physiology as a whole.

- Experiment passages in this section will feature an experiment, but you are less likely to have a passage with an organic synthesis pathway.
  - The data will be less numerical, but you will have to analyze figures and data to understand how a process influences the overall physiology of the organism.
- Information passages will also focus more on the biological side of biochemistry.
  - Expect that information passages that appear to be more biology in scope may also be accompanied by questions regarding biochemistry concepts.

Biochemistry in its Different Sections		
	Chemical and Physical Foundations of Biological Systems	**Biology and Biochemical Foundations of Living Systems**
Experiment Passages	Incorporate an organic chemistry synthesis or general chemistry concepts. Experiment is likely to focus on biochemistry at the molecular, cellular, or tissue level rather than the organism as a whole.	Heavy in biological concepts, often physiology. Experiment is likely to focus on how a biochemical process affects the organism as a whole.
Information Passages	Will be a combination of concepts from general chemistry, organic chemistry, and biochemistry, and a grasp of these subject areas will be required in order to determine the goal of the passage.	Also heavy in biological concepts, passages may be defined as both biochemistry and biology, with little distinction between the two.
Scope	From the molecular to the tissue level.	From the molecular to the entire organism.
Images	May involve molecular structures, chemical equations, graphs and charts representing data, and illustrations of biochemical processes at the molecular and cellular level.	Less likely to involve molecular structure, but physiological pathways may predominate. Chemical equations will represent physiology. Illustrations will focus on biochemical processes at the level of the organism.

OUTLINING THE PASSAGE

Regardless of the section, biochemistry passages are approached in the same way, using the Kaplan way.

Scan for Structure

The structure of biochemistry passages will be somewhat dependent on the passage type and the section. Passages in the Chemical and Physical Foundations of Biological Systems section are more likely to be accompanied by molecular structures and organic synthesis pathways, while passages in the Biology and Biochemical Foundations of Living Systems section are more likely to be accompanied by images of organisms or cells. As you scan the passage, note what is present. Unlike the physics section, data is more likely to be represented graphically or visually rather than numerically. After scanning and determining the subject area, decide whether this passage is one to do now or one to do later.

Read Strategically

Reading strategically in the biochemistry section requires that you take notice of the type of passage you are reading. Like all other sciences tested on the MCAT, experiment passages will require that you identify the hypothesis, procedure, and outcomes, as these are likely targets for questions. However, in the biochemistry section you should also be aware of the relationships between the chemistry and the biology. In the Biology and Biochemical Foundations of Living Systems section, take note of how the biochemistry affects the physiology. This topic is likely to be tested in the questions.

In the Chemical and Physical Foundations of Biological Systems section, pay special attention to the connections between the chemistry and the biology/biochemistry. Questions on the MCAT often focus on how well you can make connections between topics. If you read such that you pay attention to these questions, you will be able to anticipate where the questions are going to come after a passage.

Label Each Component

After you have read, it is time to make your outline. Identify the purpose of each paragraph and figure. Then, write it down on your outline. For biochemistry, it is also important to note specific concepts within a paragraph and where else these concepts are discussed. If a figure shows the steps in an organic chemistry synthesis and the next paragraph indicates how the products of that synthesis were used to study some aspect of biochemistry, make a note about that connection. When you create your outline by labeling each paragraph, it is also helpful to note the concept of the paragraph or figure. This will help you to identify where to find information when you start answering questions.

Reflect on Your Outline

This is, of course, where you determine the goal of the passage. What process was described? If it was an experiment passage, what biochemical process is represented and what was the outcome? How did the outcome affect the organism or change the molecular structure of an enzyme? Jot this down on your outline, as it will come in handy as you further interpret the passage while answering questions. Remember, biochemistry passages on the MCAT are aiming to test how well you can extrapolate the effects of changes at the molecular level to predict effects on the cell, tissue, and/or organism.

9.2 Answering the Questions

Like other sciences tested on the MCAT, there will be four types of biochemistry questions:

Discrete questions
- Likely to focus on single topics, or integration of two topics

Questions that stand alone from the passage
- Accompany a passage, but the passage is not required to answer the question
- Likely to be a topic related to the passage

Questions that require data from the passage
- Less likely to involve a calculation on biochemistry passage
- Data will either be found in the passage or represented in graph or chart form
- These questions will likely require you to analyze the data presented in a graph or chart

Questions that require the goal of the passage
- Will require an understanding of the passage as a whole as well as the purpose of the passage
- Will often test your ability to make connections between different topics within the passage
- Most likely related to your ability to understand biochemistry on the tissue or organismal level

DETERMINING THE PURPOSE OF THE QUESTION

Biochemistry questions on the MCAT are likely to target multiple "skills." Two of these skills include statistical data analysis and research design. Given that biochemistry is likely to be the most tested topic on Test Day, it is probable that some passages and questions will cover concepts related to biochemistry research. However, questions like this can also be answered using a systematic approach. We have already introduced the Kaplan way to approach questions. Now we will focus on how to use that strategy to your advantage on biochemistry questions.

1. Assess the question

- Read the question, but do not read the answers.
- Determine whether this is a question to do now or do later. If it is a question to do now, proceed to planning your attack.

2. Plan your attack

- Biochemistry passages are less likely to involve math, but more likely to involve reasoning and analysis.
- Identify the task of the question. That is, what is the question asking you to do?
- Tasks in biochemistry are likely to involve analysis of data in graph or chart form, analysis of information in the passage, or identification of how a biochemical process will affect the organism or another process.
- Many of the questions will require you to apply your knowledge of other subject areas such as biology, organic chemistry, and/or general chemistry to biochemical concepts.

3. Execute your plan

- Carry out your plan, going back to the passage and locating required information, analyzing the data, or determining the results and impact of a biochemical process.

4. Answer the question by matching, eliminating, or guessing

- Match your answer determined in the previous step with the answer choices.
- Some questions will give you graphics in the answer choices instead of words. When approaching a set of answer choices like this, be sure to eliminate ones that simply are not possible or sensible in the context of the question. For example, there may be images representing structures that do not exist. Do not doubt your knowledge about what is possible. Just because something appears as an answer choice does not mean it is possible.
- If guessing is required, then try to get down to two answers before making a guess. Then, make your best guess. Just because you guess doesn't mean that you don't know the material; many test-takers achieving top scores did a substantial amount of guessing during their test too!

9.3 Getting the Edge in Biochemistry

Getting a high score on Test Day requires a very solid foundation in biochemistry, as this subject area is heavily tested. However, it is important to develop a grasp of biochemistry in the context of the other sciences, especially biology, organic chemistry, and general chemistry. Many of the passages you encounter on Test Day will require you to make connections between the other sciences and biochemistry. In addition, biochemical processes do not occur in isolation. Many of the passages and questions will focus on how changes at the molecular level results in changes in the entire organism's physiology.

On Test Day, biochemistry passages will feature a variety of figures, including graphs, charts, molecular structures, chemical equations, and visual representations of biochemical concepts. Be prepared to analyze a variety of different images, as you will be repeatedly asked to do so on Test Day.

9.4 Step-By-Step Guide to Biochemistry Passages

OUTLINING THE PASSAGE

- **Scan for structure**
  - ○ Determine whether to do this passage now or later.
  - ○ Identify the structure of the passage, including charts, graphs, chemical equations, synthesis pathways, metabolic pathways, and images.
- **Read strategically**
  - ○ Identify the type of passage
  - ○ Pay special attention to the relationships between concepts
  - ○ In an experiment passage, determine the hypothesis, procedure, and outcome
  - ○ In an information passage, identify how the information in each paragraph fits together to present a unified picture
  - ○ Identify what information is presented in each figure or image
- **Label each component**
  - ○ Write down the purpose of each paragraph and figure
  - ○ Identify any connections between concepts within the passage
- **Reflect on your outline**
  - ○ Determine the goal of the passage and write it down
  - ○ Identify the concepts within the passage in an effort to anticipate questions

ANSWERING THE QUESTIONS

1. Assess the question
- Determine whether this question should be done now or later.
- Identify the topic and the degree of difficulty.
- Good questions to do now in biochemistry are ones that stand alone from the passage or do not require extensive data analysis in order to determine the correct answer.

2. Plan your attack
- Determine what you already know, and what information you need.
- Identify where to find the required information: the passage, the question, your outline, or your own knowledge.
- If you have to go back to the passage, determine where to find the required information by using your outline.
- If data analysis is required, identify the correct data set, as there may be multiple data representations.

3. Execute your plan
- Analyze the data, go back to the passage, and carry out your plan.
- If you get stuck analyzing data, remember that the trend of the data is often enough to yield a correct answer choice.

4. Answer the question by matching, eliminating, or guessing
- Match your answer to the answer choices.
- If there is not match, eliminate incorrect answer choices. Some of the answer choices may not make sense; eliminate those first.
- If elimination does not provide a clear answer, guess between two probable answers.

9.5 Preparing for the MCAT: Biochemistry in the Chemical and Physical Foundations of Biological Systems Section

These are the biochemistry topics that you are likely to see on Test Day within the Chemical and Physical Foundations of Biological Systems section.

ACID/BASE EQUILIBRIA

- Definition and identification of acids/bases, their conjugates, and their strengths
- Description of common buffering systems and equilibrium constants

IONS IN SOLUTIONS

- Define anions, cations, and recognize common ions, including ammonium and phosphate, etc.
- Understand hydration and the hydronium ion

SEPARATIONS AND PURIFICATIONS

- Basic concepts of separation and purification of proteins and peptides
- The process of electrophoresis and the substances that can be separated using this method
- Quantitative analysis of yields from separations and purifications
- The mechanism of chromatography and the specific types of chromatography, including size-exclusion, ion-exchange, and affinity

NUCLEOTIDES AND NUCLEIC ACIDS

- Definitions and compositions of nucleotides and nucleosides
- The characteristics and structure of the sugar phosphate backbone
- Structures and identities of pyrimidines and purines
- Basic chemistry of nucleotides and nucleic acids
- Additional functions of nucleotides and nucleic acids

AMINO ACIDS, PEPTIDES, AND PROTEINS

- Describing amino acids in terms of absolute configuration at the α position
- The definition of dipolar ions
- Classification of amino acids as acidic, basic, hydrophilic, or hydrophobic
- Reactions of peptides and proteins
- Identification and purpose of sulfur linkages for cysteine and cystine
- Definition and identification of peptide linkages within polypeptides and proteins
- Definition and outcome of hydrolysis
- Structure of proteins, including primary, secondary, and tertiary structures
- Definition and use of the isoelectric point

THREE-DIMENSIONAL PROTEIN STRUCTURE

- Creation and maintenance of conformational stability, including hydrophobic interactions and solvation layers (entropy)
- Definition and characteristics of quaternary structure
- Changes in protein structure as a result of denaturing and folding

NON-ENZYMATIC PROTEIN FUNCTION

- Protein functions that are not enzymatic in nature, including binding, immunity, and motor functions

LIPIDS

- Types of lipids, including those used for storage, structure, and signaling/cofactors
- Identification of storage lipids, including triacyl glycerols
- Identification of free fatty acids
- Saponification and its uses
- Identification of structural lipids, including phospholipids, phosphatides, and sphingolipids
- Identification and purpose of waxes
- Identification of signaling lipids and cofactors, including fat-soluble vitamins, steroids, and prostaglandins

CARBOHYDRATES

- Definitions and characteristics of disaccharides and polysaccharides

PHENOLS

- Oxidation and reduction reactions of phenols, including hydroquinones and ubiquinones
- Identification of biological $2e^-$ redox centers

POLYCYCLIC HETEROCYCLIC AROMATIC COMPOUNDS

- Identification and understanding of biological aromatic heterocycles

ENZYMES

- Classification of enzymes by reaction type
- Mechanisms of enzymes, including substrates and enzyme specificity, cofactors, coenzymes, and vitamins
- Theories of enzyme function, including the active site model and the induced-fit model
- Kinetics of enzymes, including catalysis, Michaelis–Menten, enzyme cooperativity, and effects of local conditions on enzyme function
- Mechanisms of enzyme inhibition
- Regulation of enzymes by allosteric binding and covalent modification

PRINCIPLES OF BIOENERGETICS

- Thermodynamics and bioenergetics, including free energy, K_{eq}, and the relationship between bioenergetics and concentration
- Bioenergetics of phosphorylation and ATP, including identification of the ΔG of ATP hydrolysis as much less than 0
- ATP group transfers
- Identification of biological oxidation–reduction reactions, including half-reactions, soluble electron carriers, and flavoproteins

9.6 Preparing for the MCAT: Biochemistry in the Biological and Biochemical Foundations of Living Systems Section

These are the biochemistry topics that you are likely to see on Test Day within the Biological and Biochemical Foundations of Living Systems section.

AMINO ACIDS

- Describing amino acids in terms of absolute configuration at the α position
- The definition of dipolar ions
- Classification of amino acids as acidic, basic, hydrophilic, or hydrophobic
- Reactions of amino acids, peptides, and proteins
- Identification and purpose of sulfur linkages for cysteine and cystine
- Definition and identification of peptide linkages within polypeptides and proteins
- Definition and Products of hydrolysis

PROTEIN STRUCTURE

- Definitions and components of primary, secondary, and tertiary structures of proteins
- The role of proline, cystine, and hydrophobic bonding in the formation and maintenance of tertiary structure
- Definition and characteristics of quaternary structure of proteins
- Factors that contribute to conformational stability
- Changes in structure as a result of denaturing and folding
- The role of hydrophobic interactions in the maintenance of conformational stability
- Definition of the solvation layer and how entropy relates to protein conformation
- Identification of techniques used to separate proteins, including isoelectric point and electrophoresis

NON-ENZYMATIC PROTEIN FUNCTION

- Protein functions such as binding, immunity, and motors

ENZYME STRUCTURE AND FUNCTION

- The role of enzymes in biological reactions
- Classification of enzymes by the type of reaction catalyzed
- Definition of activation energy and identification of how enzymes lower the activation energy
- Enzyme specificity for a certain substrate and how this contributes to biological reactions
- Models of enzyme function, including the active site model and the induced-fit model
- The role and function of zymogens cofactors, coenzymes, and water-soluble vitamins
- How local conditions can alter enzyme function

CONTROL OF ENZYME ACTIVITY

- Enzyme kinetics, including the role of enzymes in catalysis, Michaelis–Menten, and cooperativity
- Definition and role of feedback inhibition
- Definitions of the types of inhibition, including competitive, noncompetitive, mixed, and uncompetitive inhibition
- The role and function of regulatory enzymes, such as allosteric enzymes and covalently modified enzymes
- The role and function of zymogens

NUCLEIC ACID STRUCTURE AND FUNCTION

- Overall description of nucleic acids and how these substances function in living systems
- Definitions of nucleotides and nucleosides, including the sugar phosphate backbone, purines, and pyrimidines
- Identification of the structure of DNA, including the double helix and the Watson–Crick model of DNA structure
- Identification of proper base pairing; A with T, G with C
- Changes in DNA structure as a result of denaturation, reannealing, and hybridization

PRINCIPLES OF BIOENERGETICS

- General concepts of bioenergetics and thermodynamics
- The definition of free energy and K_{eq}, the equilibrium constant
- How the equilibrium constant is related to the Gibbs free energy
- The role of concentration on bioenergetics and thermodynamics, especially with regards to Le Châtelier's principle
- Identification and characteristics of endothermic and exothermic reactions
- The definition and significance of Gibbs free energy, ΔG
- The role of $\Delta G°$ in determining spontaneity of a reaction
- The thermodynamics of phosphoryl group transfers and ATP
- The role of ΔG in ATP hydrolysis, ΔG is much less than 0; ATP group transfers
- Identification and understanding of biological oxidation–reduction reactions, and the roles of half-reactions, soluble electron carriers, and flavoproteins

CARBOHYDRATES

- Proper nomenclature, classification, and common names when discussing carbohydrates
- Identification of the absolute configuration of carbohydrates
- The conformations of hexoses, including their cyclic structure
- Identification of anomers and epimers
- The glycosidic bond and hydrolysis
- Definitions and structures of monosaccharides, disaccharides, and polysaccharides

GLYCOLYSIS, GLUCONEOGENESIS, AND THE PENTOSE PHOSPHATE PATHWAY

- Pathways of glycolysis under aerobic conditions including their substrates and products
- Pathways that feed into glycolysis, especially glycogen and starch metabolism
- Fermentation under anaerobic conditions
- Gluconeogenesis
- Pentose phosphate pathway
- The results of respiration, including the net molecules formed and net energy

PRINCIPLES OF METABOLIC REGULATION

- Identification of how metabolic pathways are regulated, as well as how the body is maintained in a dynamic steady state
- How the pathways of glycolysis and gluconeogenesis are regulated
- Pathway of glycogen metabolism
- How glycogen synthesis and breakdown is regulated based on conditions within the body, including allosteric and hormonal mechanisms
- Definition of metabolic control and analysis of the mechanisms that enable metabolic control

CITRIC ACID CYCLE

- Production of acetyl-coA by conversion of pyruvate by the pyruvate dehydrogenase complex
- The reactions of the citric acid cycle, including substrates and products
- How the cycle is regulated by conditions within the body
- Molecules required for the citric acid cycle as well as net energy and products

METABOLISM OF FATTY ACIDS AND PROTEINS

- Identification of the components and characteristics of fatty acids
- Fat transport, digestion, and mobilization
- Fatty acid oxidation of both saturated fats and unsaturated fatty acids
- Production and use of ketone bodies

OXIDATIVE PHOSPHORYLATION

- The structure and role of the electron transport chain in oxidative phosphorylation
- Substrates and products of the oxidative phosphorylation pathway
- General features of oxidative phosphorylation
- The process of electron transfer in mitochondria and the use of electron carriers (NADH, NADPH), flavoproteins, and cytochromes
- Function and structure of ATP synthase and the role of chemiosmotic coupling in oxidative phosphorylation
- How oxidative phosphorylation is regulated
- The role of mitochondria in apoptosis and oxidative stress

HORMONAL REGULATION AND INTEGRATION OF METABOLISM

- How hormone structure and function are integrated at a higher level
- Metabolism specific to certain tissues
- Regulation of fuel metabolism by hormones
- Body mass regulation and obesity

PLASMA MEMBRANE

- General function and composition
- Identification and role of lipids and proteins in the plasma membrane
- Lipid components, including phospholipids, phosphatides, steroids, and waxes
- Fluid mosaic model of plasma membrane structure
- Dynamics of the plasma membrane
- Transport of solutes across the plasma membrane, including thermodynamic considerations, osmosis, passive transport, and active transport
- Function and role of the sodium–potassium pump
- Description of membrane channels, membrane potential, and membrane receptors
- The roles of exocytosis and endocytosis in membrane traffic

MEMBRANE-BOUND ORGANELLES AND DEFINING CHARACTERISTICS OF EUKARYOTIC CELLS

- The structure of the mitochondrial inner and outer membrane

BIOSIGNALLING

- The role of oncogenes
- The process of apoptosis
- Types of gated-ion channels, including voltage-gated and ligand-gated channels
- Identification and function of G-protein-coupled receptors
- Identification and roles of receptor enzymes

LIPIDS

- Structure and description of lipids, including steroids, terpenes, and terpenoids

9.7 Biochemistry Worked Examples

PASSAGE I: OXIDATIVE PHOSPHORYLATION

Mitochondrial function is heavily regulated by calcium ions. When cytosolic $[Ca^{2+}]$ levels increase, that increase is transmitted to the mitochondria, where Ca^{2+} stimulates the activity of α-ketoglutarate dehydrogenase, isocitrate dehydrogenase, and pyruvate dehydrogenase. Excessive mitochondrial $[Ca^{2+}]$, however, can trigger mitochondrial release of cytochrome *c*. Derangements of mitochondrial $[Ca^{2+}]$ are believed to play a role in the damage to heart muscle that results from the changes in blood flow that occur in heart attacks.

Several proteins are involved in regulating mitochondrial calcium levels. One of these is the *mitochondrial calcium uniporter*, or mCU. mCU, which has low affinity for Ca^{2+} but a high capacity, allows passive transport of Ca^{2+} into the mitochondrial matrix. This occurs because there is a large voltage gradient across the inner mitochondrial membrane (approximately –200 mV on the matrix side).

Another protein that regulates mitochondrial $[Ca^{2+}]$ is the *sodium–calcium exchanger*, or NCX. This antiport protein is found both in the inner mitochondrial membrane and in the plasma membrane of cardiac myocytes. In its normal "forward" mode, NCX removes one Ca^{2+} ion from the mitochondrial matrix and allows three Na^+ to enter. In its "reverse" mode, NCX brings one Ca^{2+} ion into the matrix and removes three Na^+.

The flow of sodium ions across the inner mitochondrial membrane is intimately linked to the flow of protons by the *sodium–proton exchanger* (NHE), which can also run in reverse. Therefore, the flow of calcium also affects the flow of protons across the inner mitochondrial membrane, as depicted schematically in Figure 1. Note that because of pores in the outer mitochondrial membrane, ion concentrations in the intermembrane space are essentially identical with those in the cytosol.

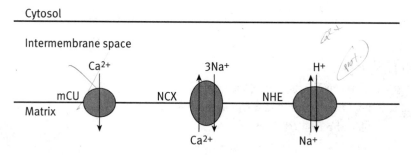

Figure 1. Ion carriers in the inner mitochondrial membrane

P1.

P2.

P3.

P4.

F1.

1. Based on information in the passage, which of the following is the most likely explanation for why the forward mode of NCX transports three sodium ions into the matrix for every one calcium ion it transports out?

   A. As a result, the antiporter does not consume ATP.
   B. NCX evolved from the Na^+/K^+ ATPase.
   C. It reduces the tendency of Ca^{2+} to re-enter the matrix. ✓
   D. It enhances ATP synthase's ability to produce ATP.

2. Based on information in the passage, mCU most likely has:

   A. a relatively high K_m value and a relatively high v_{max}. ✓
   B. a relatively high K_m value and a relatively low v_{max}.
   C. a relatively low K_m value and a relatively high v_{max}.
   D. a relatively low K_m value and a relatively low v_{max}.

3. A recently discovered protein in the intermembrane space of mitochondria in rat cardiac myocytes binds both Ca^{2+} and ATP synthase. A biochemist studying its function in isolated mitochondria found the following:

Intermembrane Ca/ATPase-binding protein concentration, μM	Intermembrane Ca^{2+} concentration, μM	ATP synthase activity (arbitrary units)
0.0	0.0	12.5
0.1	0.0	9.4
0.5	0.0	1.5
0.5	2.0	11.9

Which of the following conclusions regarding this protein is most reasonable?

   A. When the protein binds calcium ions, it binds to ATP synthase, increasing ATP synthase activity.
   B. The protein, which normally binds ATP synthase, loses its ability to bind ATP synthase when it binds to calcium. ✗
   C. The protein has a higher affinity for calcium than it does for ATP synthase. ✓
   D. The protein is one of the calcium-activated dehydrogenases mentioned in the passage.

4. A biochemist studying mCU has two samples of mitochondria. To one, the biochemist adds enough ruthenium red, a known mCU inhibitor, to completely inhibit mCU. Both samples are given radiolabeled glucose. The biochemist could most reasonably predict that the ruthenium red sample, compared to the control, would:

   A. exhibit complete cessation of ATP synthesis.
   B. have increased production of radiolabeled carbon dioxide. ✓
   C. exhibit a long-term decrease in ATP synthesis. ✗
   D. have increased production of radiolabeled ATP.

5. During a heart attack, cytosolic Ca^{2+} levels often increase. An increase in Ca^{2+} in the intermembrane space of mitochondria would most likely cause:

   A. increased ATP synthesis as a result of H^+ flow into the mitochondrial matrix.
   B. increased ATP synthesis as a result of H^+ flow out of the mitochondrial matrix.
   C. decreased ATP synthesis as a result of H^+ flow into the mitochondrial matrix. ✗
   D. decreased ATP synthesis as a result of H^+ flow out of the mitochondrial matrix ✓

Key Concepts

Skill 2—Scientific Reasoning and Problem-Solving

Membrane Potential
Oxidative Phosphorylation

Biochemistry Passage I Explanation:

USING THE KAPLAN METHODS

P1. Calcium affects mitochondrial activity

P2. mCU moves calcium into matrix

P3. NCX antiporter: 3 Na^+ for 1 Ca^{2+}

P4. NHE antiporter: 1 Na^+ for 1 H^+

Fig.1 Ion carriers in inner mitochondrial membrane

---

1. Based on information in the passage, which of the following is the most likely explanation for why the forward mode of NCX transports *three* sodium ions into the matrix for every *one* calcium ion it transports out?

   A. As a result, the antiporter does not consume ATP.
   B. NCX evolved from the Na^+/K^+ ATPase.
   C. It reduces the tendency of Ca^{2+} to re-enter the matrix.
   D. It enhances ATP synthase's ability to produce ATP.

 Assess the question

The words *most likely* in the question stem are a sign that we are expected to reason out the answer to this question. This question wants to know the reason *why* NCX exhibits a 3:1 charge ratio. When we see a *why* question, we should always ask ourselves two questions about the correct answer: *Is it true? Is it relevant?* If the answer to either question is no, we can eliminate that answer choice.

 Plan your attack

As the question stem notes, NCX normally ejects one Ca^{2+} ion for every *three* Na^+ ions that enter the matrix. The net result of this is that each time NCX operates in the forward mode, it moves a charge *into* the matrix.

Paragraph 2 of the passage states that there is large gradient across the inner mitochondrial membrane, with the matrix side at −200 mV, and that this drives the passive flow of Ca^{2+} into the matrix through the mCU.

Execute the plan

Combining these two facts, we can predict that each time the NCX fires in its forward mode, the inner mitochondrial membrane is *depolarized*: the gradient becomes smaller. Our correct answer should deal, in some way, with this decrease in the membrane potential.

 Answer by matching, eliminating, or guessing

Let's cycle through the answer choices. **(A)** is true, but it is irrelevant; the question asks *why* NCX works the way it does. **(B)** says that NCX evolved from the sodium–potassium pump. This might sound tempting—after all, the sodium–potassium pump moves three sodium ions out of the cell to move two potassium ions into the cell. It's a stretch, though, to reach the conclusion that NCX evolved from it.

Choice (C), however, fits the bill. If we're ejecting Ca^{2+} from the matrix, we don't want it to just re-enter the matrix again. Depolarizing the membrane would reduce the tendency of Ca^{2+} to enter the matrix via the mCU, which would prevent that from happening.

(D), on the other hand, is simply false. The chemiosmotic hypothesis states that ATP synthesis depends on the existence of a gradient across the inner mitochondrial membrane. Depolarizing that membrane would tend to reduce ATP synthase's ability to make ATP, not increase it.

Takeaways

When a science question asks for the *most likely* explanation, expect to combine facts.

Things to Watch Out For

Watch out for superficial similarities. While the sodium–potassium pump has the same charge balance as NCX, that's not proof that the NCX evolved from it.

Key Concepts

Skill 1—Scientific Reasoning and Problem-Solving

Enzyme Kinetics

2. Based on information in the passage, mCU most likely has:

A. a relatively high K_m value and a relatively high v_{max}.

B. a relatively high K_m value and a relatively low v_{max}.

C. a relatively low K_m value and a relatively high v_{max}.

D. a relatively low K_m value and a relatively low v_{max}.

 Assess the question

This is a Skill 1 question, asking us to simply identify two facts about mCU. First, does mCU have a relatively high value for K_m (the Michaelis constant), or a relatively low value? Second, does mCU have a relatively high v_{max} (maximum velocity), or a relatively low v_{max}?

 Plan your attack

mCU is discussed in paragraph 2, where we're told that mCU has a *low affinity* for calcium ions, but a *high capacity*.

The passage doesn't tell us, though, how that correlates to K_m and v_{max}, so we'll need to pull those from memory.

 Execute the plan

Of the two, v_{max} is simpler, so let's start there. In enzyme kinetics, v_{max} is a measure of how fast an enzyme can convert its substrate to product. Since we're told that mCU has a *high capacity*, we can assume that it can carry out its function quickly, which means it should have a high value for v_{max}.

K_m, the Michaelis constant, represents the substrate concentration at which the enzyme's velocity is one-half of v_{max}. Since the passage says that mCU has a *low affinity* for calcium ions, that means it does *not* bind Ca^{2+} very well. We would expect that it would take a relatively high concentration of Ca^{2+} to reach v_{max}, so K_m should also be relatively high.

4 **Answer by matching, eliminating, or guessing**

Once we know that v_{max} should be relatively high, we can eliminate **(B)** and **(D)**. The fact that K_m should also be relatively high eliminates the one remaining wrong answer choice, **(C)**, leaving **choice (A)** as the correct answer.

Takeaways

When questions have multipart answers, you should start eliminating wrong answers choice as soon as you've figured out one part.

Key Concepts

Skill 4—Data-Based and Statistical Reasoning

Enzyme Binding
Enzyme Inhibition

3. A recently discovered protein in the intermembrane space of mitochondria in rat cardiac myocytes binds both Ca^{2+} and ATP synthase. A biochemist studying its function in isolated mitochondria found the following:

Intermembrane Ca/ATPase-binding protein concentration, μM	Intermembrane Ca^{2+} concentration, μM	ATP synthase activity (arbitrary units)
0.0	0.0	12.5
0.1	0.0	9.4
0.5	0.0	1.5
0.5	2.0	11.9

Which of the following conclusions regarding this protein is most reasonable?

A. When the protein binds calcium ions, it binds to ATP synthase, increasing ATP synthase activity.

B. The protein, which normally binds ATP synthase, loses its ability to bind ATP synthase when it binds to calcium.

C. The protein has a higher affinity for calcium than it does for ATP synthase.

D. The protein is one of the calcium-activated dehydrogenases mentioned in the passage.

Assess the question

The presence of a table in the question stem should immediately tell you that this is a Skill 4 question, asking you for data-based reasoning. The question stem is asking us to draw the most reasonable conclusion among the four listed; there might be better ones, but those four are the only ones that matter on Test Day.

Moreover, this question talks about a completely new experiment that is only tangentially related to the topic of the passage, making it a good candidate for triaging. Finally, looking at the answer choices, we can see that our conclusions address the function of the protein that binds Ca^{2+} ions and ATP synthase.

Plan your attack

There doesn't appear to be any information in the passage that will help us answer this question. To answer it, we'll need to examine the table and see how changes in calcium and protein concentrations affect the activity of ATP synthase. Then we'll need to use our understanding of enzyme binding to draw a conclusion.

 Execute the plan

The first trial is our control; with zero protein and zero calcium, ATP synthase has a relatively high activity. In the second and third trials, the biochemist increases the concentration of the ATP synthase-binding protein, but leaves out calcium. What happens? ATP synthase activity drops, and the more protein we add, the more it drops. So we can reasonably conclude that the protein inhibits ATP synthase.

Looking at the last trial, though, the biochemist adds a lot of calcium to the inter-membrane space while also adding a lot of the protein. What happens now? ATP synthase activity is nearly normal! This suggests that calcium acts as an *antagonist* to this protein, preventing it from inhibiting ATP synthase activity. Now that we know what happens in this trial, we can look for an answer choice that matches our findings.

 Answer by matching, eliminating, or guessing

Scanning the answers, only one—**choice (B)**—agrees with our analysis. All of the others fail in some significant way.

(A) might be tempting, since ATP synthase activity does rise when calcium is added in the fourth trial, but it doesn't explain why ATP synthase activity decreases when the protein is added in the absence of calcium.

We don't have enough information to adequately decide on **(C)**. We know that 2.0 μM of calcium ions is enough to more-or-less completely restore ATP synthase ac-tivity, but, for all we know, that could be an enormous excess. Moreover, we can't be sure what the protein's affinity for ATP synthase is; even when we add 0.5 μM of protein, that's not enough to completely inhibit ATP synthase.

(D) suffers from the same problem as **(A)**: while that might be a reasonable infer-ence from the last two trials, it doesn't explain the overall data. Even worse, the dehydrogenases mentioned in the passage are part of the Krebs cycle, which takes place in the mitochondrial matrix. The question stem clearly states that this protein was discovered in the intermembrane space, not the matrix.

Things to Watch Out For

When a question asks *Which of the fol-lowing is most likely?*, remember that you're limited to the four choices in the answer question. Don't waste time try-ing to come up with the "best" possible conclusion!

Key Concepts

Skill 3—Reasoning about the Design and Execution of Research

Krebs Cycle
Electron Transport Chain
Oxidative Phosphorylation

---

4. A biochemist studying mCU has two samples of mitochondria. To one, the biochemist adds enough ruthenium red, a known mCU inhibitor, to completely inhibit mCU. Both samples are given radiolabeled glucose. The biochemist could most reasonably predict that the ruthenium red sample, compared to the control, would:

A. exhibit complete cessation of ATP synthesis.

B. have increased production of radiolabeled carbon dioxide.

C. exhibit a long-term decrease in ATP synthesis.

D. have increased production of radiolabeled ATP.

 Assess the question

This is an example of a Skill 3 question, which gives you details of a new experiment, and then asks what the researcher could predict. Two of the answers deal with decreases in ATP synthesis, while the other two deal with the radiolabeled carbon.

 Plan your attack

The first step here is to figure out what effect completely inhibiting mCU would have on the mitochondrion. That information is in paragraph 2, which says that mCU transports calcium into the matrix. But what effect does that have on the mitochondrion? To answer that question, we need to look at paragraph 1, which says that calcium ions upregulate the activity of dehydrogenases in the Krebs cycle.

So now we need to consider how the Krebs cycle feeds into ATP synthesis in oxidative phosphorylation. That information is not in the passage, so it'll need to come from our knowledge of aerobic respiration. We may also need to use our knowledge of how ATP synthase makes ATP.

 Execute the plan

If we inhibit mCU completely, that would reduce Ca^{2+} levels in the mitochondrial matrix. According to paragraph 1, that would reduce flux through the Krebs cycle, which would mean less NADH and $FADH_2$ would be produced. If we have less NADH and $FADH_2$, that necessarily means that we have *less* substrate available for the electron transport chain, and therefore we would expect a *decrease* in ATP synthesis.

4 **Answer by matching, eliminating, or guessing**

Scanning the answer choices, we can eliminate two answers immediately. **(B)** can't be the answer, because it would require *increased* flux through the Krebs cycle. **(D)** also doesn't work: not only would it require ATP synthesis, but the carbons from glucose are not directly incorporated into ATP during ATP synthesis.

That leaves two choices: **(A)**, which says that ATP synthesis stops completely, and **(C)**, which says it decreases. To decide which is correct, we need to look at paragraph 1, which says that Ca^{2+} *stimulates* enzymes in the Krebs cycle. *Stimulates* means that calcium increases their activity, but is not *required* for their activity. Thus, we can predict that a lack of calcium should slow down these enzymes, not shut them down. ATP synthesis should therefore decrease, not stop, so the correct answer is **choice (C)**.

MCAT Expertise

For Test Day, you are responsible for understanding ATP synthesis at the level of detail presented in an introductory biochemistry course, which would include the fact that carbons from glucose are not directly incorporated into ATP. You are *not* required, however, to know how adenosine and other nucleotides are actually synthesized.

Takeaways

When answer choices cover two (or more) different topics, you may need to consider multiple issues to determine the correct answer.

Key Concepts

Skill 2–Scientific Reasoning and Problem-Solving

Electron Transport Chain
Oxidative Phosphorylation

5. During a heart attack, cytosolic Ca^{2+} levels often increase. An increase in Ca^{2+} in the intermembrane space of mitochondria would most likely cause:

   A. increased ATP synthesis as a result of H^+ flow into the mitochondrial matrix.

   B. increased ATP synthesis as a result of H^+ flow out of the mitochondrial matrix.

   C. decreased ATP synthesis as a result of H^+ flow into the mitochondrial matrix.

   D. decreased ATP synthesis as a result of H^+ flow out of the mitochondrial matrix.

 Assess the question

This is a classic Skill 2 question, asking what would happen if cytosolic Ca^+ increases. The answers ask about whether ATP synthesis will increase or decrease, and the direction of flow of protons across the inner mitochondrial membrane.

 Plan your attack

To answer this question, we'll need two pieces of information. First, we need to figure out what effect increased Ca^{2+} levels have in the intermembrane space. The answer to that question will come from Figure 1.

The second piece of information is the effect of that flow on ATP synthesis. We'll need to pull that from our knowledge of the electron transport chain and oxidative phosphorylation.

 Execute the plan

According to Figure 1, the mCU brings Ca^{2+} in the intermembrane space into the matrix. When Ca^{2+} builds up in the matrix, NCX exchanges the extra calcium for sodium ions, so Na^+ will accumulate in the matrix. According to paragraph 4, the NHE exchanges Na^+ for H^+. So when Ca^{2+} builds up in the intermembrane space, the net result is the flow of protons *into* the mitochondrial matrix.

But does that help or hurt ATP synthesis? According to the chemiosmotic hypothesis, ATP synthase utilizes the proton gradient across the inner mitochondrial membrane as the energy source for ATP synthesis, and sends protons *into the matrix* to do so. (The electron transport chain uses the energy from oxidation of NADH and $FADH_2$ to move protons into the intermembrane space.) The flow of protons as a result of calcium buildup is the same as the flow of protons in ATP synthesis. We can conclude that the two processes compete for the same pool of protons, so ATP synthesis should decline.

 ## 4 Answer by matching, eliminating, or guessing

Once we predict that protons should flow into the mitochondrial matrix, we can immediately eliminate **(B)** and **(D)**. Knowledge of the chemiosmotic hypothesis allows us to confidently pick **choice (C)** as the correct answer.

MCAT Expertise

Many MCAT questions have two-part answers. Once you predict half the answer, it's worth checking the answer choices. Sometimes, only one answer choice has that part correct!

BIOCHEMISTRY PASSAGE II: METABOLIC REGULATION

In humans, the enzyme *isocitrate dehydrogenase* (IDH) exists in multiple forms; one form, IDH1, is found in the cytosol, while two others, IDH2 and IDH3, are expressed in the mitochondria. IDH3 exists as a heterotrimer of three subunits. In *E. coli,* a facultative anaerobe, only one IDH exists: it is a dimer of 416-subunit residues. The percentage of residues in *E. coli* IDH that are equivalent to those in any form of human IDH is less than 15 percent. Unlike all human IDH forms, *E. coli* IDH is inhibited by phosphorylation. Moreover, unlike most enzymes regulated by phosphorylation, *E. coli* IDH undergoes phosphorylation at its active site.

IDH phosphorylation is critical in *E. coli* because decreased IDH activity increases flow through the *glyoxylate cycle*, an alternative metabolic pathway shown schematically in Figure 1. The glyoxylate cycle, which is also found in plants, is used to bypass parts of the citric acid cycle when the organism is depending on fatty acids and/or acetyl-CoA as its primary source of energy. In the glyoxylate cycle, *isocitrate lyase* converts isocitrate to glyoxylate and succinate. *Malate synthase* then combines glyoxylate and a molecule of acetyl-CoA to form malate. Isocitrate lyase and malate synthase are not known to exist in humans, although recent evidence suggests that at least some vertebrates may produce them.

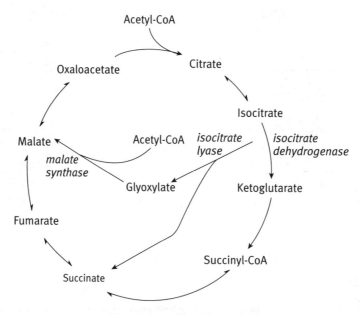

Figure 1. Glyoxylate cycle

To study IDH regulation, researchers cultured cells, as shown in Table 1, in media containing ^{31}P. After lysing the cells, SDS-PAGE was run on an aliquot from each sample. A Western blot, which gives a spot (a positive result) when a protein capable of binding a particular antibody is present, was performed on Samples 1–4 using an antibody that detects *E. coli* IDH.

Sample	Cells used	Carbon source used
1	E. coli	0.4% glucose
2	E. coli	0.4% sodium acetate
3	Human hepatocytes	0.4% glucose
4	Human hepatocytes	0.4% sodium acetate
5	E. coli	0.2% sodium acetate
6	E. coli	0.4% sodium acetate + 0.4% glucose

Table 1. Cell cultures used to study IDH activity

P1.

P2.

F1.

P3.

T1.

1. Which of the following most likely shows the result of the Western blot experiment described in the passage? (Note: the numbers 1 through 4 correspond to the samples in Table 1.)

A.
```
1  2  3  4


–  –  –  –
```

B.
```
1  2  3  4


        –  –
–  –  –  –
```

√C.
```
1  2  3  4



–  –
```

D.
```
1  2  3  4



   –
```

2. In *E. coli*, which of the following would be expected to increase as a consequence of a drop in IDH activity?

   I. Pyruvate kinase activity
   II. Acetyl-CoA levels
   III. CO_2 production

A. I only
B. II only
C. I and III only
D. I, II, and III

3. A biochemist decides to perform autoradiography, which can quantify the amount of a radioactive isotope present, on the samples described in Table 1. Based on information in the passage, he would predict that IDH from:

A. only Sample 1 would exhibit ^{31}P activity.
B. only Samples 2 and 5 would exhibit ^{31}P activity.
C. only Samples 2, 5, and 6 would exhibit ^{31}P activity.
D. all the IDH samples in Table 1 would exhibit ^{31}P activity.

4. Based on information in the passage, which of the following is the most likely explanation for how phosphorylation inhibits IDH in *E. coli*?

A. Phosphorylation causes allosteric changes to the active site that prevent isocitrate from binding.
B. Phosphorylation causes electrostatic repulsion of the negatively charged isocitrate.
C. Phosphorylation targets IDH for destruction by lysosomes.
D. Phosphorylation results in the dissociation of the IDH dimer.

5. In humans, IDH3 is NAD$^+$-dependent, while IDH1 and IDH2 are dependent on NADP$^+$. Which of the following would be LEAST likely to be true?

A. Expression of IDH1 is regulated by mechanisms that have no effect on IDH3 expression.
B. The values of K_m and V_{max} for IDH1 and IDH2 are likely to differ significantly from those for IDH3.
C. The gene for IDH1 and the gene for IDH3 are located on different chromosomes.
D. In vitro, the equilibrium ratio of isocitrate to α-ketoglutarate using IDH1 equals the ratio for IDH3.

Key Concepts

Skill 4—Data-Based and Statistical Reasoning

Non-Enzymatic Protein Function

Biochemistry Passage II Explanation:

USING THE KAPLAN METHOD

P1. Isocitrate dehydrogenase different in humans, *E. coli*

P2. Glyoxylate cycle

F1. Glyoxylate cycle and Krebs cycle

P3. IDH regulation experiment

T1. Cell cultures used in IDH regulation experiment

---

1. Which of the following most likely shows the result of the Western blot experiment described in the passage? (Note: the numbers 1 through 4 correspond to the samples in Table 1.)

A.

| 1 | 2 | 3 | 4 |

_ _ _ _

B.

| 1 | 2 | 3 | 4 |

_ _
= =
_ _ = =

C.

| 1 | 2 | 3 | 4 |

_ _

D.

| 1 | 2 | 3 | 4 |

_

 Assess the question

The AAMC has said the new MCAT will have an increased focus on testing your ability to interpret data. This Skill 4 question illustrates one way of doing that—giving you figures to interpret as the answer choices. The question stem is asking which of these four gels best corresponds to the results of the Western blot experiment in the passage. Note, though, that in every case, Sample 2 gives a positive result.

Plan your attack

To answer this question, we need the brief description of how Western blots work given in paragraph 3. We also need to know whether human IDH will respond to an antibody specific for *E. coli* IDH; to answer that question, we'll need information in paragraph 1.

Execute the plan

First, based on paragraph 3, a Western blot produces a spot whenever there's a protein capable of binding to the antibody. In this case, we're using an antibody for *E. coli* IDH.

To answer the second question, we need to know if the human IDH will bind the antibody. According to paragraph 1, there's less than a 15 percent match between the sequences of *E. coli* IDH and human IDH. If there's that little similarity, then it's reasonable to conclude that the antibody for *E. coli* IDH will *not* be able to bind human IDH. That means Samples 3 and 4 should give no response.

Answer by matching, eliminating, or guessing

If we look at the answer choices, we can immediately eliminate both (**A**) and (**B**): they show spots for lanes 3 and 4, where there shouldn't be any.

That leaves us with two choices, (**C**) and (**D**). To decide which one is correct, we need to ask: *Does* E. coli *always produce IDH?* The answer to this question is yes. Paragraph 1 tells us *E. coli* is a *facultative* anaerobe, which means it is capable of performing aerobic respiration if oxygen is present. In order to do that, it needs to have the enzymes of the Krebs cycle available. Both lanes 1 and 2 should thus yield a spot on a Western blot, so the answer is **choice (C)**.

Takeaways

Don't fall into the trap of "compartmentalizing" knowledge on Test Day. Some MCAT questions integrate knowledge from multiple areas.

Key Concepts

Skill 2—Scientific Reasoning and Problem-Solving

Principles of Metabolic Regulation
Citric Acid Cycle

2. In *E. coli*, which of the following would be expected to increase as a consequence of a drop in IDH activity?

   I.   Pyruvate kinase activity
   II. Acetyl-CoA levels
   III. CO_2 production

   A. I only
   B. II only
   C. I and III only
   D. I, II, and III

Assess the question

This is a Roman numeral question that asks us which of these three things *increases* when IDH activity *decreases*.

Plan your attack

To answer this question, we'll need to use Figure 1 and our knowledge of the Krebs cycle to figure out what happens when IDH activity drops. Since this is a Roman numeral question, though, we should check the answer choices *before* we start assessing the statements.

Since item I shows up three times, we should start there: if it's wrong, *we're done*. To determine if item I is true, we need to figure out what happens to pyruvate kinase activity. To do that, we'll need our knowledge of what pyruvate kinase does and how it's regulated.

If item I is true, then we should look at III, CO_2 production. Answering that will require our knowledge of the Krebs cycle. Finally, we might need to consider item II, acetyl-CoA levels. Acetyl-CoA shows up in Figure 1, so we'll need to look there.

Takeaways

With Roman numeral questions, checking the answer choices *before* considering the statements can save valuable time.

Execute the plan

According to Figure 1, if IDH doesn't convert isocitrate to α-ketoglutarate, it'll enter the glyoxylate cycle, where it'll be turned into glyoxylate and succinate. That means we bypass the formation of α-ketoglutarate and succinyl-CoA. This is important because both of those steps produce NADH, which is used to produce ATP. So less IDH activity means less ATP.

Pyruvate kinase, the last enzyme in glycolysis, produces ATP as it converts phosphoenolpyruvate (PEP) into pyruvate. Since ATP is a product of the reaction, Le Châtelier's principle says that low levels of it should *increase* pyruvate kinase's activity. Item I is therefore true.

Looking at item III, CO_2 production, isocitrate has six carbons, while succinate has four carbons. So where do the other two carbons go in the Krebs cycle? To CO_2! Less IDH activity means less CO_2 is produced, so item III is false.

 ### Answer by matching, eliminating, or guessing

Because item I is true, we can eliminate (**B**). Item III is false, which allows us to eliminate (**C**) and (**D**). So the correct answer must be **choice (A)**, and we don't even need to look at item II. That said, it's worth understanding *why* item II is false. According to the passage, when IDH activity drops, glyoxylate forms. Glyoxylate combines with acetyl-CoA to form oxaloacetate. So each time a molecule of isocitrate enters the glyoxylate cycle, a molecule of acetyl-CoA is *consumed*, not produced.

Key Concepts

Skill 3—Reasoning about the Design and Execution of Research

Citric Acid Cycle

3. A biochemist decides to perform autoradiography, which can quantify the amount of a radioactive isotope present, on the samples described in Table 1. Based on information in the passage, he would predict that IDH from:

A. only Sample 1 would exhibit ^{31}P activity.

B. only Samples 2 and 5 would exhibit ^{31}P activity.

C. only Samples 2, 5, and 6 would exhibit ^{31}P activity.

D. all the IDH samples in Table 1 would exhibit ^{31}P activity.

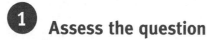 **Assess the question**

You might have been wondering why the passage mentioned ^{31}P but then didn't mention it again. Or you might have wondered why Table 1 includes six samples, while the Western blot experiment only used the first four. The first thing that should come to your mind in such cases is *There's probably a question coming up on that!* In this case, we have a Skill 3 question, asking us to formulate a hypothesis about incorporation of ^{31}P into IDH.

 **Plan your attack**

To answer this question, we'll need to synthesize the information in the passage on IDH phosphorylation—which is in paragraphs 1 and 2—with our understanding of how organisms regulate metabolic pathways.

 **Execute the plan**

Paragraph 2 states that IDH is phosphorylated when *E. coli* uses either fatty acids or acetyl-CoA as its primary fuel source. Paragraph 1 tells us that human IDH doesn't undergo phosphorylation. So we shouldn't expect any ^{31}P activity from Samples 3 and 4.

What does "primary fuel source" mean? Practically speaking, it means that no glucose is available. So we would predict that *E. coli* will phosphorylate IDH in the absence of glucose. Looking at Table 1, that's Samples 2 and 5.

4 Answer by matching, eliminating, or guessing

Choice (B) matches our prediction exactly.

(D) is wrong because human IDH is not regulated by phosphorylation. **(A)** doesn't work because Sample 1 relies on glucose as its primary source. Similarly, **(C)** is wrong because Sample 6 contains both acetate *and* glucose. Glucose is the preferred fuel source, and cells will almost invariably use that first when it's available.

Things to Watch Out For

Experiments with several trial groups are a great source of questions on Test Day.

Key Concepts

Skill 2—Scientific Reasoning and Problem-Solving

Control of Enzyme Activity

4. Based on information in the passage, which of the following is the most likely explanation for how phosphorylation inhibits IDH in *E. coli*?

   A. Phosphorylation causes allosteric changes to the active site that prevent isocitrate from binding.
   B. Phosphorylation causes electrostatic repulsion of the negatively charged socitrate.
   C. Phosphorylation targets IDH for destruction by lysosomes.
   D. Phosphorylation results in the dissociation of the IDH dimer.

① Assess the question

This is a Skill 2 question, asking us to figure out how phosphorylation causes inhibition of IDH in *E. coli*.

② Plan your attack

To answer this question, we need to draw on our knowledge of enzyme function and inhibition. We'll also need to know what the passage tells us about phosphorylation of IDH in *E. coli*; that information is in paragraph 1.

Things to Watch Out For

On Test Day, if an MCAT passage notes that a particular phenomenon is unusual, pay attention to it. This is often a signal that you'll be tested on that concept!

③ Execute the plan

Enzyme inhibition means that the activity of the enzyme drops. Paragraph 1 tells us that in *E. coli*, IDH *undergoes phosphorylation at its active site*. That tells us that whatever happens, it must involve a change at the active site.

4 **Answer by matching, eliminating, or guessing**

Cycling through the answer choices, the only one that could plausibly involve the active site is **choice (B)**.

(A) is what we might predict if we didn't look at paragraph 1; most enzymes that are regulated by phosphorylation undergo allosteric changes. **(C)** can't be true because we're talking about *E. coli*, which is a bacterium—and bacteria don't have organelles such as lysosomes. **(D)** *could* be true, but we're looking for the *most likely* explanation, and the passage doesn't give us any information that suggests that IDH *must* be dimerized to be active.

Similar Question

Based on information in the passage, the inhibition of IDH in *E. coli* most closely resembles:

A. reversible competitive inhibition.

B. irreversible competitive inhibition.

C. reversible noncompetitive inhibition.

D. irreversible noncompetitive inhibition.

Since the passage states that the phosphate group binds to the active site, we're dealing with a form of competitive inhibition. Since phosphorylation involves formation of a *covalent* bond, rather than a temporary electrostatic association between the substrate and active site, the inhibition is considered irreversible. The correct answer is **choice (B)**.

Key Concepts

Skill 2–Scientific Reasoning and Problem-Solving

Principles of Metabolic Regulation
Enzyme Activity

---

5. In humans, IDH3 is NAD$^+$-dependent, while IDH1 and IDH2 are dependent on NADP$^+$. Which of the following would be LEAST likely to be true?

A. Expression of IDH1 is regulated by mechanisms that have no effect on IDH3 expression.

B. The values of K$_m$ and V$_{max}$ for IDH1 and IDH2 are likely to differ significantly from those for IDH3.

C. The gene for IDH1 and the gene for IDH3 are located on different chromosomes.

D. In vitro, the equilibrium ratio of isocitrate to α-ketoglutarate using IDH1 equals the ratio for IDH3.

 Assess the question

This question tells us something new: IDH1 in humans uses NADP$^+$, while IDH3 uses NAD$^+$. The question then asks us, as a Skill 2 question often does, to draw a conclusion. But this question is more difficult because it asks us to identify the conclusion that is *least* likely to be true. Looking at the answer choices, there's no common theme running among them.

 Plan your attack

Questions that ask what is *LEAST likely to be true* are often more difficult because it's hard to predict what the correct answer will be. Our best bet will be to look at paragraph 1 to figure out what the passage tells us about IDH1, IDH2, and IDH3. We'll also need to use our knowledge of enzyme activity to answer this question.

3 **Execute the plan**

Paragraph 1 tells us that IDH1 is expressed in the cytosol, while IDH3 is expressed in the mitochondria, and that all three forms of IDH carry out the conversion of isocitrate to α-ketoglutarate. But, since IDH3 uses NAD$^+$ while IDH1 and IDH2 use NADP$^+$, we can conclude that the mechanism used by IDH3 is *different* from the mechanism used by IDH1 and IDH2. (Note: we can't say if IDH1 and IDH2 have the same mechanism or not.)

MCAT Expertise

The interface on Test Day allows you to highlight text in the passage, but it does *not* let you highlight question stems. If you want to make notes on questions, you'll need to write them down on your scratch paper.

At this point, it's useful to look through the answer choices one at a time. Since we're looking for the statement that is *LEAST likely*, anything that we can reasonably assume to be true can be eliminated; we want to select the answer that is either implausible or outright impossible.

 ## Answer by matching, eliminating, or guessing

Let's start with **(A)**. Can we think of a plausible scenario where IDH1 and IDH3 are regulated in different mechanisms? Absolutely. There's a great analogy in glucokinase and hexokinase. Both carry out the first step in glycolysis, but they are regulated in different ways. So **(A)** is likely to be true, and we can eliminate it.

(B) tests our understanding of enzyme kinetics. Should we expect IDH1 and IDH3 to have different values for v_{max}, the maximum velocity for the enzyme, and K_m, the substrate concentration at which it is half-saturated? Continuing our glucokinase/hexokinase discussion, absolutely. Glucokinase has a lower affinity for glucose than hexokinase, and therefore different values for K_m and v_{max}. So it's reasonable to expect the same thing to be true here.

(C) is actually the easiest of the four; nothing in the passage gives us any reason to believe that IDH1 and IDH3 should have their genes on the same chromosome, so **(C)** is also likely to be true. Even the genes for the α and β subunits of hemoglobin are located on different chromosomes!

By process of elimination, that leaves **(D)**. At first blush, this might seem to be true: enzymes *speed up* reactions, but they do not affect the *equilibrium* yield, since K_{eq} depends only on the relative stability of the reactants and products. But do IDH1 and IDH3 catalyze the same reaction? No! Since IDH1 depends on $NADP^+$, while IDH3 requires NAD^+, they don't. Thus they have two different expressions for K_{eq}, and we can't reasonably expect that the ratio of isocitrate to α-ketoglutarate will be the same. Since **choice (D)** is likely to be *false*, it's the answer that earns us a point.

9.8 Biochemistry Practice

PASSAGE III (QUESTIONS 1–5)

Peptide synthesis is a common target for antimicrobial compounds. Many such drugs, including chloramphenicol, work by directly inhibiting peptide bond synthesis. Another category, the macrolides, do not inhibit peptide bond formation, but instead block the channel through which newly synthesized peptides exit the ribosome, the nascent peptide exit tunnel (NPET).

Macrolides are molecules with lactone rings containing 14 to 16 atoms, and include erythromycin; a newer, more potent subclass called ketolides includes telrithromycin. Macrolides were long thought to act like a "plug" in the NPET, blocking so much of the tunnel that peptides cannot pass through. More recent evidence, however, suggests this theory is incorrect.

First, neither drug completely inhibits protein synthesis. At least some proteins can exit the NPET, and undergo complete translation, even in their presence. The likelihood of a protein being synthesized depends on its N-terminal sequence. Most sequences cause blockage of the NPET and an early end to protein synthesis, while some sequences permit complete synthesis of a protein. A sequence allowing full synthesis is shown in Figure 1; proteins with relatively homologous chains are also known to allow full synthesis. Moreover, a hybrid mRNA in which the sequence in Figure 1 precedes a chain that would normally be blocked also tends to be fully translated.

AUG	AGC	GAA	GCA	CUU	AAA	AUU	CUG	AAC	AAC	AUC	CGU
Met	Ser	Glu	Ala	Leu	Lys	Ile	Leu	Asn	Asn	Ile	Arg

Figure 1. A peptide sequence capable of escaping from a macrolide-bound NPET, along with its corresponding mRNA sequence

Second, telrithromycin is actually less effective than erythromycin at inhibiting synthesis: cells exposed to telrithromycin synthesize more proteins than do those exposed to erythromycin. Some proteins are fully expressed, while synthesis of some ends after just a few residues; in such cases, the nascent peptide falls out of the ribosome before the ribosome ever reaches a stop codon. (The human genetic code is depicted in Figure 2.)

Second letter

		U	C	A	G	
First letter	U	UUU } Phe UUC UUA } Leu UUG	UCU UCC } Ser UCA UCG	UAU } Tyr UAC UAA Stop UAG Stop	UGU } Cys UGC UGA Stop UGG Trp	U C A G
	C	CUU CUC } Leu CUA CUG	CCU CCC } Pro CCA CCG	CAU } His CAC CAA } Gln CAG	CGU CGC } Arg CGA CGG	U C A G
	A	AUU AUC } Ile AUA AUG Met	ACU ACC } Thr ACA ACG	AAU } Asn AAC AAA } Lys AAG	AGU } Ser AGC AGA } Arg AGG	U C A G
	G	GUU GUC } Val GUA GUG	GCU GCC } Ala GCA GCG	GAU } Asp GAC GAA } Glu GAG	GGU GGC } Gly GGA GGG	U C A G

(column on far right labeled **Third letter**)

Figure 2. The human genetic code for RNA molecules

P1.

P2.

P3.

F1.

P2.

F2.

1. A researcher cultures a bacterium sensitive to both erythromycin and telrithromycin on three agar plates. Plate 1 has erythromycin, plate 2 has telrithromycin, and plate 3 is a control. Based on information in the passage, the researcher would predict that the percentage of partially translated proteins would be:

   A. highest on plate 1 and lowest on plate 2.
   B. highest on plate 2 and lowest on plate 1.
   C. highest on plate 1 and lowest on plate 3.
   D. highest on plate 2 and lowest on plate 3.

2. Which of the following changes in the mRNA sequence shown in Figure 2 would most likely lead to the greatest inhibition in protein synthesis?

   A. Changing AGC to AGU in codon 2
   B. Changing GAA to GAG in codon 3
   C. Changing CUG to UUG in codon 8
   D. Changing AAC to AGC in codon 10

3. Based on information in the passage, which of the following changes is most likely to be observed in the first few minutes after erythromycin administration in a bacterium susceptible to it?

   A. A decrease in the concentration of charged tRNAs
   B. Covalent binding of 30S and 50S ribosomal subunits
   C. Mutations attaching the sequence in Figure 1 to other genes
   D. An increase in the concentration of peptidyl-tRNAs

4. The graph below shows protein synthesis in an *E. coli* cell culture in the absence of antibiotics.

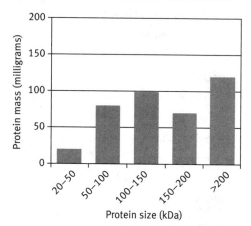

Which of the following graphs most likely represents the results obtained in the presence of telrithromycin? (Note: All vertical scales are the same as the graph above; peptides <20 kDa were not measured.)

A.

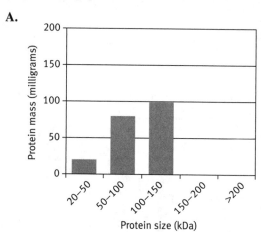

✓ **B.**

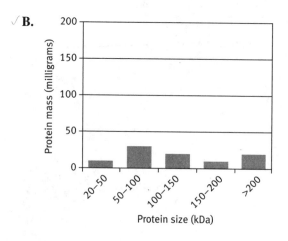

C.

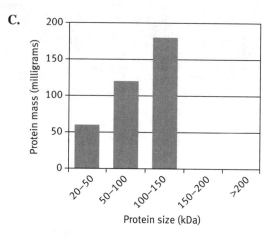

D.

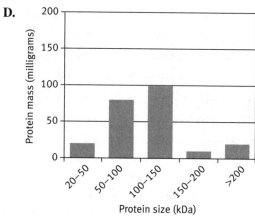

5. An *E. coli* cell is given methionine radiolabeled with ^{31}S. Five minutes later, which of the following is most likely to be true?

✓ **A.** Most proteins synthesized in that five-minute period will express the radiolabel at their N-terminus.

B. Most proteins synthesized in that five-minute period will express the radiolabel, but not at their N-terminus.

C. Most proteins synthesized in that five-minute period will express the radiolabel at both their N-terminus and at interior positions.

D. Both newly synthesized and already-existing proteins will exhibit the radiolabel.

This chapter continues on the next page ▶ ▶ ▶

Biochemistry Practice Passage Explanations

P1. Macrolide antibiotics

P2. "Plug in a bottle" mechanism probably wrong

P3. Still have protein synthesis

F1. Sequence that can evade macrolides, exit ribosome

P4. Erythromycin inhibits protein synthesis *more* than telrithromycin

F2. Human genetic code

1. (C)

The key to this question is a careful reading of the question stem and the passage. The question stem asks us which plate will have the highest and lowest percentages of *partially translated proteins*. Paragraph 2 tells us that telrithromycin is more potent than erythromycin, so we might be led to predict that the order is plate 2 (telrithromycin) > plate 1 (erythromycin) > plate 3 (control). That would lead us to **(D)**—which is a trap.

Paragraph 3 tells us that while telrithromycin is *more potent* as an antibiotic, it is actually *worse* at inhibiting synthesis than erythromycin is! So the correct answer is actually plate 1 > plate 2 > plate 3, which matches **choice (C)**.

2. (D)

Paragraph 3 states that the mRNA sequence shown in Figure 2 makes a peptide macrolide-resistant: it can escape the tunnel even if erythromycin or telrithromycin is bound. If we want the greatest *increase* in inhibition, then we need a significant change in the sequence of that peptide. To answer this question, we'll need to use the genetic code in Figure 2, and look for a mutation that would lead to a *different amino acid*. Cycling through the choices, we find that the correct answer is **choice (D)**: AAC codes for asparagine, while AGC codes for serine.

(A) Proximity to the start codon does not, by itself, increase the likelihood that a mutation would affect inhibition by macrolides.

(B) The third nucleotide in a codon is in the *wobble* position, which tends to be the most likely nucleotide to result in a *silent* mutation when altered.

(C) might look promising: it changes the *first* nucleotide in the codon. A look at the genetic code, though, shows us this is one of the few cases where such a mutation is actually silent; both CUG and UUG code for leucine.

3. (D)

We're looking for a change likely to happen in the presence of erythromycin. According to paragraph 4, erythromycin can cause the nascent peptide to fall out of the ribosome. However, since this happens without a stop codon, the nascent peptide

MCAT Expertise

With the exception of the start and stop codons, you are *not* expected to memorize the genetic code for Test Day. On the other hand, the MCAT will not ask a question that punishes superior knowledge. If you were asked this same question *without* being given the genetic code, the AAMC would not use CUG/UUG in an answer choice.

is not released from the tRNA, so we would expect a buildup of peptidyl-tRNA, or peptides still bound to tRNA molecules. This matches **choice (D)**.

(A) Since protein synthesis decreases, we would not expect the concentration of charged tRNAs to drop; if anything, they would increase.

(B) This would be true if erythromycin bound the two ribosomal subunits together, but nowhere does the passage imply this happens.

(C) Paragraph 4 states that this kind of mutation results in the expression of proteins that would normally be stopped by erythromycin. However, it is unlikely that such a mutation would happen spontaneously in the first few minutes after erythromycin administration.

4. (B)

The graph in the question stem represents the products of protein synthesis in normal *E. coli* cells. The graphs in the answer choices represent possible protein synthesis in *E. coli* after exposure to telrithromycin. According to paragraph 3, the inhibition of synthesis is determined only by the nature of the N-terminal sequence of the peptide. Since we have no reason to believe that there is a specific correlation between N-terminal sequence and protein size, we would expect an overall decrease in protein synthesis at *all* molecular masses. This matches **choice (B)**.

(A) This would be correct if the inhibition were based solely on molecular size (in this case, inhibiting synthesis of proteins >150 kDa in mass).

(C) The total amount of protein produced is the same; according to paragraph 4, protein synthesis drops when macrolides are given.

(D) This choice shows partial inhibition, as the passage states, but only for proteins with high molecular weights; as with **(A)**, we have no reason to believe the inhibition is limited to certain molecular weights.

5. (B)

Where would we find radiolabeled methionine after five minutes? *Every* peptide chain begins with methionine—the only codon for Met is also the start codon. But the majority of finished peptides do *not* have Met at their N-terminus; in most proteins, that initial Met, along with other N-terminal residues, are removed in post-translational processing. Among other things, that N-terminus sequence is often involved in signaling the destination of a protein (for example, whether it should end up in the cell membrane). There's also no mechanism for exchanging methionine in existing proteins, so the correct answer is **choice (B)**.

(A) Most initial methionines are lost in post-translational processing.

(C) Most proteins have internal methionines, but most of the initial methionines are removed.

(D) There is no mechanism for exchanging amino acids in existing proteins with new amino acids.

CHAPTER TEN

Biology

MCAT test-takers usually view biology as their strongest area, as many students taking the MCAT are majoring in or have earned degrees in the biological sciences. However, the MCAT does not seek to test biological knowledge; it aims to test the scientific thinking and reasoning skills required for success in medical school. While biology knowledge is important, it is how well you are able to use that knowledge that earns points on Test Day.

When encountering an MCAT biology passage, many students try to apply the same strategies they used when studying for undergraduate biology courses, including reading the passage for understanding and focusing on details in the passage. However, the MCAT is more like an open-book test and memorizing the details wastes time and doesn't necessarily result in correct answers. In this chapter, we will discuss the Kaplan approach to biology passages and questions.

10.1 Reading the Passage

One of the trademarks of MCAT biology passages is that the topic itself will be familiar, but the context will be unfamiliar. For example, a passage on action potential transmission may discuss rare diseases associated with derangements in neural transmission. The job of the test-taker is to apply what he or she already knows about the topic to new situations. The ability to use what you know in new ways is a significant part of succeeding as a medical student and a physician.

One of the biggest movements in modern medicine is the practice of evidence-based medicine. What this means is that a physician uses current studies and information as a guide to diagnosis and treatment. Thus, the MCAT has shifted to test these skills by presenting information in the context of a study, and asking questions about experimental design. In the Biological and Biochemical Foundations of Living Systems section, the areas tested include organic chemistry, biochemistry, and biology, with a small amount of general chemistry. Since experiments in chemistry do not typically involve control groups, population studies, or statistical analysis, you can expect that passages in biology will seek to test your skills in analyzing statistical data and evaluating experiment design. To that end, biological passages will require you to apply your knowledge in these areas.

PASSAGE TYPES

The passage types related to biology on the MCAT are the same as in the other sciences. However, there are specific differences related to the field of biology.

Information Passages

- Contain prose similar to that found in a textbook.
- A typical passage might discuss a particular disease, describe its symptoms, and include a discussion about the pathophysiology (how a disease occurs), including genetics, environmental factors, and derangements at the molecular level.
- In addition to a recounting of information, these passages may also describe previous studies within this field, providing statistical data from a particular study.
- A very large amount of detail may be present. Note that the details are present, and then move on. Avoid getting caught up in understanding every detail.

Experiment Passages

- Include one or more experiments and a description of the results in the form of a chart, graph, table, or diagram.
- Background information is generally presented to provide context.
- Experiments may be laboratory-based or population-based.
- Pay special attention to the hypothesis, experimental design, and results.

Remember, your goal is to get through a passage as quickly as possible but still read the passage critically enough to allow you to answer questions. Be careful not to spend so much time digesting a passage that you run out of time when answering questions. MCAT biology passages may contain a tremendous amount of information and data. However, it is important to remember that the passage will always be there to go back to, if needed.

	Passage Types in Biology	
	Information Passages	**Experiment Passages**
Scope	Discuss a particular phenomenon, disease, or study.	Discuss an experiment.
How to Read It	Read to get the gist of each paragraph; avoid getting caught up in the details.	Read to obtain the hypothesis, experimental design, and results.
Common Pitfalls	Spending too much time trying to understand and analyze the details.	Spending too much time trying to understand the procedure and results before the questions ask for it.

OUTLINING THE PASSAGE

Biology passages are often highly detailed, and integrate multiple concepts within biology. With the addition of biochemistry on the MCAT in 2015, the scope will also include biochemical concepts as well as organic and general chemistry. With the integration of a large number of possible topics and content areas, MCAT biology passages have the potential to be exceptionally detailed. While the details are important, there are no points awarded for one's ability to memorize and recall details. However, some sense of the details is required in order to answer the questions correctly. The key to a high score on Test Day is to find a balance between investing enough time into the passage to develop a solid understanding and reading quickly enough so that all of the questions may be answered in a timely manner. The most efficient way to do this is to read quickly, but critically, using the Kaplan way.

Scan for Structure
- Look at the passage, taking note of the presence of charts, graphs, tables, or diagrams.
  - Determine the topic and degree of difficulty.
  - Triage the passage, deciding whether to do it now or later.

Read Strategically
- Identify the type of passage.
- Actively read every paragraph, asking, "What is being said here? Why is this information here?"
- If you see lists of details or the passage becomes exceptionally detailed, move quickly, taking note of the presence of details, not the actual identity of those details.
- Do not stop to analyze how the details fit or what the details mean.
- Keep moving, but get the gist of each paragraph.

Label Each Component
- Write down the purpose of each paragraph, chart, graph, table, or diagram.
- If an image has a relationship with a paragraph, be sure to note that.
- If it was an experiment passage, be sure to note the hypothesis, procedure, and outcome.
- If it was an information passage, identify the general subject area.
- Note any lists of details so that these can be identified quickly.
- Keep your outline simple, just enough so that you can find required information.

Reflect on Your Outline
- Identify the goal of the passage. Why was this passage written?

10.2 Answering the Questions

Like the other sciences, biology questions follow the four basic types of questions.

Discrete questions
- Questions that are not based on a passage.
- Often preceded by a warning such as, "Questions 12–15 are not based on a descriptive passage."
- Most likely to ask a question about either a piece of information that you already know or a concept that will require you to apply your knowledge.

Questions that stand alone from the passage
- Questions that are within a block of passage-based questions but do not actually require the passage to determine the answer.
- Usually are related to the topic of the passage, but will likely ask you to apply your knowledge to a new situation.

Questions that require data from the passage
- These questions may require information or data from the passage.
- Very likely to ask you to apply your knowledge to a new situation.
- May involve statistical analysis, evaluation of experimental design, interpretation of data and/or information, or identification of a relationship between concepts.

Questions that require the goal of the passage
- Common goals of these questions include evaluation of the validity of a hypothesis, identification of supporting or refuting evidence, comparison of related topics, or interpretation/analysis of a theory given a new piece of evidence.
- Interpretation of data from a table, chart, or graph may also be required.

DETERMINING THE PURPOSE OF THE QUESTION

MCAT biology covers a tremendous amount of topics. In addition, an understanding of several background concepts may be required in order to answer the question. Answering the questions quickly, efficiently, and correctly requires a solid passage outline and a systematic approach to ensure that essential details are not missed.

1. Assess the Question

- Read the question but avoid reading the answers.
- Determine the type of question and the degree of difficulty.
- Make a judgment regarding how much work the question will require. Does it appear to require extensive information from the passage or a large amount of analysis?
- Decide whether to do the question now or later.

2. Plan Your Attack

- Identify the question task. What is this question asking you to do? Analyze data or experiment design? Evaluate concepts or data with respect to a new piece of information?
- Using the task of the question, determine what must be done in order to arrive at an answer. Does the question require data or information from the passage?

3. Execute Your Plan

- Carry out the plan as determined in the previous step.
- Use your outline to find required information or to remind yourself of the passage goal.
- Look up the required information, analyze the data, evaluate new information presented.

4. Answer the Question by Matching, Eliminating, or Guessing

- Match your answer to the answer choices.
- If there is no clear match, start by eliminating the incorrect answers.
- Incorrect answers often come in the form of answers that simply do not make sense. Critically read the answer choices and determine which answer choices do not make sense.
- If a clear answer does not emerge, do your best to eliminate at least two answers, and guess between the remaining two answers.
- Avoid blind guessing: the best guesses are ones that are educated, with a reason for choosing a particular answer.

10.3 Getting the Edge in Biology

Success on MCAT biology passages requires a quick, but thorough, reading of the passage coupled with an excellent passage outline. MCAT biology passages will often cover a wide range of topics, with a large amount of detail. Learning to identify the location of the detail without investing time in the interpretation of those details is an essential reading skill for Test Day success. This is often very difficult for students to learn how to do as it runs counter to how most students study for their undergraduate classes. But, the MCAT is not like the tests administered in undergraduate classes, as it requires much more than memorization of concepts and details; the MCAT requires interpretation and evaluation of the concepts and details, but only when required by a question.

Answering questions on MCAT biology passages requires quick location of information using a passage outline. In addition, the questions require students to think critically about both the question stem and the answer choices. Approaching the question stem and answer choices with confidence and a critical eye will allow you to identify the correct question task and eliminate incorrect answer choices.

10.4 Step-By-Step Guide to Biology Passages

OUTLINING THE PASSAGE

- **Scan for structure**
  - Determine whether to do this passage now or later.
  - Identify the structure of the passage, including charts, graphs, tables, diagrams, and/or large blocks of text.

- **Read strategically**
  - Identify the type of passage.
  - Pay special attention to the relationships between concepts.
  - In an experiment passage, determine the hypothesis, procedure, and outcome.
  - In an information passage, identify how the information in each paragraph fits together to present a unified picture.
  - Identify what information is presented in each figure or image.

- **Label each component**
  - Write down the purpose of each paragraph, chart, table, graph, or diagram.
  - If a paragraph and image are related, be sure to note this, as paragraphs may be entirely devoted to describing a diagram or chart.
  - If a paragraph discusses experiment procedure or study design, be sure to make a note of it, as biology passages are ripe for evaluation of these research concepts.
  - Identify any connections between concepts within the passage.
  - Make sure each part of your outline identifies the topic, as your outline will help you to make sense of a potentially wide range of concepts within a biology passage.

- **Reflect on your outline**
  - Determine the goal of the passage and write it down.
  - Identify the concepts within the passage in an effort to anticipate questions.
  - Identify any relationships between the concepts within the passage.

ANSWERING THE QUESTIONS

1. Assess the Question

- Determine whether this question should be done now or later.
- Identify the topic and the degree of difficulty.
- Good questions to do now in biology are those that do not require extensive integration of information or data from the passage. These are often the questions that stand alone from the passage.

2. Plan Your Attack

- Determine what you already know, and what information you need.
- Identify where to find the required information: the passage, the question, your outline, or your own knowledge.
- If you have to go back to the passage, determine where to find the required information by using your outline.
- If data analysis is required, identify the data set.
- If analysis of experimental procedure or data is required, identify where that information can be found.

3. Execute Your Plan

- Analyze the data, go back to the passage, and carry out your plan.
- If you get stuck analyzing data, remember that the trend of the data is often enough to yield a correct answer choice.
- If you are analyzing study design, be sure to identify the variables and the control group, as well as the hypothesis or reason for the study.

4. Answer the Question by Matching, Eliminating, or Guessing

- Match your answer to the answer choices.
- If there is no match, eliminate incorrect answer choices. Some of the answer choices may not make sense; eliminate those first.
- If elimination does not provide a clear answer, guess between two probable answers.

10.5 Preparing for the MCAT: Biology

These are the biology topics that you are likely to see on Test Day. Note this list does not include topics for which biochemistry knowledge is also required; those topics are listed in Section 9.6.

PROTEIN STRUCTURE

- Recognition of the different levels of structure and conformational stability

NONENZYMATIC PROTEIN FUNCTION

- Within the immune system and as motors

ENZYME STRUCTURE AND FUNCTION

- Applying the different models of enzymatic structure and function and defining control of enzyme activity

NUCLEIC ACID STRUCTURE AND FUNCTION

- The role of nucleic acids in the transmission of genetic information

DNA REPLICATION

- The process and mechanism of DNA replication, including strand separation, and coupling of nucleic acids
- Definition of replication as a semi-conservative process
- Identification of specific enzymes involved in replication
- Definition and identification of origins of replication; the existence of multiple origins of replication in eukaryotes
- The process and significance of replication of the ends of DNA molecules

REPAIR OF DNA

- Mechanisms of DNA repair during replication
- Mechanisms of mutation repair

GENETIC CODE

- The Central Dogma of molecular biology, the flow of information from DNA to RNA to protein
- The genetic code as triplets
- The relationship between codons and anticodons
- The concept of a degenerate code and the role of wobble pairing
- The definition and significance of missense and nonsense codons
- The definition, role, and structure of mRNA (messenger RNA)
- The use of initiation and termination codons in the genetic code

TRANSCRIPTION

- The definition and role of transfer RNA (tRNA)
- The definition and role of ribosomal RNA (rRNA)
- The mechanism of transcription
- The process and significance of mRNA processing in eukaryotes, including introns and exons
- The roles of ribozymes, spliceosomes, small nuclear ribonucleoproteins, and small nuclear RNA (snRNAs)
- The definition and function of introns, and their evolutionary significance

TRANSLATION

- Definitions and roles of mRNA, tRNA, and rRNA
- Structure and role of ribosomes
- Cofactors required for initiation and termination
- Modification of proteins after translation

EUKARYOTIC CHROMOSOME ORGANIZATION

- Proteins associated with chromosomes
- Definitions, significance, and differences between single-copy *vs.* repetitive DNA
- Definition and significance of supercoiling
- Differences between heterochromatin and euchromatin
- Identification and roles of centromeres and telomeres

CONTROL OF GENE EXPRESSION IN PROKARYOTES

- The concept of operons and the Jacob–Monod model of operon function
- Mechanisms and function of gene repression in bacteria
- Mechanisms of positive control in bacteria

CONTROL OF GENES EXPRESSION IN EUKARYOTES

- Regulation of genes at the level of transcription
- The role and function of DNA-binding proteins and transcription factors
- Amplification and duplication of genes
- Concept of gene splicing, including introns and exons
- Control of gene expression at the post-transcriptional level
- Process by which a failure of normal cellular controls results in cancer, including the roles of tumor-suppressor genes and oncogenes
- Chromatin structure regulation
- Methylation of DNA
- Definition and role of noncoding RNAs

RECOMBINANT DNA AND BIOTECHNOLOGY

- The process of gene cloning
- The definition and use of restriction enzymes
- Characteristics and formation of DNA libraries
- Process used for the generation of cDNA
- The process of hybridization
- The process by which cloned genes are expressed
- The process and general use of the polymerase chain reaction
- The procedures and use of gel electrophoresis and Southern blotting
- Mechanism of DNA sequencing
- The process of gene expression analysis
- How gene functions are determined
- The definition, role, and significance of stem cells
- DNA technology for practical use, including medical applications, human gene therapy, pharmaceuticals, forensic evidence, environmental cleanup, and agriculture
- Safety and ethical considerations in DNA technology

EVIDENCE THAT DNA IS GENETIC MATERIAL

- Understanding of experiments that have shown that DNA is inherited and expressed to create a particular phenotype.

MENDELIAN CONCEPTS

- Definitions of phenotype and genotype and how the concepts are related
- Definitions of gene and locus
- The role of alleles; definition of single allele and multiple alleles
- Definitions of homozygosity and heterozygosity
- Definition of wild type
- Concepts of recessiveness, complete dominance, codominance, incomplete dominance, leakage, penetrance, and expressivity
- The definition of hybridization and the concept of hybrid viability
- Definition and significance of the gene pool

MEIOSIS AND OTHER FACTORS AFFECTING GENETIC VARIABILITY

- The process and significance of meiosis
- Comparison of meiosis and mitosis, including significant differences
- The process of gene segregation, including independent assortment and linkage
- Gene recombination, including single crossovers, the double crossovers, synaptonemal complex, and tetrad formation
- Concept, identification, and definition of sex-linked characteristics
- The Y chromosome and its lack of genetic information
- How sex is determined
- The definition, patterns, and process of cytoplasmic/extranuclear inheritance
- Mutations, including the general concept of mutations as an errors in DNA sequence
- Types of mutations and consequences, including random, translation error, transcription error, base substitution, inversion, addition, deletion, translocation, and mispairing
- The definitions and roles of advantageous and deleterious mutations
- Definition and significance of inborn errors of metabolism
- The relationship between mutagens and carcinogens
- Definition and consequences of genetic drift
- The mechanism of crossing over or synapsis for increasing genetic diversity

ANALYTIC METHODS IN GENETICS

- Definition and application of the Hardy–Weinberg principle
- Use and role of a test cross or backcross, including the concepts of the parental, F1, and F2 generations
- Using crossover frequencies to create a gene map
- Statistical methods used to study biological phenomena; biometry

EVOLUTION

- The concept of natural selection as related to fitness and selection by differential reproduction
- The concepts of natural and group selection
- Measuring evolutionary success as an increase in the percent representation of alleles in the gene pool of the next generation
- Speciation as a result of polymorphism, adaptation, and specialization
- Definitions, roles, and characteristics of outbreeding, inbreeding, and bottlenecks
- Measuring evolutionary time by gradual random changes in the genome

METABOLISM OF FATTY ACIDS AND PROTEINS

- Fat anabolism
- Biosynthesis of lipids and polysaccharides as a non-template synthesis mechanism
- Protein metabolism

PLASMA MEMBRANE

- Junctions between cells, including gap junctions, tight junctions, and desmosomes

MEMBRANE-BOUND ORGANELLES AND DEFINING CHARACTERISTICS OF EUKARYOTIC CELLS

- Characteristics of eukaryotic cells, including membrane-bound nucleus, presence of organelles, and mitotic division
- Structure and function of the nucleus, including compartmentalization, storage of genetic information, the nucleolus, nuclear envelope, and nuclear pores
- Location and function of the nucleolus
- Mitochondria as the site of ATP production
- Structure of the inner and outer membrane of mitochondria
- Mitochondrial self-replication
- Characteristics of lysosomes as a membrane-bound vesicle containing hydrolytic enzymes
- Structure and role of the endoplasmic reticulum, including rough and smooth components; ribosome relocation to the ER; double membrane structure, role in membrane biosynthesis; and role in secretion of proteins
- Structure and function of the Golgi apparatus, especially in packaging and secretion
- Function of peroxisomes as a hydrogen-peroxide containing organelle

CYTOSKELETON

- General function of the cytoskeleton in cell support and movement
- Composition of microfilaments, and their role in cleavage and contractility
- Composition of microtubules and their role in and transport
- Role of intermediate filaments in support
- Function and composition of flagella and cilia
- Microtubule organizing centers and centrioles

TISSUES FORMED FROM EUKARYOTIC CELLS

- Connective tissue cells
- Epithelial cells

CELL THEORY

- The history and development of cell theory
- How cell theory changed biology

CLASSIFICATION AND STRUCTURE OF PROKARYOTIC CELLS

- Prokaryotic domains, including Archaea and Bacteria
- Classification of bacteria by shape, including bacilli (rod-shaped), spirilli (spiral-shaped), and cocci (spherical)
- Characteristics and structure of prokaryotic cells, including the lack of a nuclear membrane, mitotic apparatus, and typical eukaryotic organelles
- Composition and presence of cell wall in bacteria
- Characteristics and mechanism of flagellar propulsion

GROWTH AND PHYSIOLOGY OF PROKARYOTIC CELLS

- Prokaryotic mechanism of reproduction by fission
- Prokaryotic genetic adaptability and the relationship with acquisition of antibiotic resistance
- Growth characteristics, including exponential growth
- Definition and fundamental characteristics of anaerobes and aerobes
- Definitions of parasitic and symbiotic relationships
- Bacterial movement and chemotaxis

GENETICS OF PROKARYOTIC CELLS

- Extragenomic DNA and plasmids
- Definition and significance of transformation as a mechanism by which DNA fragments from the external medium are incorporated into the bacterial genome
- Definition and significance of conjugation
- The role and function of transposons

VIRAL STRUCTURE

- General structure of viruses, including nucleic acid, protein, presence or absence of an envelope, and the lack of organelles or a nucleus
- Structure of a typical bacteriophage
- Variations in the contents of the viral genome (RNA or DNA)
- The relative size of viruses compared to bacteria and eukaryotic cells

VIRAL LIFE CYCLE

- Viral reproduction as a self-replicating biological unit that requires the machinery of a host cell for reproduction
- The general life cycles of phages and animal viruses, including attachment to host, penetration of cell membrane or cell wall, entry of viral genetic material, replication of viral components using the machinery of the host cell, and self-assembly and release of new viral particles
- Definition and significance of transduction as a transfer of genetic material by viruses
- The life cycle of retroviruses, including integration into host DNA; the purpose of reverse transcriptase
- The HIV life cycle
- Subviral particles, including prions and viroids

MITOSIS

- The process of mitosis, including the stages of prophase, metaphase, anaphase, telophase, and interphase
- Identification and role of structures involved in mitosis, including centrioles, asters, spindles, chromatids, centromeres, kinetochores, nuclear membrane (both breakdown and reorganization), and chromosomes (especially movement patterns)
- Identification and significance of each portion of the cell cycle, including G0, G1, S, G2, and M phases
- Mechanism and purpose of growth arrest
- Mechanisms and role of cell-cycle control
- Significance of loss of cell-cycle controls in cancer cells

REPRODUCTIVE SYSTEM

- The process of gametogenesis by meiosis
- Compare and contrast ovum and sperm with regard to differences in formation, morphology, and relative contribution to the next generation
- Identification of the reproductive sequence, including fertilization, implantation, development, and birth

EMBRYOGENESIS

- Identification and processes occurring during early embryological development, including fertilization, cleavage, blastula formation, gastrulation, and neurulation
- The process of gastrulation, including first cell movements and the formation of the primary germ layers (endoderm, mesoderm, and ectoderm)
- Identification of major structures arising from the primary germ layers
- Identification and significance of the neural crest
- Interactions between the environment and genes during development

MECHANISMS OF DEVELOPMENT

- Mechanisms of cell specialization, including determination and differentiation and how these processes result in different tissue types
- Identification of cell–cell communication mechanisms during development
- Patterns of cell migration
- The definition of pluripotency and how it relates to stem cells
- Regulation of genes during development
- The role of programmed cell death (apoptosis) during development
- Definition of regenerative capacity and its existence in certain species
- Definition of senescence and how it applies to aging

NERVOUS SYSTEM: STRUCTURE AND FUNCTION

- Identification of the major functions of the nervous system, including high level control and integration of body systems and adaptive capability to external influences
- Identification of the basic organization of the nervous system
- The roles and relationship between sensor and effector neurons
- Roles, functions, and antagonistic control of the sympathetic and parasympathetic nervous system
- Identification of reflexes, including the feedback loop and reflex arc as well as the role of the spinal cord and supraspinal circuits
- Identification of feedback control and integration of the nervous system with the endocrine system

NERVE CELL

- Identification of the cell body and the structures it contains, including the nucleus and organelles
- Structure and role of the dendrites as branched extensions of the cell body
- Structure and function of the axon
- Identification of the myelin sheath as produced by Schwann cells and its function as an insulator of the axon**
- The process by which saltatory conduction occurs to propagate the nerve impulse and the role of nodes of Ranvier**
- Identification of the synapse as the site of impulse propagation between cells
- The role of transmitter molecules in synaptic activity
- Identification and role of the resting potential and the function of the electrochemical gradient
- Transmission of nerve impulses by the action potential, including the threshold potential, all-or-nothing conduction of impulses, and the role of the sodium–potassium pump
- The purpose and relationship between excitatory and inhibitory nerve fibers; frequency of firing
- The definition of summation
- The purpose of glial cells and neuroglia

**This topic can also be tested on the Chemical & Physical Foundations of Biological Systems section.

ENDOCRINE SYSTEM: HORMONES AND THEIR SOURCES

- The function of the endocrine system and how it exerts specific chemical control at the cell, tissue, and organ level
- Definitions of endocrine gland and hormone
- The names, locations, and products of major endocrine glands
- Major types of hormones
- Neuroendocrinology as the study of the relationship between neurons and hormonal systems

ENDOCRINE SYSTEM: MECHANISMS OF HORMONE ACTION

- Mechanisms of hormone action at the cellular level
- Blood supply and the transport of hormones to target tissues
- Hormone specificity and its relationship to the target tissue
- Nervous system integration and feedback control regulation by second messengers

RESPIRATORY SYSTEM

- General functions of the respiratory system, including gas exchange, thermoregulation, protection against disease, and particulate matter filtration
- Identification of the structure of lungs and alveoli
- Mechanisms of breathing, including the roles of the diaphragm, rib cage, differential pressure, resiliency, and surface tension effects
- Function of the respiratory system in thermoregulation, including the roles of the nasal and tracheal capillary beds, evaporation, and panting
- Function of the respiratory system in particulate filtration, including the roles of nasal hairs and the mucus/cilia system in lungs
- Mechanism of alveolar gas exchange, including diffusion and differential partial pressure
- Control of pH using respiration
- Regulation of respiration by nervous control, including CO_2 sensitivity

CIRCULATORY SYSTEM

- Functions of the circulatory system, including circulation of oxygen, nutrients, hormones, ions, and fluids and the removal of metabolic waste
- The role of the circulatory system in thermoregulation
- Structure and function of the four-chambered heart
- Identification and role of endothelial cells
- Definitions of systolic and diastolic pressures and which parts of the circulatory cycle are represented by each
- Circulation, including the pulmonary and systemic circulations
- Structure and functional differences between the arterial and venous systems**
- Structures of the arterial (arteries, arterioles) and venous (venules, veins) systems
- Differences between the pressure and flow characteristics of the arterial and venous systems
- The mechanisms of gas and solute exchange and heat exchange in the capillary beds
- The capillary beds as a source of peripheral resistance
- The composition of blood, including plasma, chemicals, and blood cells
- Production of erythrocytes in the bone marrow and destruction of erythrocytes in the spleen
- Regulation of plasma volume
- Mechanisms of coagulation and clotting
- Transport of oxygen by blood, including the role of hemoglobin and the definition of hematocrit
- Oxygen content, affinity, and transport of blood; modification of oxygen affinity as related to conditions and location (tissues or lungs)
- Transport and level of carbon dioxide in blood
- Control of the circulatory system by the nervous and endocrine systems

LYMPHATIC SYSTEM

- General structure of the lymphatic system
- Functions of the lymphatic system, including equalization of fluid distribution, transport of proteins and large glycerides, production of lymphocytes involved in immune reactions, and return of materials to the blood

**This topic can also be tested on the Chemical & Physical Foundations of Biological Systems section.

IMMUNE SYSTEM

- Definitions and targets of the innate (nonspecific) and adaptive (specific) immunity
- Cells of the adaptive immune systems, including T-lymphocytes and B-lymphocytes
- Cells of the innate immune system, including macrophages and phagocytes
- Major tissues of the immune system including the spleen, bone marrow, thymus, and lymph nodes
- Definition of antigen and antibody
- How antigens are presented in the immune system
- Clonal selection
- Antigen-antibody recognition
- The structure of antibodies
- Autoimmune disease and the process by which the immune system distinguishes self from non-self
- The role of the major histocompatibility complex

DIGESTIVE SYSTEM

- The process of ingestion, including saliva as lubricant and source of enzymes, and the role of the esophagus and esophageal transport
- Structure and role of the stomach, including storage, churning of food, production of digestive enzymes, and site of digestion
- The role of low pH and gastric juice in digestion, and mucosal protection against self-destruction
- The structural relationship of the liver within the gastrointestinal system and the roles of the liver, including production of bile, blood glucose regulation, and detoxification
- Function of bile and its storage in the gall bladder
- The role of the pancreas in digestion, including production of enzymes and transport of enzymes to the small intestine
- The structure (including divisions) and role of the small intestine in digestion, including absorption of food molecules and water, production of enzymes, site of digestion, and neutralization of stomach acid
- Function and structure of villi within the small intestine
- The gross structure and function of the large intestine, including absorption of water and location of bacterial flora
- The role of the rectum in storage and elimination of waste and feces
- Muscular control of the gastrointestinal system, including the role and nature of peristalsis
- Endocrine control of the gastrointestinal system by hormones and target tissues
- The enteric nervous system and how it exerts nervous control over functions of the gastrointestinal system

EXCRETORY SYSTEM

- Roles of the excretory system in homeostasis, including blood pressure regulation, osmoregulation, acid–base balance, and removal of soluble nitrogenous waste
- Structure of the kidney, including the cortex and medulla
- Structure of the nephron, including the glomerulus, Bowman's capsule, proximal convoluted tubule, loop of Henle, distal convoluted tubule, and collecting duct
- Urine formation including the concepts of glomerulus filtration, secretion and reabsorption of solutes, concentration of urine, and the counter-current multiplier system
- Storage and elimination of urine by the ureter, bladder, and urethra
- Osmoregulation and the role of capillary resorption of H_2O, amino acids, glucose, and ions
- Muscular control of urination, including the sphincter muscle

REPRODUCTIVE SYSTEM

- Structure and function of the male and female reproductive systems, including gonads and genitalia
- Differences between male and female structures
- Control of reproduction by hormones, including male and female sexual development, female reproductive cycle, pregnancy, parturition (birth), lactation, and integration with nervous control

MUSCLE SYSTEM

- Functions of the muscle system, including support for mobility, peripheral circulatory assistance, and thermoregulation by the shivering reflex
- Identification and structure of the three basic muscle types, including striated, smooth, and cardiac muscle
- Structure of muscle, including the T-tubule system, contractile apparatus, sarcoplasmic reticulum, and fiber type; control of contraction
- Contractile velocity of different muscle types
- Cardiac muscle contraction and regulation
- Fatigue and oxygen debt
- Nervous control within the muscle system, including motor neurons, neuromuscular junction, motor end plates, sympathetic and parasympathetic innervation, and voluntary and involuntary muscles

SPECIALIZED CELL–MUSCLE CELL

- Structure and characteristics of striated, smooth, and cardiac muscle cells
- Significant quantities of mitochondria in red muscle cells to produce a ready ATP source
- Identification and organization of contractile elements within muscles, including actin and myosin filaments, crossbridges, and the sliding filament models
- Structures within sarcomeres, including the "I" and "A" bands, "M" and "Z" lines, and the "H" zone
- Role and presence of troponin and tropomyosin
- Regulation of contraction by calcium

SKELETAL SYSTEM

- Functions of the skeletal system, including structural rigidity and support, calcium storage, and physical protection
- Structure of the skeleton, including specialization and structures of bone types, joint structures, and endoskeleton *vs.* exoskeleton
- Structure of bones, including the calcium/protein matrix and the cellular composition of bone
- Structure and function of cartilage
- Definitions and roles of ligaments and tendons
- Endocrine control of the skeletal system

SKIN SYSTEM

- Structure of the skin system, including layer differentiation, cell types, and relative impermeability to water
- Functions of the skin system in homeostasis and osmoregulation
- Functions of the skin system in thermoregulation, including hair and erectile musculature, fat layer for insulation, sweat glands located in the dermis, and vasoconstriction/vasodilation in surface capillaries
- Functions of the skeletal system in physical protection, including nails, calluses, hair, and protection against abrasion and disease organisms
- Hormonal control of the skin system, including sweating, vasodilation, and vasoconstriction

This chapter continues on the next page ▶ ▶ ▶

10.6 Biology Worked Examples

PASSAGE I: THE NERVOUS SYSTEM

During development, oligodendrocyte progenitor cells are formed, which further differentiate into the glial cells responsible for creating the myelin sheaths of the nervous system. Multiple sclerosis (MS) is characterized by damage to, or destruction of, myelin sheaths in the central nervous system (CNS). This results in symptoms that vary from physical to mental manifestations. There is currently no cure for this disease and its cause is still not completely clear.

The most widely accepted theory for the onset of MS has consistently been the classical *autoimmune hypothesis*. Recent research reports evidence that nonspecific T-cells in the cervical lymph nodes, which drain the CNS, become exposed to cells with myelin-like characteristics. These T-cells then become specific against the myelinating oligodendrocytes. After entry into the CNS, an inflammatory response is induced, signaling other leukocytes and macrophages to migrate through the blood–brain barrier. The attack mounted by these cells effectively kills the oligodendrocytes and degrades the myelin sheaths. Figure 1 outlines this process.

Another theory is the *oligodendropathy hypothesis*. According to the researchers supporting this postulation, unexplained reasons cause oligodendrocytes to undergo apoptosis (spontaneous self destruction). Death of the glial cells then leads to myelin degradation. The inflammatory immune response by macrophages is simply a means to clean away the already destroyed myelin debris. Figure 2 outlines this process.

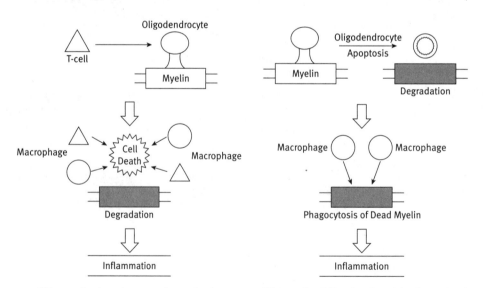

Figure 1. Autoimmune hypothesis **Figure 2.** Oligodendropathy hypothesis

P1.

P2.

P3.

F1.

1. The propagation of action potentials in the CNS of a patient with multiple sclerosis compared to a control subject would be:

    A. faster, because there is less matter to inhibit its path down the axon.

    B. faster, because the lack of myelin allows ions to more easily cross the cell membrane.

    C. slower, because of the decreased number of Schwann cells.

    D. slower, because conduction is no longer saltatory. ✓

2. The sequence in Figure 2 would be best supported over that of Figure 1 by which of the following?

    A. The CNS of a patient with multiple sclerosis was observed to have many scars and lesions.

    B. T-cells from a mouse with multiple sclerosis are transferred to a normal mouse that over time begins to display symptoms of multiple sclerosis.

    C. A study was conducted that showed large numbers of immune cells were observed to first enter the CNS only after signs of myelin degradation had been noted. ✓

    D. Unusually high numbers of macrophages are found in the CNS of patients with multiple sclerosis.

3. In Guillain–Barré syndrome, demyelination occurs in the peripheral nervous system only. A patient with this condition would be LEAST likely to exhibit a decrease in:

    A. motor coordination. ✓

    B. autonomic function.

    C. efferent motor responses.

    D. afferent sensory responses.

4. Researchers develop a drug that slows the progression of multiple sclerosis by stimulating production of myelin in the CNS. This treatment addresses the primary cause of the condition described by:

    A. the autoimmune hypothesis only. t-cell recruit mac

    B. the oligodendropathy hypothesis only. spont. degrad.

    C. both hypotheses.

    D. neither hypothesis. ✓

5. The diagram below depicts a somatic reflex arc.

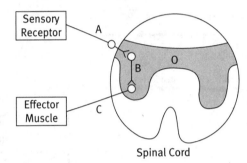

    In a patient with multiple sclerosis, the reflex arc would most likely:

    A. remain unchanged.

    B. exhibit a delay at neuron A.

    C. exhibit a delay at interneuron B. ✓

    D. exhibit a delay at neuron C.

Biology Passage I Explanation:

Sample Passage Map

P1: Multiple sclerosis

P2: autoimmune; T-cells kill oligodendrocytes

P3: oligodendropathic; apoptosis then macrophages

F1: Autoimmune hypothesis

F2: Oligodendropathy hypothesis

Key Concepts

Myelin sheath, Action potentials

---

1. The propagation of action potentials in the CNS of a patient with multiple sclerosis compared to a control subject would be:

   A. faster, because there is less matter to inhibit its path down the axon.

   B. faster, because the lack of myelin allows ions to more easily cross the cell membrane.

   C. slower, because of the decreased number of Schwann cells.

   D. slower, because conduction is no longer saltatory.

① Assess the question

The question wants to know whether multiple sclerosis speeds up or slows down action potentials, as well as why.

② Plan your attack

We'll need to look at the description of how multiple sclerosis damages the nervous system in paragraph 1, and then use our knowledge of the nervous system to find the correct answer.

③ Execute the plan

Paragraph 1 tells us that in MS, neurons in the CNS lose their myelin sheaths. The myelin sheath serves a number of functions, but its most notable one is to speed up conduction of action potentials. Without the myelin sheath, conduction speed decreases dramatically, so we would predict that conduction should slow down in its absence.

Specifically, the myelin sheath speeds up conduction because conduction becomes *saltatory*—ion exchange across the membrane becomes necessary only at the nodes of Ranvier, the periodic gaps in the myelin sheath. So a loss of myelin should result in a loss of saltatory conduction.

 Answer by matching, eliminating, or guessing

Choice (D) matches both parts of our prediction, and is the correct answer. **(C)** might seem tempting, but read it carefully: it refers to a decrease in *Schwann cells*, which are found only in the *peripheral* nervous system. Since MS involves the *central* nervous system, that answer is a trap.

Things to Watch Out For

Some trap answers on Test Day are designed to be so tempting that test-takers will pick them and move on before ever reading the correct answer. Critical thinking will help you avoid those traps!

Key Concepts

Nerve cell, Myelin sheath

2. The sequence in Figure 2 would be best supported over that of Figure 1 by which of the following?

   A. The CNS of a patient with multiple sclerosis was observed to have many scars and lesions.

   B. T-cells from a mouse with multiple sclerosis are transferred to a normal mouse that over time begins to display symptoms of multiple sclerosis.

   C. A study was conducted that showed large numbers of immune cells were observed to first enter the CNS only after signs of myelin degradation had been noted.

   D. Unusually high numbers of macrophages are found in the CNS of patients with multiple sclerosis.

 Assess the question

This question asks us for a new finding that would support the oligodendropathy theory depicted in Figure 2 *over* the autoimmune hypothesis in Figure 1. That means the correct answer must be true *only* of the oligodendropathy theory.

 Plan your attack

We'll need to examine the two figures to find the key differences. We'll then need to find an answer choice that illustrates one of those differences.

 Execute the plan

Looking at the two figures, the key difference is how the cells die. In the autoimmune hypothesis (Figure 1), the T-cells kill the oligodendrocytes; in the oligodendropathy hypothesis (Figure 2), the cells undergo apoptosis *first* (for unknown reasons), and *then* the T-cells attack. Our correct answer should illustrate the latter theory *only*.

 Answer by matching, eliminating, or guessing

For (**A**), the presence of scars and lesions in the central nervous system could fit with either hypothesis—it is simply an effect of demyelination in general, however it occurred. (**A**) is incorrect.

Next, look at (**B**). Here, a previously normal mouse develops MS after it is exposed to T-cells from an affected mouse. This suggests that the T-cells caused the onset of multiple sclerosis. Figure 1 shows this is the first step of the autoimmune hypothesis, so (**B**) is out.

Choice (C) describes a scenario in which demyelination has already occurred before the immune cells arrive. This matches what Figure 2 shows us, and contradicts Figure 1. **Choice (C)** must be our answer.

Choice (D) is too general. Both figures show macrophages in the CNS, so this cannot be the answer.

Key Concepts

Nervous system structure and function

> **3.** In Guillain–Barré syndrome, demyelination occurs in the peripheral nervous system only. A patient with this condition would be LEAST likely to exhibit a decrease in:
>
> **A.** motor coordination.
> **B.** autonomic function.
> **C.** efferent motor responses.
> **D.** afferent sensory responses.

 Assess the question

This question is testing the functions of the peripheral and central nervous systems. Note that since this is a LEAST question, we're looking for the one answer that doesn't fit.

 Plan your attack

This is a pseudodiscrete question; we don't need any information from the passage, but we will need our knowledge of the functions of the central and peripheral nervous systems. In particular, we're looking for the one function that is *not* part of the peripheral nervous system.

 Execute the plan

The central nervous system includes the brain and spinal cord, while the peripheral nervous system contains the sensory and motor systems. So we're looking for an answer involving the brain and/or spinal cord.

 Answer by matching, eliminating, or guessing

Motor coordination takes place in the cerebellum of the brain, which is part of the CNS. Thus **choice (A)** is correct, and we can stop.

Things to Watch Out For

Read questions carefully to catch keywords, such as "NOT" or "EXCEPT."

For completeness' sake, let's look at the other answers. Autonomic function is controlled by both the CNS and PNS, so **(B)** is wrong. Efferent motor responses and afferent sensory responses are both relayed by the peripheral nervous system (and processed in the CNS), so we can eliminate **(C)** and **(D)**.

> **4.** Researchers develop a drug that slows the progression of multiple sclerosis by stimulating production of myelin in the CNS. This treatment addresses the primary cause of the condition described by:
>
> **A.** the autoimmune hypothesis only.
> **B.** the oligodendropathy hypothesis only.
> **C.** both hypotheses.
> **D.** neither hypothesis.

Key Concepts

Nerve cell, Myelin sheath

 Assess the question

This question asks us to determine whether the phenomenon described in the question stem supports the theories described in the passage.

 Plan your attack

To answer this question, we'll need to see if stimulating CNS production of myelin supports the autoimmune hypothesis, by checking paragraph 2; and/or the oligodendropathy hypothesis, by checking paragraph 3.

③ **Execute the plan**

Paragraph 2 tells us that, according to the autoimmune hypothesis, multiple sclerosis is triggered by T-cells attacking myelin-producing oligodendrocytes. Would creating more myelin prevent this attack? No. So the drug does not treat the cause, according to this theory.

Paragraph 3 describes the oligodendropathy hypothesis, which argues that MS is triggered by apoptosis, or spontaneous self-destruction, of oligodendrocytes. Would creating more myelin prevent this from happening? No; myelin does not play a role in apoptosis. So the new drug wouldn't treat the cause in this theory, either.

④ **Answer by matching, eliminating, or guessing**

Once we know that the drug's action doesn't treat the cause according to the autoimmune hypothesis, we can eliminate (**A**) and (**C**). Knowing that it doesn't treat the cause in the oligodendropathy hypothesis either means we can also eliminate (**B**), leaving **choice (D)** as the correct answer.

Takeaways

Whenever a passage discusses multiple processes or theories, be sure to understand the key features of each, as well as their key similarities and differences.

Key Concepts

Nervous system structure and function,
Reflexes

5. The diagram below depicts a somatic reflex arc.

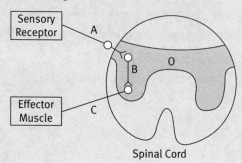

In a patient with multiple sclerosis, the reflex arc would most likely:

A. remain unchanged.
B. exhibit a delay at neuron A.
C. exhibit a delay at interneuron B. ✓
D. exhibit a delay at neuron C.

 Assess the question

This question gives us a diagram of a reflex arc, and then asks us how MS would affect the diagram. Note that one of the choices is "no change," so we shouldn't ignore that possibility.

2 Plan your attack

We'll need the description of multiple sclerosis in paragraph 1, as well as our knowledge of reflex arcs, to answer this question.

3 Execute the plan

Multiple sclerosis only affects the central nervous system—that is, the brain and spinal cord—according to paragraph 1. That means it does *not* affect the peripheral nervous system, with its motor and sensory components. As a result, we can predict that MS would affect a neuron that is part of the central nervous system, if there is one. If there isn't, then there should be no change.

Answer by matching, eliminating, or guessing

In the diagram, neuron A is a sensory neuron, while neuron C is a motor neuron. Both of these are part of the peripheral nervous system, so we can eliminate (**B**) and (**D**). Neuron B, however, is an interneuron, which is part of the *central* nervous system. Therefore we would expect it to be involved, so **choice (D)** is the correct answer.

choice (C)

BIOLOGY PASSAGE II: THE ENDOCRINE SYSTEM

Aldosterone release from the adrenal cortex plays a key role in controlling blood pressure. This important hormone is regulated as shown in Figure 1:

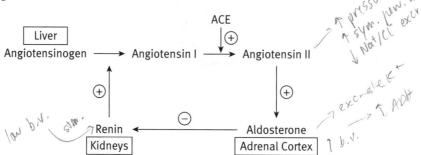

Figure 1. The renin-angiotensin feedback system

Low blood volume through the kidneys triggers juxtaglomerular cells to secrete renin into circulation. Angiotensinogen released from the liver is converted by this enzyme into the peptide angiotensin I. Angiotensin-converting enzyme (ACE) then converts angiotensin I into angiotensin II, which stimulates the adrenal cortex to release aldosterone. The ultimate increase in blood volume caused by aldosterone shuts off the secretion of renin from the juxtaglomerular cells. Angiotensin II also increases arteriolar vasoconstriction, sympathetic nervous activity, and reabsorption of sodium and chloride. Aldosterone, in addition to its effects on sodium, also increases potassium excretion.

Researchers at a pharmaceutical company are investigating the use of compounds thought to inhibit steps in the renin-angiotensin-aldosterone system as a means of treating hypertension. A clinical trial has been approved to test the effects of four such drugs. Eighty subjects, each exhibiting chronic hypertension with systolic pressures above 160 mm Hg and diastolic pressures above 100 mm Hg, were recruited; the subjects were divided into four groups of 20 patients each. Each group received a 10 mg daily dose of one of the four drugs. Blood pressure, urine volume, and concentration of urine potassium were measured every day for each patient in each group. At the end of the trial, the average results of these measurements over the last week of the trial were calculated; the results are shown in Table 1.

	Average Systolic/Diastolic Blood Pressure (mm Hg)	Average Daily Urine Volume (L)	Average Daily Urine Potassium Concentration (mEq/L)
Drug A	118/75	2.5	175
Drug B	145/95	2.2	50
Drug C	116/80	2.5	40
Drug D	122/78	1.1	135
Normal ranges	120 – 80	0.8–2.0	25–125

Table 1. Results of a clinical trial of four drugs to treat hypertension

P1.

F1.

P2.

P3.

Table 1.

1. Based on the results in Table 1, which of the following conclusions about Drug A and Drug C is most reasonable?

    A. Drug A inhibits renin release and Drug C inhibits ADH release.
    B. Drug A inhibits ADH release and Drug C inhibits ACE release. ✓
    C. Drug A inhibits ACE release and Drug C inhibits renin release.
    D. Drug A inhibits aldosterone release and Drug C inhibits ADH release.

2. Suppose that a certain substance is capable of preventing binding of *all* hormones to receptors on the cell membrane. Such a drug would influence the function of:

    A. ADH, but not aldosterone. ✓
    B. aldosterone, but not ADH.
    C. both ADH and aldosterone.
    D. neither ADH nor aldosterone.

3. A successful inhibitor of the renin-angiotensin-aldosterone system could reasonably be expected to cause all of the following EXCEPT:

    A. increased dilation of arterioles.
    B. decreased urine sodium concentration. ✓
    C. decreased pupil dilation. ✗
    D. increased urine volume. ✗

4. While Drug B was the least successful for treating hypertension, the results obtained suggest it would be most useful in treating:

    A. hypotension. ✗
    B. dehydration. ✗
    C. edema. ✓
    D. hyperkalemia (high plasma K^+ levels). ✗

5. A researcher believes she knows the mechanism by which Drug D lowers blood pressure. To confirm her hypothesis, she should perform an experiment, with appropriate controls, to measure:

    A. angiotensinogen release from the liver.
    B. renin release from the kidneys.
    C. arteriolar pressure increases caused by angiotensin II. ✓
    D. concentration of ACE in the plasma.

Takeaways

When a passage presents an experiment, expect questions testing your ability to interpret the results, especially if the passage doesn't draw any conclusions for you.

Key Concepts

Osmoregulation, Secretion and reabsorption of solutes

Biology Passage II Explanation:

USING THE KAPLAN METHODS

P1: Aldosterone

F1: Renin-angiotensin-aldosterone system

P2: Hormone functions

P3: Exp: inhibit RAA pathway to lower blood pressure

T1: Exp results; 4 drugs

> 1. Based on the results in Table 1, which of the following conclusions about Drug A and Drug C is most reasonable?
>
>   **A.** Drug A inhibits renin release and Drug C inhibits ADH release.
>   **B.** Drug A inhibits ADH release and Drug C inhibits ACE release.
>   **C.** Drug A inhibits ACE release and Drug C inhibits renin release.
>   **D.** Drug A inhibits aldosterone release and Drug C inhibits ADH release.

Assess the question

All the answer choices deal with inhibiting release of hormones, so our job is to figure out which hormones Drug A and Drug C inhibit, out of renin, ADH, ACE, and aldosterone.

Plan your attack

To answer this question, we'll need to examine the differences in Table 1 between Drug A and Drug C; we'll also need to use Figure 1, which shows how the various hormones are regulated, and paragraph 3, which gives us the normal urine output and potassium content. We may also need paragraph 2, which describes the functions of some of these hormones.

Execute the plan

Looking at Table 1, the average blood pressure for patients taking Drug A and patients taking Drug C is approximately the same. The average urine output is the same for both drugs, and is elevated in both cases. The only difference in the table is the urine concentration of K^+ ions; the urine of Drug A patients has an elevated potassium level, while Drug C patients have a potassium level at the low end of the average range. Our correct answer thus needs to explain how Drug A causes K^+ excretion to rise, but Drug C does not.

The key to answering this question is tucked into the end of paragraph 2: increased K^+ excretion is caused by aldosterone. Therefore, Drug A's effects should *not* include inhibiting aldosterone.

 Answer by matching, eliminating, or guessing

We can immediately eliminate (**D**), since we've established that would not result in elevated urine K^+. Renin (**A**) and ACE (**C**) are both needed to stimulate aldosterone release. Inhibiting either of them should result in reduced aldosterone activity, which would make it unlikely that Drug A would cause elevated urine potassium levels. Eliminating those answers leaves **choice (B)** as the correct answer.

Note that we didn't even need to consider Drug C here, but if it were inhibiting ACE, we'd expect to see decreased aldosterone activity, which doesn't contradict the information in the table.

Things to Watch Out For

Watch out when an experimental passage presents results for multiple variables. Odds are there will be at least one problem that requires a conclusion to be drawn from a comparison of those results.

Key Concepts

Cellular mechanisms of hormone action

2. Suppose that a certain substance is capable of preventing binding of *all* hormones to receptors on the cell membrane. Such a drug would influence the function of:

   A. ADH, but not aldosterone.
   B. aldosterone, but not ADH.
   C. both ADH and aldosterone.
   D. neither ADH nor aldosterone.

1 Assess the question

While it's hard to envision that a substance such as the one suggested by the question stem could even exist, that doesn't matter. We assume it's true and go on from there. The answer choices ask whether this substance would affect ADH, aldosterone, both, or neither.

2 Plan your attack

This is actually a pseudodiscrete question, as we don't need any information directly from the passage. In fact, we only need two pieces of information: an understanding of what hormones bind to cell membrane receptors, and the hormone classes to which ADH and aldosterone belong. Then we can apply that information to the new scenario in the question stem.

3 Execute the plan

There are two major classes of hormones: steroid hormones and peptide (amino acid) hormones. Steroid hormones have *intracellular* receptors, because steroids are permeable and cross the cell membrane. Peptide hormones, however, have membrane-bound receptors, because amino acids are too polar to cross the cell membrane.

So if our hypothetical compound can block *all* hormone binding at the cell membrane, then it would affect peptide hormones, but it should not affect steroid hormones. Aldosterone, like all adrenal cortex hormones, is a steroid; ADH, like all hormones produced in the hypothalamus, is a peptide. Keeping this in mind, we would expect the drug to affect only ADH, and not aldosterone.

4 Answer by matching, eliminating, or guessing

Choice (A) matches our prediction.

3. A successful inhibitor of the renin-angiotensin-aldosterone system could reasonably be expected to cause all of the following EXCEPT:

    A. increased dilation of arterioles.

    B. decreased urine sodium concentration.

    C. decreased pupil dilation.

    D. increased urine volume.

Key Concepts

Osmoregulation, Secretion and reabsorption of solutes, Sympathetic and parasympathetic nervous systems

1 Assess the question

We are being asked to consider the effects of blocking the renin-angiotensin-aldosterone (RAA) pathway and to identify the answer that does not fit that picture.

2 Plan your attack

Figure 1 shows the various steps of the pathway, while paragraph 2 describes the effects of the hormones.

3 Execute the plan

Since we're looking for something that blocking the pathway will *not* cause, the wrong answers are things that inhibiting the pathway *will* cause. The correct answer will therefore be either a normal effect of the renin-angiotensin-aldosterone pathway, *or* something that is not affected by it at all.

4 Answer by matching, eliminating, or guessing

Paragraph 2 tells us that angiotensin II increases arteriole vasoconstriction. So, inhibiting RAA would mean a *lack* of constriction—in other words, we expect vasodilation. That means (**A**) *would* happen, and is therefore incorrect.

The end effect of the RAA pathway is release of aldosterone, which *increases* sodium reabsorption in the kidney. Inhibiting the pathway would mean *decreased* sodium reabsorption, and therefore *higher* excretion. **Choice (B)** says we'd expect *lower* sodium excretion; this is the "normal" RAA effect we predicted we'd see as the correct answer.

Things to Watch Out For

Watch out for when a question stem uses the word EXCEPT. This becomes even more important when a question effectively contains a double negative, as this one does. When selecting your answer choice, make sure it satisfies the question.

Paragraph 2 tells us that angiotensin II increases sympathetic nervous activity. Pupil dilation is a sympathetic effect, so inhibiting RAA would decrease dilation. Rule out **choice (C)**.

Because aldosterone increases sodium reabsorption, it also indirectly increases water reabsorption. We would thus expect the RAA pathway to decrease urine volume. **Choice (D)** is also incorrect.

4. While Drug B was the least successful for treating hypertension, the results obtained suggest it would be most useful in treating:

A. hypotension
B. dehydration.
C. edema.
D. hyperkalemia (high plasma K^+ levels).

Key Concepts

Osmoregulation, Mechanisms of hormone action, Feedback control regulation

1 Assess the question

This question is fairly straightforward: which of these conditions would Drug B be best at treating?

2 Plan your attack

To answer this question, we'll need to look at the results for Drug B in Table 1, and then use our knowledge of the conditions in the answer choices.

3 Execute the plan

Looking at Table 1, patients taking Drug C had slightly elevated urine output, but normal urine potassium levels. So the correct answer will be a condition that can be treated solely by increasing urine output.

4 Answer by matching, eliminating, or guessing

Looking at the answer choices, the only one that can be treated solely by increasing urine output is edema, which is an accumulation of fluid in interstitial spaces. The correct answer is **choice (C).**

(**A**) might sound tempting; if Drug B doesn't reduce blood pressure, maybe it can be used to raise blood pressure. However, the passage told us that the patients involved in the trial have blood pressures above 160/100, so Drug B still managed to reduce blood pressure, and this cannot be the answer. To treat dehydration, (**B**), we would want a drug that increases water retention in the body. Drug B resulted in high urine volume, so it would not increase water retention.

In hyperkalemia, (**D**) plasma potassium levels are elevated. Drug B did not elevate urine potassium levels, so it is unlikely that it would be effective in ridding the body of excess potassium.

Takeaways

If you're not familiar with a concept in an answer choice, don't reflexively select *or* reject that answer.

Key Concepts

Mechanisms of hormone action,
Feedback control regulation

5. A researcher believes she knows the mechanism by which Drug D
lowers blood pressure. To confirm her hypothesis, she should perform
an experiment, with appropriate controls, to measure:

A. angiotensinogen release from the liver.
B. renin release from the kidneys.
C. arteriolar pressure increases caused by angiotensin II.
D. concentration of ACE in the plasma.

 Assess the question

This is a Skill 3 question, asking what test would confirm the mechanism of action
for Drug D. All of the choices involve hormones shown in Figure 1.

 Plan your attack

To answer this question, we need to know how Drug D works. That information isn't
explicitly given to us in the passage, so we'll need to use the data in Table 1 to help
us figure out how Drug D works. Then we can use our knowledge of the hormones
in the answer choices to determine the correct answer.

 Execute the plan

In Table 1, patients on Drug D had significantly reduced blood pressure, but they
also had *high* urine potassium levels and *normal* urine volume. We're therefore looking for an answer that doesn't involve excess urine excretion.

 Answer by matching, eliminating, or guessing

Looking at the answer choices, the most promising answer is **choice (C)**, which
doesn't directly involve the kidneys at all. Angiotensin II, according to paragraph 2,
causes vasoconstriction; inhibiting angiotensin II could directly result in vasodilation.

Changes in angiotensinogen release **(A)** and renin release **(B)** should both alter aldosterone levels, so it would not be likely that these would produce a decrease in
blood pressure *without* increasing urine volume. Finally, while **(D)** sounds tempting, the actual *concentration* of ACE is irrelevant; what matters is its *activity*. It is
possible that there are large amounts of ACE in the blood, but the vast majority of it
could be inhibited.

This chapter continues on the next page ▶ ▶ ▶

10.7 Biology Practice

BIOLOGY PASSAGE III (QUESTIONS 1–6)

Yeasts, which are unicellular fungi, can reproduce by budding, or by performing mitosis and meiosis. *S. cerevisiae*, for example, will undergo mitosis when resources are plentiful, but can undergo meiosis to form haploid spores when the primary fuel sources support fermentation rather than aerobic respiration.

Both mitosis and meiosis depend on formation of a complex, Cdk1-Clb, between the proteins Cdk1 and cyclin B to activate spindle formation. In mitosis, Cdk1-Clb is activated within minutes, while in meiosis it typically takes at least three hours. The human analog of Cdk1, Cdc2, can substitute for Cdk1 in yeast.

The entry of yeast into meiosis I depends on the expression of Ndt80, a transcription factor expressed only during meiosis, which triggers formation of the meiotic spindle and disassembly of synaptonemal complexes. It is regulated in part by positive feedback: Ndt80 acts as an activator for its own gene. Another required protein is Ama1, which activates the anaphase-promoting complex (APC/C), which is required for the cell to enter anaphase I. During prophase I, APC/C suppresses the signals that cause yeast cells to undergo mitosis; it also helps inhibit entry into S phase.

In an experiment, a researcher cultured *S. cerevisiae* cells in glucose-rich medium. One population was mutated to lack the gene for Ndt80; the other lacked genes for both Ndt80 and Ama1. Two hundred cells from each sample were then transferred to media designed to induce meiosis. The researcher then counted the number of cells in each sample that exhibited the presence of a meiotic spindle; the results are shown in Figure 1.

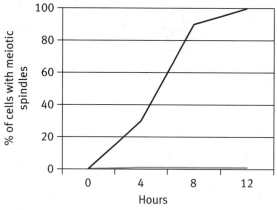

Figure 1. Development of the meiotic spindle in −Ndt80 and
−Ndt80 −Ama1 cells

P1.

P2.

P3.

P4.

F1.

1. Suppose researchers discover a compound that prevents binding of Cdk1 to cyclin B. While they use the drug in their research, they do not pursue using it as a treatment for fungal infections. Which of the following would be the most likely reason for that decision?

   A. The drug might not quantitatively kill fungal cells.

   B. The drug might be too expensive to mass produce.

   C. The drug might pose too great a risk to subjects.

   D. The drug might cause dangerous genetic mutations in the yeast cells.

2. Based on information in the passage, which of the following is most likely to be true of meiotic cells lacking Ndt80 and Ama1?

   A. Cells lacking Ndt80 only will arrest in prophase I; cells lacking both proteins will arrest in anaphase I.

   B. Cells lacking Ndt80 only will arrest in anaphase I; cells lacking both proteins will arrest in metaphase I.

   C. Cells lacking Ndt80 only will arrest in prophase I; cells lacking both proteins will arrest in metaphase I.

   D. Cells lacking Ndt80 only will arrest in metaphase I; cells lacking both proteins will arrest in anaphase I.

3. Which of the following, if true, would be the best explanation for how Ama1 is regulated prior to entry into anaphase?

   A. The cell can detect chromosomes not attached to spindle fibers, and produces a signal that inhibits Ama1 when it does.

   B. The cell can detect chromosomes not attached to spindle fibers, and produces a signal that activates Ama1 when it does.

   C. The cell can detect the attachment of chromosomes to spindle fibers, and produces a signal that activates Ama1 when it does.

   D. The cell can detect the attachment of chromosomes to spindle fibers, and produces a signal that inhibits Ama1 when it does.

4. A sample of *S. cerevisiae* grown in a medium containing only acetate and no glucose would most likely exhibit:

   A. formation of Cdk1-Clb in less than an hour.

   B. activation of APC/C in prophase I.

   C. exclusively mitosis.

   D. decreased expression of Ndt80.

5. A certain yeast cell is unable to proceed to metaphase I of meiosis *and* unable to proceed to metaphase I of mitosis. It most likely contains a mutation in the gene for:

   A. Ama1.

   B. Ndt80.

   C. tubulin.

   D. Cdc2.

6. Based on information in the passage, is it reasonable to conclude that after telophase I:

   I.   APC/C remains active into meiosis II.

   II. Ndt80 remains active into meiosis II.

   III. Additional Ama1 must be synthesized.

   A. II only

   B. I and II only

   C. I and III only

   D. I, II, and III only

Biology Practice Passage Explanations

P1. Yeast do both mitosis and meiosis (nutrient shortage)

P2. Timing of Cdk1-Clb complex critical

P3. Proteins that induce meiosis

P4. Ndt80/Ama1 knockout experiment

Fig1. Results of experiment

1. (C)

One of the keys to antimicrobial therapy, in general, is that it must be relatively safe for the host, and attack a mechanism that the infected organism's cells do not use. For example, the bacterial ribosome is not identical to the human ribosome, so drugs that target the bacterial ribosome generally pose little threat to humans. Here, however, paragraph 2 tells us that the human analog of Cdk1, Cdc2, *can work like Cdk1 in yeast cells.* That implies there is a high degree of homology between the yeast pathway and the mitotic pathway in humans and other mammals. As a result, such a drug would be likely to affect both the yeast cells and human cells; it could cause damage to organs that require frequent cell divisions (such as the stomach). **Choice (C)** is the best answer.

(A) This might be true, but even if it could kill the yeast cells (and perhaps *especially* if it could kill the yeast cells!), it would still pose a risk to the subjects.

(B) Even if this were true, it would not be the best reason to avoid testing the drug.

(D) Formation of the mitotic spindle is independent of DNA synthesis, and there is no information in the passage that suggests the drug would be capable of causing mutations in the yeast cells.

2. (C)

First, note that all of the answers state that the cells will arrest at some stage of meiosis. To answer this question, then, we need to know the key events of prophase I and metaphase I. To exit prophase I, chromosomes must condense, the nuclear envelope needs to disintegrate, and the spindle bodies need to form. According to Figure 1, in cells lacking Ndt80 only, the spindle never forms; in cells lacking both Ndt80 and Ama1, though, it *does* form. Therefore, we can conclude that Ndt80 cells should arrest in prophase I. According to paragraph 3, Ama1 activates APC/C, which is needed for entry into anaphase I. Therefore, it is most reasonable to conclude that in the absence of Ama1, the cells will arrest in metaphase I. This matches **choice (C)**.

(A) Ndt80 cells will arrest in prophase I, but the lack of Ama1 prevents activation of APC/C, which is needed for entry into anaphase I.

(B) Without Ndt80, the spindle never forms, so cells cannot leave prophase I.

(D) Without Ndt80, the spindle never forms, so cells cannot leave prophase I; moreover, without Ama1, cells cannot enter anaphase I.

3. (A)

During anaphase, the cell needs to avoid nondisjunction, the incorrect separation of chromosomes during cell division. To do this, the cell needs to make sure that every chromosome is attached to a spindle fiber. Since the number of chromosomes in cells varies widely, the easiest way to do this would be to depend on a signal that disappears when all chromosomes have been attached, rather than one that appears when chromosomes are attached; as a result, we can eliminate **(C)** and **(D)**. Since paragraph 3 tells us that Ama1 *activates* APC/C, which initiates anaphase, then we would expect that the signal should be an inhibitory one; once all the chromosomes have attached, the inhibitory signal disappears, and Ama1 will become active. This matches **choice (A)**.

4. (B)

Paragraph 1 states that when fermentable fuel sources predominate, yeast cells are more likely to undergo sporulation. Acetate would be an example of such a fuel source, especially in the absence of glucose. Thus, we would expect the yeast to undergo meiosis, and the only answer choice that corresponds to induction of meiosis is **choice (B)**.

(A) According to paragraph 2, Cdk1-Clb forms within minutes in *mitosis*, not meiosis.

(C) We would expect to see exclusively *meiosis*, not mitosis.

(D) Ndt80 is required for meiosis, so this would be a signal for mitosis.

5. (C)

According to the information in Figure 1, neither Ama1 nor Ndt80 is necessary for formation of the meiotic spindle. That rules out both **(A)** and **(B)**. A close reading of paragraph 2 shows that Cdc2 is a gene found in *humans*, not in yeast, which eliminates **(D)**. That leaves **choice (C)**, tubulin, as the correct answer; tubulin is the protein required for actual formation of the spindle fibers.

6. (B)

This question tests your understanding of meiosis II. In particular, to answer this correctly, you need to know that there is no S phase preceding meiosis II, as there is preceding meiosis I. Therefore, we would expect that APC/C (item I) would remain active to prevent the cell from undergoing S phase. That eliminates **(A)**. We would also expect that Ndt80 (item II) would be active, since a second meiotic spindle is needed for meiosis II, so we can eliminate **(C)**. On the other hand, we have no reason to conclude that *additional* Ama1 is needed to activate the APC/C (item III); it is possible that Ama1's activation of APC/C during prophase I lasts throughout meiosis I and meiosis II. **Choice (B)** is the best answer.

Things to Watch Out For

Item III is incorrect here because the question asks if it is reasonable to conclude that it *is* true. If the question had asked *which of the following* could *be true*, then it would be correct, since it's at least possible.

CHAPTER ELEVEN

General Chemistry

One of the main characteristics of the MCAT is that all of the questions, even in the physical sciences, will be related to living systems. Thus, passages presenting an inorganic chemical reaction with stoichiometry questions will be far less likely. Any questions related to general chemistry will also involve biochemistry or biology. In addition, general chemistry will appear in both the Chemical and Physical Foundations of Biological Systems and the Biological and Biochemical Foundations of Living Systems sections. Approximately 5 percent of the questions in the Biological and Biochemical Foundations of Living Systems section will be strictly general chemistry, while approximately 30 percent of the questions in the Chemical and Physical Foundations of Biological Systems section will be general chemistry. However, it is important to remember that knowledge in general chemistry concepts is essential to success in organic chemistry and biochemistry. As such, fewer questions in general chemistry does not necessarily mean that less knowledge is required; it simply means that the testmaker is likely to be more creative in testing general chemistry concepts in the context of organic chemistry or biochemistry.

11.1 Reading the Passage

One of the most difficult aspects of the MCAT is reading the passages. Test-takers tend to waste a lot of time reading passages the same way as one would read a textbook or newspaper; by attempting to completely understand every argument made and every detail given. However, the goal of the MCAT is NOT reading the passages: it is answering questions by using the passage as a piece of reference material. MCAT science passages are full of data that will always be there if required to answer questions. When you read a passage, take a broad look at what is happening and think about the basic science concepts that are being applied to situations presented within the passage. No more than two minutes should be spent on a single passage; in fact, most efficient test-takers read MCAT passages in 90 seconds or less. General chemistry passages on the MCAT will require the ability to read quickly, focusing on the goal of the passage, and then answering the questions with a keen eye toward the task in the question.

PASSAGE TYPES

As in the other sciences, there are two types of general chemistry passages on the MCAT: information and experiment. However, the content of the passages has changed drastically on the most current revision of the MCAT in 2015. Previously, passages in general chemistry would focus on inorganic chemistry alone; formation of compounds, balancing equations, and the basic general chemistry one might see in an introductory level course. However, the new MCAT will be presenting general chemistry in the context of living systems. This means that each passage will require knowledge and the ability to apply the fundamental concepts of biology and biochemistry within the context of general chemistry. Since only 5 percent of the questions in the Biological and Biochemical Foundations of Living Systems section will be related to general chemistry, it is unlikely that any single passage in that section will be strictly general chemistry. That being said, passages that are strictly general chemistry are more likely to be found in the Physical and Chemical Foundations of Biological Systems section.

Information passages

- Read like a textbook or journal article.
- Usually explain the general chemistry behind a natural phenomenon.
- May be associated with one or more figures, such as a reaction, equation, table, chart, graph, or diagram. The text of the passage usually describes these figures.

Experiment

- Consists of brief background information, most likely linking the chemical process presented in the experiment with a biological process.
- The procedure will be described, and results will be presented.
- The hypothesis of the experiment is usually stated fairly early in the passage.
- Numerical results may be presented in a table or a graph.

General Chemistry in the Biology and Biochemical Foundations of Living Systems section and the Chemical and Physical Foundations of Biological Systems section		
	Biology and Biochemical Foundations of Living Systems	**Chemical and Physical Foundations of Biological Systems**
Percent of questions in general chemistry	5%	33%
Passages	Possibly one, but unlikely to see a passage that is strictly general chemistry	More than one, general chemistry topics are also likely to be mixed with biochemistry and physics
Questions	Very few questions that will require only general chemistry knowledge. Many more questions may require you to integrate general chemistry concepts with other sciences.	Some questions will only require general chemistry knowledge, but all will discuss living systems. Expect to integrate general chemistry with biochemistry and organic chemistry.

OUTLINING THE PASSAGE

Almost all general chemistry passages, regardless of the section, will involve one or more graphical representations, especially graphs and tables. Thus, your outline must reflect these images in order to accurately represent the passage. However, this only requires very slight changes to the Kaplan way of reading and outlining general chemistry passages.

Scan for Structure

- Scan the passage for structure, noting the presence of charts, graphs, tables, diagrams, and text.
- Determine the degree of difficulty and the level of time commitment required.
- Decide whether to do this passage now or later.

Read Strategically

- Read each paragraph as a critic, asking, "What is this paragraph doing here? What is the message that is being conveyed?"
- Identify each chart, graph, table, or diagram and determine what is represented in each one. There is no need to interpret the image—simply identify the relationship between the image and the text within the passage.
- If a paragraph explains an image or provides definitions for a list of variables, this is a cue that you may skim this information because it appears in two places within the passage.
- Often the purpose of a chart or graph is specifically stated in the title of the figure.

Label Each Component

- Outline each paragraph, stating the purpose of each paragraph.
- Write down the purpose of each image presented with the passage.
- Identify any relationships between the text and the image. For example, an entire paragraph may be devoted to explaining variables or results of an experiment. These same ideas may also be represented visually, meaning that there is a direct relationship.

Reflect on Your Outline

- Determine the goal of the passage.
- Write it down, and move on to the questions.

11.2 Answering the Questions

Similar to the other sciences, general chemistry questions will fall into one of four categories.

Discrete questions

- Questions not associated with a descriptive passage.
- Will be preceded by a warning such as, "Questions 12–15 are NOT based on a descriptive passage."
- Likely to ask for you to recall a specific piece of information or apply your knowledge to a new situation.
- NOT likely to require analysis of an experiment.

Questions that stand alone from the passage

- Questions associated with a passage, but the passage is not required to answer the question.
- Often thematically related to the passage, but often designed to test an additional aspect of the topic that is not mentioned in the passage.

Questions that require data from the passage

- Often will require data analysis or conceptual understanding of ideas presented in the passage.
- You will be required to apply your knowledge to information within the passage.
- Does not require the goal of the passage.

Questions that require the goal of the passage

- Will require a deeper understanding of the passage as a whole, especially the overall goal of the passage.
- Usually the most time-consuming of the question types in general chemistry.

DETERMINING THE PURPOSE OF THE QUESTION

Each question is designed to test a specific skill and information set. The MCAT is designed to test your ability to apply your knowledge in a logical manner in order to answer questions. The Kaplan way provides you with a logical method for applying your knowledge to maximize your points on Test Day.

1. Assess the Question

- Identify the topic and degree of difficulty of the question.
- Decide whether this question is one to do now or later.

2. Plan Your Attack

- Determine what information is required to answer the question.
- If a specific image is required to answer the question, identify what kind of information is summarized within the image. Then, identify the type of analysis required. Is the analysis large based on the results of an experiment? Is a calculation required? Are you being asked to identify a trend?
- Locate the information required to answer the question.
- Identify the task of the question. What are being asked to do? The more specific you are with identifying the task, the easier it will be to carry out your plan.

3. Execute Your Plan

- Go back to the passage, figure, or question stem to find required information.
- Analyze, calculate, recall the information—carry out your plan.

4. Answer the Question by Matching, Eliminating, or Guessing

- Match your answer with the answer choices.
- If there is no clear answer, start by eliminating answer choices that are obviously incorrect.
- After obviously incorrect answer choices are eliminated, identify any answer choices that simply do not make sense.
- If you cannot get down to a single answer choice, choose between two probable answer choices.

11.3 Getting the Edge in General Chemistry

Over the years, the amount of general chemistry on the MCAT has declined and shifted in scope. Currently, the only general chemistry tested on the MCAT is that which has a direct application to the life sciences. Thus, performing calculations using the Henderson–Hasselbalch equation is still important, but only as it is applied to determining how changes in the concentration of bicarbonate and carbonic acid affect the pH of blood. On Test Day, you can expect that general chemistry concepts will be tested in the context of biological systems. This is often vastly different from what is seen in undergraduate general chemistry courses, as the purpose of these courses is to provide a foundation in general chemistry that can be applied to more specific types of chemistry. Therefore, the type of learning required to succeed on general chemistry passages is different.

General chemistry passages will often feature multiple images, and you will be required to interpret these images. However, interpretation is only necessary if a question requires it. Note the image, what it summarizes, and move on. No need to interpret it when reading the passage. The questions will likely ask you to perform a calculation or analysis in the context of biology. For example, Le Châtelier's principle is likely to be tested along with knowledge of the carbonic acid blood buffer system, rather than as a topic in which substances are added to a beaker.

Mastering general chemistry on the MCAT means being able to apply the principles of general chemistry to living systems. This requires practice, and top scoring test-takers often refine their skills by reading passages and answering questions about the topic at hand. Reading a textbook or review book is helpful, but the MCAT requires you to apply knowledge, not to memorize it.

11.4 Step-By-Step Guide to General Chemistry Passages

OUTLINING THE PASSAGE

Scan for structure
- Determine whether to do this passage now or later.
- Identify the structure of the passage, including charts, graphs, chemical equations, synthesis pathways, metabolic pathways, and images.

Read strategically
- Identify the type of passage.
- Pay special attention to the relationships between concepts.
- In an experiment passage, determine the hypothesis, procedure, and outcome.
- Identify relationships between the text and the figures presented with the passage.

Label each component
- Write down the purpose of each paragraph and figure
- Determine the type of information presented in all of the figures and the connections with the information within the text of the passage.

Reflect on your outline
- Determine the goal of the passage and write it down.
- Identify the concepts within the passage in an effort to anticipate questions.

ANSWERING THE QUESTIONS

1. Assess the question

- Determine whether this question should be done now or later.
- Identify the topic and the degree of difficulty.
- Good questions to do now in general chemistry are ones that do not require a lot of data or experimental analysis from the passage.

2. Plan your attack

- Determine what you already know, and what information you need.
- Identify where to find the required information: the passage, the question, your outline, or your own knowledge
- If you have to go back to the passage, determine where to find the required information by using your outline
- If data analysis is required, identify the correct data set, as there may be multiple data representations.
- Determine the task of the question. Paraphrase the question, if required, in order to ensure that your plan is designed to actually answer the question.

3. Execute your plan

- Analyze the data, go back to the passage, and carry out your plan.
- If you get stuck analyzing data, remember that the trend of the data is often enough to yield a correct answer choice.

4. Answer the question by matching, eliminating, or guessing

- Match your answer to the answer choices.
- If there is not a match, eliminate incorrect answer choices. Some of the answer choices may not make sense; eliminate those first.
- If elimination does not provide a clear answer, guess between two probable answers.

11.5 Preparing for the MCAT: General Chemistry

These are the general chemistry topics that you are likely to see on Test Day. All of the following topics appear in the Chemical and Physical Foundations of Biological Systems section except those labeled otherwise.

PRINCIPLES OF BIOENERGETICS

- Transfers of phosphoryl groups and ATP, including the concept that ΔG of ATP hydrolysis is much less than 0

GAS PHASE

- Definition of absolute temperature and the application of the Kelvin (K) scale
- Definition of pressure and the function of a simple mercury barometer
- Identification of that the molar volume of an ideal gas at 0°C and 1 atm is 22.4 L/mol
- Definition of an ideal gas and the application of the ideal gas law ($PV = nRT$), Boyle's law (PV = constant), Charles's Law (V/T = constant), and Avogadro's law (V/n = constant)
- Fundamental concepts of the kinetic molecular theory of gases
- Concept that behavior of a real gas may deviate from the ideal gas law, including qualitative and quantitative (Van der Waals equation) analysis
- Identification and calculation of partial pressure and mole fraction
- Application of Dalton's law to calculate composition from partial pressures

ELECTROCHEMISTRY

- Definition and characteristics of an electrolytic cell, including electrolysis, anode, cathode, and electrolyte
- Application of Faraday's law related to the amount of elements deposited or gas liberated at an electrode to current
- Identification of electron flow, oxidation, and reduction at the electrodes of an electrolytic cell
- Definition and characteristics of galvanic or voltaic cells, including half-reactions, reduction potentials, cell potential, and direction of electron flow
- Characteristics of a concentration cell**
- The direction of electron flow and application of the Nernst equation in concentration cells*
- Fundamental characteristics of batteries, including electromotive force, voltage, lead-storage batteries, and nickel-cadmium batteries

MOLECULAR STRUCTURE AND ABSORPTION SPECTRA

- Absorption of visible light by compounds, including the concept of the color reflected and the effects of structural changes on absorption (as in indicators)

ATOMIC NUCLEUS

- Definitions and applications of atomic number and atomic weight
- Characteristics of neutrons, protons, and isotopes
- Identification of nuclear forces and binding energy
- Concepts of radioactive decay, including α, β, and γ decay as well as half-life, exponential decay, and semi-log plots
- Function of a mass spectrometer

ELECTRONIC STRUCTURE

- General orbital structure of the hydrogen atom, definition of the principal quantum number, and the number of electrons per orbital
- Definitions and characteristics of ground state and excited states
- Definition and application of absorption and emission line spectra
- Application of the Pauli exclusion principle
- Concepts of paramagnetism and diamagnetism
- Characteristics of the Bohr atom
- Definition and concepts related to the Heisenberg uncertainty principle
- Calculation of effective nuclear charge
- Identification of the photoelectric effect

*This concept is *only* tested on the Biological and Biochemical Foundations of Living Systems section.

**This concept can also be tested on the Biological and Biochemical Foundations of Living Systems section.

THE PERIODIC TABLE–CLASSIFICATION OF ELEMENTS INTO GROUPS BY ELECTRONIC STRUCTURE

- Identification and characteristics of specific groups on the periodic table, including alkali metals, alkaline earth metals, halogens. Identification and characteristics of representative elements, transition metals, metals, and non-metals

THE PERIODIC TABLE–VARIATIONS OF CHEMICAL PROPERTIES WITH GROUP AND ROW

- Fundamental concepts of valence electrons
- Definition of the first and second ionization energy, as well as predicting first and second ionization energy from electronic structure for elements in different groups or rows
- Definition of electron affinity and variation with group and row
- Definition of electronegativity and comparative values for some representative elements and important groups
- Relationship between electron shells and sizes of atoms and ions

STOICHIOMETRY

- Definition and calculation of molecular weight
- The difference between the empirical and molecular formula
- Identification of metric units commonly used in chemistry
- Using percent mass to determine composition of a compound
- Application of the mole concept and Avogadro's number N_A
- Definition and application of density
- Identification and application of the oxidation number, including common oxidizing and reducing agents; disproportionation reactions
- Use of chemical equations to describe reactions, including conventions for writing chemical equations; balancing equations, including redox equations; determining limiting reactants; and calculating theoretical yields

ACID/BASE EQUILIBRIA

- Definition of an acid and a base according to Brønsted–Lowry
- Characteristics of the ionization of water, including the application and value of K_w ($K_w = [H^+][OH^-] = 10^{-14}$ at 25° C and 1 atm)
- Definition and application of pH, including the pH of pure water
- Identification of conjugate acids and bases
- Identification of strong acids and bases
- Identification and characteristics of weak acids and bases, including dissociation of weak acids and bases with or without added salt; hydrolysis of salts of weak acids or bases; calculation of pH of solutions of salts of weak acids or bases (Henderson–Hasselbalch equation)
- Application of the equilibrium constants K_a and K_b; application of pK_a, pK_b
- Definition and fundamental concepts of a buffer, including common buffer systems and the influence of a buffer system on a titration curve

IONS IN SOLUTION

- Definitions of anion and cation
- Identification of common names, formulas, and charges for familiar ions such as ammonium, phosphate, and sulfate
- The concept of hydration and the hydronium ion

SOLUBILITY

- Identification of the units of concentration such as molarity
- Application of the solubility product constant and the equilibrium expression K_{sp}
- Characteristics of the common ion effect and its use in laboratory separation; complex ion formation
- Relationships between complex ions and solubility; solubility and pH
- The role of colligative properties and osmotic pressure in the transfer of substances across the plasma membrane*
- Application of Henry's law of gas solubility, especially in terms of alveolar gas exchange*

TITRATION

- Use and identification of common indicators
- Fundamental concepts of neutralization
- Interpretation of titration curves
- Characteristics of redox titrations

*This concept is *only* tested on the Biological and Biochemical Foundations of Living Systems section.

COVALENT BOND

- Fundamental concepts of Lewis electron dot formulas, including resonance structures, formal charge, and Lewis acids and bases
- Definition of partial ionic character, including the role of electronegativity in determining charge distribution and dipole moment
- Definitions and characteristics of σ and π bonds, including hybrid orbitals (sp^3, sp^2, sp) and respective geometries; valence shell electron pair repulsion and prediction of shapes of molecules such as NH_3, H_2O, and CO_2; structural formulas for molecules involving H, C, N, O, F, S, P, Si, and Cl; delocalized electrons and resonance in ions and molecules
- Concepts of multiple bonding, including effect on bond length, bond energies, and rigidity of molecular structure

LIQUID PHASE–INTERMOLECULAR FORCES

- Role of hydrogen bonding, dipole interactions, and Van der Waals forces (London dispersion forces) in intermolecular interactions in the liquid phase

ENERGY CHANGES IN CHEMICAL REACTIONS–THERMOCHEMISTRY, THERMODYNAMICS

- The concept of a thermodynamic system and state function
- The zeroth law of thermodynamics and the concept of temperature
- First law of thermodynamics: $\Delta E = Q - W$ (conservation of energy)
- Second law of thermodynamics: concept of entropy as a measure of disorder, and the identification of relative entropy for gas, liquid, and crystal states
- Measurement of heat changes (calorimetry), heat capacity, and specific heat
- Fundamental differences between endothermic and exothermic reactions, including enthalpy (H), standard heats of reaction and formation, and Hess's law of heat summation
- Relationship between bond dissociation energy and heats of formation
- The concept of free energy: G**
- Relationship between $\Delta G°$ and spontaneity of reaction
- Definitions and application of the heat of fusion and heat of vaporization
- Fundamental concepts of the phase diagram, including pressure and temperature

**This concept can also be tested on the Biological and Biochemical Foundations of Living Systems section.

RATE PROCESSES IN CHEMICAL REACTIONS—KINETICS AND EQUILIBRIUM

- Concept of the reaction rate and its dependence upon reactant concentration, rate law, rate constant, and reaction order
- Concept and determination of the rate-limiting step
- Impact of temperature on the reaction rate, including activation energy and use of the Arrhenius equation
- Identification of the activated complex or transition state and interpretation of energy profiles showing energies of reactants, products, activation energy, and ΔH for the reaction
- Comparison of kinetic control and thermodynamic control of a reaction
- Use and purpose of catalysts
- Reversible chemical reactions and the role of equilibrium, including the law of mass action, equilibrium constant, and application of Le Châtelier's principle**
- Relationship between the equilibrium constant and $\Delta G°$**

**This concept can also be tested on the Biological and Biochemical Foundations of Living Systems section.

This chapter continues on the next page ▶ ▶ ▶

11.6 General Chemistry Worked Examples

PASSAGE I: ACIDS AND BASES

Carbon dioxide gas is a by-product of metabolism in the human body. After diffusing out of metabolically active tissue, the majority of carbon dioxide will enter red blood cells, where it is rapidly hydrated by the enzyme carbonic anhydrase, as shown in Reaction 1.

$$H_2O\ (aq) + CO_2\ (g) \rightleftharpoons H_2CO_3\ (aq) \rightleftharpoons HCO_3^-\ (aq) + H^+\ (aq)$$

Reaction 1

The apparent equilibrium constant for the dissociation of carbonic acid is $K'_a = 7.9 \times 10^{-7}$ and the concentration of carbonic acid is proportional to the amount of carbon dioxide, as shown below.

$$[H_2CO_3] = k_{H\,CO_2} \times pCO_2$$

Where k_H is the Henry's law constant for carbon dioxide solubility, approximately $0.03\ \dfrac{\text{mmol}}{\text{L} \cdot \text{mm Hg}}$, and pCO_2 is the partial pressure of CO_2 in the blood. The latter varies with location in the circulatory system, but typically measures between 35–44 mm Hg for arterial blood and 39–52 mm Hg for venous.

Bicarbonate ions are transported out of red blood cells where they help maintain a constant serum pH. During transport, bicarbonate ions are exchanged for chloride ions. Equilibrium keeps bicarbonate and chloride ion serum levels at approximately 25 mM and 100 mM, respectively. This buffer system, along with the body's compensatory mechanisms, results in a normal arterial pH stabilized at 7.40.

Acidosis is a condition in which the body's arterial pH drops below 7.35. Respiratory acidosis is a specific condition that occurs when pCO_2 is too great. Metabolic acidosis is a similar condition in which an acid is being either over-produced by the body or insufficiently excreted by it.

Conversely, alkalosis is a condition in which the body's pH rises above 7.45. Respiratory alkalosis is a specific condition that can develop when carbon dioxide is removed too quickly from the body, such as hyperventilation during periods of significant stress—which commonly exacerbates this condition. Metabolic alkalosis also has many causative agents, including bicarbonate ion and chloride ion imbalances. In general, metabolic imbalances can be compensatory mechanisms for respiratory abnormalities.

P1.

R1.

P2.

E1.

P3.

P4.

P5.

1. Which of the following provides the best approximation for the pH of venous blood in a physiologically normal individual?

   A. $pH = -\log(7.9 \times 10^{-7}) + \log\left(\dfrac{25}{0.03 \times 35}\right)$

   B. $pH = -\log(7.9 \times 10^{-7}) + \log\left(\dfrac{0.03 \times 35}{25}\right)$

   C. $pH = -\log(7.9 \times 10^{-7}) + \log\left(\dfrac{0.03 \times 44}{25}\right)$ ✓

   D. $pH = -\log(7.9 \times 10^{-7}) + \log\left(\dfrac{25}{0.03 \times 44}\right)$

2. Why is the chloride ion required by the cell for Reaction 1 to continue?

   A. Chloride ions act as catalysts for the system.
   B. Anion exchange prevents the accumulation of products.
   C. Chloride ions relieve the excessive charge build up. ✓
   D. The chloride ion is a base, which helps neutralize acidic products.

3. The arterial partial pressure of carbon dioxide in blood is approximately:

   A. 0.0052 kPa. 40 mm Hg
   B. 0.052 kPa.
   C. 5.3 kPa.
   D. 40 kPa.

4. Over the last century, carbon dioxide emissions have noticeably increased the carbon dioxide concentration in the atmosphere. What effect has this had on the oceans?

   A. Marine life dependent on CO_3^{2-} have proliferated.
   B. The oceans have become more basic.
   C. There has been an increase in the bicarbonate levels. ✓
   D. The rise in $[CO_2]_{atm}$ has been exacerbated by global warming.

5. Given a typical plasma volume of 5 L, a typical adult has an amount of bicarbonate with a buffering capability equivalent to how many 500 mg calcium carbonate antacid tablets?

   A. 12.5 ✓
   B. 25
   C. 125
   D. 6×10^3

   $$\dfrac{[HCO_3^-][H^+]}{[H_2CO_3]} = 7.9 \times 10^{-7}$$

   $\dfrac{25\ mmol}{L} \times \dfrac{1\ mol}{1000\ mmol} \times 5L\ ... g \times \dfrac{... g}{1\ mol\ ...}$

6. Metabolic acidosis is characterized by a:

   A. high plasma $[HCO_3^-]$, a low plasma $[H^+]$, and increased breathing rate.
   B. high plasma $[HCO_3^-]$, a high plasma $[H^+]$, and decreased breathing rate.
   C. low plasma $[HCO_3^-]$, high plasma $[H^+]$, and increased breathing rate. ✓
   D. low plasma $[HCO_3^-]$, high plasma $[H^+]$, and decreased breathing rate.

General Chemistry Passage I Explanation:

USING THE KAPLAN METHODS

P1. CO_2 metabolized to bicarbonate

R1. Reversible reaction, carbonic acid as intermediate

P2. pH varies throughout circulation

E1. Henry's law relationship for $[H_2CO_3]$

P3. Cl^- exchanged to allow R1 to continue, normal values of buffer system

P4. Acidosis described

P5. Alkalosis described

---

1. Which of the following provides the best approximation for the pH of venous blood in a physiologically normal individual?

    A. $pH = -\log\left(7.9 \times 10^{-7}\right) + \log\left(\dfrac{25}{0.03 \times 35}\right)$

    B. $pH = -\log\left(7.9 \times 10^{-7}\right) + \log\left(\dfrac{0.03 \times 35}{25}\right)$

    C. $pH = -\log\left(7.9 \times 10^{-7}\right) + \log\left(\dfrac{25}{0.03 \times 44}\right)$

    D. $pH = -\log\left(7.9 \times 10^{-7}\right) + \log\left(\dfrac{0.03 \times 44}{25}\right)$

 ## Assess the question

It is necessary to *set up* the calculations for pH. While it might be possible to make a quick guess (*slightly less than 7.4*), that is insufficient because our logarithmic calculations will not be accurate enough to differentiate between the answers. Notice the similarities within the answers: they all contain "$-\log\left(7.9 \times 10^{-7}\right)$"—this number is from the passage and can be used to help plan an attack.

 ## Plan your attack

The question requires a calculation of pH. The answer choices are all somewhat similar; it's a matter of the numerator and denominator of the second term. An attack should begin by identifying the equation being used and then using the passage to fill in the necessary terms.

Execute the plan

All of the answers include the same term; that term is the pK'_a for carbonic acid. The equation includes pH, pKa for an acid and the log of a ratio. This information and the context of the passage (buffering) leads one to the Henderson–Hasselbalch equation. The equation becomes:

$pH = pK_a + \log\left(\dfrac{[HCO_3^-]}{[H_2CO_3]}\right)$. The passage gives the bicarbonate concentration as 25 mM, but the carbonic acid concentration is more elusive. In order to solve for it, it is necessary to combine $[H_2CO_3] = k_{H CO_2} \times pCO_2$ and the given values for pCO_2.

 Answer by matching, eliminating, or guessing

Executing the plan quickly leads to the elimination of (**B**) and (**D**) because they have the concentration of bicarbonate in the denominator. The difference between (**A**) and (**C**) is the pCO_2—which can be deduced from the passage; it is either 39 mm Hg or 44 mm Hg. Using the reference values, 35 mm Hg is too low for venous blood, so the correct answer is **choice (C)**.

> **2.** Why is the chloride ion required by the cell for Reaction 1 to continue?
>
>   **A.** Chloride ions act as catalysts for the system.
>   **B.** Anion exchange prevents the accumulation of products.
>   **C.** Chloride ions relieve the excessive charge build up.
>   **D.** The chloride ion is a base, which helps neutralize acidic products.

1 Assess the question

The question asks about reasoning. The correct answer must match the role of the chloride ion and make sense, based on a fundamental chemical understanding.

2 Plan your attack

First identify the function of the chloride ion. Paragraph 3 explicitly states that an exchange of chloride ions occurs during transport of the bicarbonate ion out of the cell. The correct answer will reasonably explain why the removal of bicarbonate and/or the addition of chloride ions is necessary for the reaction to continue. Use what is known to attack each answer choice.

3 Execute the plan

Starting with **choice (A)**, chloride ion as a catalyst is not implausible, however, there is not enough information to confirm this. Because of that, and the statement that chloride is "exchanged," this a suspect answer.

For **choice (B)**, since bicarbonate is a product of Reaction 1 and the chloride ion does help remove it, this answer is plausible based on Le Châtelier's principle.

Choice (C) can be eliminated because there is no difference electrically.

Finally, in **choice (D)**, the chloride ion is the conjugate base of a strong acid (HCl), which makes it a very weak base—to the point that it is inert, so this is not correct.

Answer by matching, eliminating, or guessing

Executing the plan led to the elimination of **(A)**, **(C)**, and **(D)**, indicating that **(B)** is correct. Since the reaction is reversible it is plausible that the law of mass action would inhibit further production of bicarbonate—if it remains in the cell. This reasoning matches **choice (B)**.

MCAT Expertise

Even relatively straightforward calculations can vex many MCAT test-takers. The ability to make quick work of questions like this on Test Day will give you an advantage over your competition!

3. The arterial partial pressure of carbon dioxide in blood is approximately:

   A. 0.0052 kPa.
   B. 0.052 kPa.
   C. 5.3 kPa.
   D. 40 kPa.

 Assess the question

This question asks for pCO_2, the partial pressure of CO_2 in the blood. The answers are numbers that differ in order of magnitude, so we should pay more attention to that than the exact value. Also, the answers are in kilopascals, not mm Hg as in the passage.

 Plan your attack

To answer this question, we'll need to find information on the pressure; that information appears at the end of paragraph 2. We'll also need to convert the answer to kilopascals. To do that, we need to know the conversion factors for pressure units.

 Execute the plan

Paragraph 2 states that pCO_2 is between 35 and 44 mm Hg. Given the spacing between answer choices, we can just pick a number that is within the range and easy to use; 40 mm Hg will do.

All that's left is to convert mm Hg to kilopascals; since 1 atm = 760 mm Hg = 101.3 kPa, we get $\left(\dfrac{101.3\ kPa}{760\ mm\ Hg} \right)$, which gives **choice (C)**.

 Answer by matching, eliminating, or guessing

The only answer close to 5 kPa is **choice (C)**. Note that **(D)** assumes that 1 kPa = 1 mm Hg, which is incorrect. **(A)** and **(B)** are both based on using the conversion factor 1 atm = 760 mm Hg.

This chapter continues on the next page ▶ ▶ ▶

> **4.** Over the last century, carbon dioxide emissions have noticeably increased the carbon dioxide concentration in the atmosphere. What effect has this had on the oceans?
>
> **A.** Marine life dependent on CO_3^{2-} have proliferated.
> **B.** The oceans have become more basic.
> **C.** There has been an increase in the bicarbonate levels.
> **D.** The rise in $[CO_2]_{atm}$ has been exacerbated by global warming.

 Assess the question

This question relies on your ability to relate the partial pressure of a gas above a fluid to the pH within the fluid. This is testing Henry's law as well as the consequences given this particular system.

 Plan your attack

One of the most important concepts of Henry's law is the idea that amount of gas dissolved in a liquid is proportional to the partial pressure of the gas above the liquid. Furthermore, gases become increasingly soluble at lower temperatures. Using outside knowledge will be sufficient to make a prediction.

 Execute the plan

If the atmospheric concentration of carbon dioxide increases, then the amount of carbon dioxide dissolved in the oceans would also increase. If the amount of dissolved carbon dioxide increases, then (according to Reaction 1), so does the amount of carbonic acid and ultimately bicarbonate ions and acidity. If the acidity of the oceans increases, then the pH decreases.

 Answer by matching, eliminating, or guessing

Executing the plan led to the elimination of **(B)** and the selection of **(C)**. **(A)** can be eliminated after further consideration, because an increase in the acidity of the oceans would promote the formation of HCO_3^- from CO_3^{2-} and H^+, rendering *less* of the carbonate ion available for marine life. **(D)** relates solubility to temperature, and while the two are related, if there were to be an increase in global temperatures, then that would reduce the solubility of carbon dioxide and raise atmospheric concentrations; however this does not address the effect on the oceans, so it cannot be the correct answer.

5. Given a typical plasma volume of 5 L, a typical adult has an amount of bicarbonate with a buffering capability equivalent to how many 500 mg calcium carbonate antacid tablets?

   A. 12.5
   B. 25
   C. 125
   D. 6×10^3

 Assess the question

The question is asking about the limit of a buffer system. The answer choices and the context of the passage indicate you'll probably need to do a stoichiometry calculation to solve this problem.

 Plan your attack

First determine how much bicarbonate would be found in a typical adult. This will require some information from the passage as well as a conversion from volume and concentration to amount. Then use stoichiometry to determine the equivalent amount of antacid.

 Execute the plan

Paragraph 3 indicates that the typical level of bicarbonate is 25 mM and the question provides an average volume of 5 L, so there are 12.5 L of bicarbonate. Since bicarbonate's formula is HCO_3^- one mole can neutralize one mole of acid, and 1 mmol = 1 mEq. Therefore, we have 125 mEq of base.

To calculate the number of calcium carbonate tablets needed, we need to know that carbonate is CO_3^{2-}, so 1 mmol = 2 mEq. Now we can do a stoichiometry calculation:

$$125\,\text{mEq} \times \frac{1\,\text{mmol CaCO}_3}{2\,\text{mEq}} \times \frac{100\,\text{mg CaCO}_3}{1\,\text{mmol CaCO}_3} \times \frac{1\,\text{tablet}}{500\,\text{mg}} = 12.5\,\text{tablets}$$

Answer by matching, eliminating, or guessing

Our prediction of 12.5 tablets matches **choice (A)**. Notice common errors that may lead one to pick a wrong answer: **(B)** from incorrectly assuming that one mole of calcium carbonate neutralizes one equivalent of acid. **(C)** is the number of milliequivalents of bicarbonate in blood, and **(D)** is the milligrams of calcium carbonate required, not the number of 500-mg tablets.

6. Metabolic acidosis is characterized by a:

   A. high plasma [HCO_3^-], a low plasma [H^+], and increased breathing rate.

   B. high plasma [HCO_3^-], a high plasma [H^+], and decreased breathing rate.

   C. low plasma [HCO_3^-], high plasma [H^+], and increased breathing rate.

   D. low plasma [HCO_3^-], high plasma [H^+], and decreased breathing rate.

Assess the question

For this question it is necessary to reason through the provided information and make predictions about effects on plasma bicarbonate concentrations, pH, and breathing rate.

Plan your attack

Use passage information pertaining to "metabolic acidosis," as well as the relationships in Reaction 1, to make a prediction. Once a conclusion is reached, look to eliminate answers—this is a strategic move when there is significant repetition in the answer choices. Continue until only one answer remains.

Execute the plan

The term "acidosis" is enough to predict a decrease in pH and an increase in [H^+]—eliminate (**A**). The passage indicates that "metabolic acidosis is a similar condition in which an acid is being either overproduced by the body or insufficiently excreted by it." Use the equilibrium in Reaction 1 to determine the effect of increased acid production on bicarbonate concentrations. An increase in [H^+] would shift the equilibrium back towards water and carbon dioxide, so bicarbonate concentrations would decrease—eliminate (**B**).

Answer by matching, eliminating, or guessing

With two answer choices left, it's necessary to discern the differences between them and make a prediction. The difference is in the breathing rate. If the body experiences an increase in carbon dioxide levels, it would be expected that the ventilation rate would increase to compensate. Furthermore, the passage indicates that hyperventilation exacerbates alkalosis (presumably lowering pH, which is desired)—with a prediction in hand, look for a match, (**C**).

GENERAL CHEMISTRY PASSAGE II: SOLUBILITY

Adequate solubility of ions and macromolecules, along with their permeability in various sections of the digestive and excretory systems, helps prevent malnutrition and other dangerous conditions.

The human body needs to absorb regular doses of certain vitamins and minerals. *Vitamins* are organic molecules that an organism cannot sufficiently synthesize, and that are not broken down for energy, but are needed for normal cellular operation. Some vitamins have hormone-like functionality (vitamin D for example), while others act as antioxidants (vitamin C) or as precursors to enzyme cofactors (vitamin B_{12}).

Dietary minerals are elements (other than C, H, N, and O) required for living; *trace minerals* are dietary minerals essential only in minute quantities. Most of them must be taken as parts of compounds, because many free elements can react with substances in the digestive tract to form by-products, some of which are toxic. Approximately 30 elements are known, or suspected to be, essential to normal biological function. Most minerals are naturally occurring in the diet, although foods may be fortified.

The chemical and physical nature of required nutrients affects their solubility and permeability. It can also alter their *bioavailability*, the fraction of the ingested dose that reaches systemic circulation unaltered. Any process that alters the compound or hinders its absorption will reduce bioavailability. For example, certain food additives can alter bioavailability; for example, the fat substitute Olestra (molecular formula $C^{13}H^{14}O^{11}$) reduces vitamin K absorption. Each gram of Olestra in food can reduce absorption of vitamin K by 8 micrograms. Table 1 displays some of the nutritional and chemical characteristics of important vitamins and minerals. (Note: the average adult has a blood volume of ~5 liters.)

Nutrient Source	Oral Bioavailability	Recommended Daily Intake (RDI)	Molecular mass (g/mol)
Vitamin A Acetate	0.99	900 μg	328.49
Vitamin B_6	0.85	1.7 mg	123.11
Vitamin C	0.99	90.0 mg	176.12
Vitamins D_2 and D_3	0.99	10.0 μg	396.65
Vitamin E Acetate	0.67	15.0 mg	472.74
Vitamin K	0.90	120 μg	444.65
Potassium Chloride	0.90	4700 mg	74.55
Sodium Chloride	0.99	1500 mg	58.44
Calcium Carbonate	0.35	1300 mg	100.09
Zinc Sulfate	0.37	5.0 mg	161.47

Table 1. Nutritional and chemical characteristics

P1.

P2.

P3.

P4.

T1.

1. Vitamin C formulations are administered in a variety of ways, including pure ascorbic acid administered orally and ascorbyl palmitate (*vitamin C ester*) administered topically. How does the addition of the palmitate group affect oral and topical bioavailability of vitamin C?

Palmitic Acid

  A. The palmitate group decreases oral bioavailability via reduced solubility in the digestive tract, but increases topical bioavailability by minimizing free radicals in the epidermis.
  B. The palmitate group increases oral bioavailability via increased permeability in the digestive tract, and increases topical bioavailability by increasing vitamin C stability in topical solutions.
  C. The palmitate group decreases oral bioavailability via decreased permeability in the digestive tract, and has little effect on topical bioavailability because ascorbyl palmitate penetrates the skin as effectively as pure vitamin C.
  D. The palmitate group has little effect on oral bioavailability because the palmitate group is removed by hydrolysis in the digestive tract, and increases topical bioavailability by increasing the stability of vitamin C in topical solutions.

2. A company would like to develop an oral vitamin E supplement for diet-restricted patients. What is the minimum amount of vitamin E acetate ($K_{sp} = 1.6 \times 10^{-7}$) needed in the supplement in order to reach serum saturation levels for vitamin E? (Ignore ion contributions from other compounds.)

  A. 0.006 g
  B. 0.015 g
  C. 0.3 g
  D. 1.5 g

3. Why is the observed bioavailability of minerals generally low even though they have relatively high K_{sp} values?

  A. Some mineral ions are insoluble in aqueous solution and thus the ions cannot be digested and absorbed.
  B. Other molecules are interacting with the ions in the oral route, inhibiting absorption.
  C. Mineral ions do not have enough valence electrons to sufficiently interact with intestinal ion channels.
  D. Ions are immediately deposited in the bone and other tissue, thus measured bioavailability is low.

4. Hyperoxaluria causes CaC_2O_4 to deposit in urine. A 0.75 liter urine sample free of oxalate was collected. The calcium concentration of the urine was determined to be 1 mM, and then oxalate was added until crystals formed. If 0.15 mg was added, what is the K_{sp} of calcium oxalate?

  A. $K_{sp} = 2.9 \times 10^{-7}$
  B. $K_{sp} = 2.4 \times 10^{-9}$
  C. $K_{sp} = 2.9 \times 10^{-9}$
  D. $K_{sp} = 2.4 \times 10^{-11}$

5. Olestra ($C_{13}H_{14}O_{11}$), once a popular food additive, has been found to reduce the absorption of certain nutrients. For example, each mole of Olestra effectively removes 8 moles of vitamin K from the digestive tract. How much vitamin K must be ingested to achieve serum levels equivalent to the RDI, if 0.34 g of Olestra is taken concurrently?

  A. 3.18 g
  B. 3.31 g
  C. 3.49 g
  D. 3.81 g

General Chemistry Passage II Explanation:

USING THE KAPLAN METHODS

P1. Solubility = excretory/digestive tract section dependence

P2. Vitamins = various functions; examples

P3. Minerals ≠ C, H, O, N; description

P4. Chemical composition dictates bioavailability/absorption rates

T1. Values for minerals and vitamins

KEY Concepts

Stoichiometry is a high-yield general chemistry skill on the MCAT. This skill can also be utilized in physics and biochemistry. Be comfortable relating dimensional analysis to topics such as solubility products.

1. Vitamin C formulations are administered in a variety of ways, including pure ascorbic acid administered orally and ascorbyl palmitate (*vitamin C ester*) administered topically. How does the addition of the palmitate group affect oral and topical bioavailability of vitamin C?

Palmitic Acid

A. The palmitate group decreases oral bioavailability via reduced solubility in the digestive tract, but increases topical bioavailability by minimizing free radicals in the epidermis.

B. The palmitate group increases oral bioavailability via increased permeability in the digestive tract, and increases topical bioavailability by increasing vitamin C stability in topical solutions.

C. The palmitate group decreases oral bioavailability via decreased permeability in the digestive tract, and has little effect on topical bioavailability because ascorbyl palmitate penetrates the skin as effectively as pure vitamin C.

D. The palmitate group has little effect on oral bioavailability because the palmitate group is removed by hydrolysis in the digestive tract, and increases topical bioavailability by increasing the stability of vitamin C in topical solutions.

Assess the question

This question has long answer choices that deal with changes in oral and topical bioavailability. Each answer choice has a total of four parts (change in oral bioavailability, explanation, change in topical bioavailability, explanation). In answering this question, we'll probably want to start with just one part, rather than try to predict everything at once.

Plan your attack

The passage only mentions vitamin C in passing, in paragraph 2, where it states that vitamin C is an antioxidant. We also get data on it in Table 1; in particular, its bioavailability is a very high 99%. Beyond that, we'll need to rely on our knowledge of nutrient absorption and even a little bit of organic chemistry—namely, the behavior of esters—to answer this question.

Execute the plan

What will happen when the ester reaches the stomach? It's in an aqueous solution that contains significant amounts of acid. That's the perfect recipe for hydrolysis of the ester, which results in vitamin C and palmitic acid. As a result, vitamin C should be available in the stomach as it is in its pure form, so its bioavailability should remain approximately the same.

Answer by matching, eliminating, or guessing

Scanning the first part of each answer, only **choice (D)** matches this prediction. Looking at the remainder of the answer, the explanation matches our prediction. Moreover, the second half of the statement is correct as well: the palmitate group should increase the stability of vitamin C in topical solutions.

Let's quickly look at the wrong answers. **(B)** would be unlikely on general principle; since the oral bioavailability is already 99 percent, it's unlikely that palmitate—or anything else, for that matter—could significantly increase that percentage. On the other hand, **(A)** and **(C)** both claim a significant decrease. **(A)** claims this occurs because the ester is less soluble in water; as stated above, esters undergo hydrolysis in water, so this is incorrect. **(C)**, on the other hand, claims that it is because of decreased permeability of the ester. In fact, the reverse is true: if anything, the vitamin C ester, because of its large hydrophobic group, should be *more* permeable, not less.

Takeaways

For predictions of permeability and solubility, use the chemical structures, but be mindful of chemical reactions that could alter the physical properties.

Things to Watch Out For

Even after you've found a prediction, be sure to check all of the answers—they may contain clues that could reveal an unconsidered factor.

Key Concepts

Biological systems have evolved to interact with the inorganic world. Normal functioning relies on a harmony between the two.

2. A pharmaceutical company is developing an oral vitamin E supplement. What is the minimum oral dose of vitamin E acetate ($K_{sp} = 1.6 \times 10^{-7}$) needed to saturate the blood with vitamin E? (Assume no other sources of either ion, and that the acetate's bioavailability equals vitamin E's.)

   A. 0.15 grams
   B. 0.3 grams
   C. 1.0 grams
   D. 1.5 grams

 Assess the question

This calculation question asks for the minimum *mass* of vitamin E acetate needed to saturate the blood. The answer choices are relatively far apart, so approximations should be OK. That said, stoichiometry questions are often good candidates for triage.

 Plan your attack

To answer this question, we'll need several pieces of information. First, we need K_{sp} from the question stem. We'll also need the molecular mass from Table 1, as well as the bioavailability, since paragraph 4 tells us that not all of an oral dose reaches systemic circulation. We'll need to combine that with our knowledge of molar solubility and stoichiometry calculations.

 Execute the plan

Vitamin E ester should dissociate in water to give vitamin E and acetate ions. Since the question stem tells us we can assume there are no other sources of either ion, we can assume that x moles of the ester will yield x moles of vitamin E and x moles of acetate, since acetate is a -1 ion.

K_{sp} = [Vitamin E][Acetate]. Since the question indicates ion contributions from other compounds can be ignored, the only contributor of either ion is vitamin E acetate. Predicting a 1:1 stoichiometric ratio (the acetate ion carries a -1 charge), gives: [Vitamin E] = [Acetate] and [Vitamin E] = $\sqrt{K_{sp}}$.

At this point, round the K_{sp} value to a workable number such as 1.6×10^{-7} which allows the square root calculation to become: [Vitamin E] $= \sqrt{16} \times \sqrt{10^{-8}} = 4 \times 10^{-4}$ mol/L. *Notice that "workable" (when taking the square root of a number in scientific notation) means the significand is a perfect square and the exponent is even.*

This is the theoretical maximum concentration of vitamin E (from vitamin E acetate) that can saturate the blood. In order to determine the actual amount necessary to reach these levels, the volume is required. Use the volume of blood given in the passage to make an estimate.

$(4 \times 10^{-4} \text{ mol/L})(5 \text{ L}) = 2 \times 10^{-3} \text{ mol}$. Then use the molar mass to determine the equivalent amount in grams: $(2 \times 10^{-3} \text{ mol})(4.75 \times 10^{2} \text{ g/mol}) = \sim 10 \times 10^{-1} \text{ g} = \sim 1 \text{ g}$.

Lastly, consider the bioavailability (0.67). Only 67 percent of the ingested vitamin E acetate is actually absorbed. Therefore, in order to absorb 1 gram of vitamin E acetate $(\dfrac{1\,g}{.67} = \dfrac{1}{\frac{2}{3}} \sim = 1\,g \times \dfrac{3}{2})$, approximately 1.5 grams must be ingested.

 Answer by matching, eliminating, or guessing

Only one answer, **choice (D)**, is greater than 1 gram, so it must be our correct answer. We didn't actually need to *perform* the final bioavailability calculation, but we did need to consider it.

The wrong answers all reflect reasoning errors test takers might make. **(A)** results from taking the square root incorrectly (getting 4×10^{-3} instead of 4×10^{-4}). If you forgot to multiply by the average blood volume of 5 L, you'd get **(B)**. Finally, **(C)** results from neglecting the bioavailability.

Takeaways

Look at the answer choices and the information given. Always ensure that your calculations include units to ensure that you have achieved the answer as desired.

Things to Watch Out For

Scientific notation makes math much simpler. Dimensional analysis in these situations is critical and awareness of common ions (acetate) will ensure you utilize the K_{sp} equation properly.

Key Concepts

Stoichiometry and dimensional analyses are skills utilized in various topics.

3. Which of the following would best explain the relatively low bioavailability of zinc sulfate?

   A. Zinc sulfate is insoluble in aqueous solution and thus its ions cannot be digested and absorbed.

   B. Other substances interact with the ions in the oral route, inhibiting absorption.

   C. Zn^{2+} ions do not have enough valence electrons to sufficiently interact with intestinal ion channels.

   D. Zn^{2+} ions are immediately deposited in the bone and other tissue, thus lowering the bioavailability.

 Assess the question

This question asks us why zinc sulfate has a low bioavailability. The answers are reasons, which means we need an answer that is both scientifically plausible *and* relevant to the question at hand.

 Plan your attack

Bioavailability is defined in paragraph 4. Zinc sulfate is considered a mineral, which is discussed in the third paragraph. Table 1 confirms that zinc sulfate does, in fact, have low bioavailability.

 Execute the plan

Paragraph 4 states that processes that hinder absorption or alter a substance reduce bioavailability. Paragraph 3 notes that elements can react with molecules in the digestive tract, sometimes forming toxic by-products. It's reasonable to believe that the same might happen with ions as well as free elements. Therefore, we can predict that the correct answer should indicate either a reaction involving zinc ions or some factor that hinders absorption.

Answer by matching, eliminating, or guessing

Considering the answer choices one at a time, **(A)** is false: sulfates are generally soluble. **Choice (B)** matches our prediction: it gives us a reason why Zn^{2+} would be poorly absorbed.

(C) is incorrect; cations are drawn by electrostatic forces as a result of their positive charges, not their electrons. Finally, **(D)** is also incorrect; bone does not act as a storage pool for zinc.

Takeaways

When left with four confusing choices, eliminate the ones that are certainly wrong.

Things to Watch Out For

Solubility rules are often, but not always, necessary to solve solution problems. When in doubt, start with what you are most confident with and work from there.

Key Concepts

Questions that task you with explaining discrepancies require critical thinking and a firm understanding of the passage. If unsure how to approach these, mark them for review and return to them when you have more time.

4. Hyperoxaluria causes CaC_2O_4 to deposit in urine. A 0.75 liter urine sample free of oxalate was collected. The calcium concentration of the urine was determined to be 1 mM, and then oxalate was added until crystals formed. If 0.15 mg was added, what is the K_{sp} of calcium oxalate?

A. $K_{sp} = 2.9 \times 10^{-7}$
B. $K_{sp} = 2.4 \times 10^{-9}$
C. $K_{sp} = 2.9 \times 10^{-9}$
D. $K_{sp} = 2.4 \times 10^{-11}$

 Assess the question

This is clearly a calculation question. In order to solve for the K_{sp} it will be necessary to determine the ion product at the time of precipitation. This will involve calculating the concentrations of both ions present. The question provides the calcium concentration, and the concentration of oxalate can be calculated from the information in the question stem.

 Plan your attack

It will be necessary to have the K_{sp} expression for CaC_2O_4 (which can be derived from the balanced reaction) and the concentrations of each of the ions in the equation.

The calcium concentration is given and the concentration of oxalate can be calculated from the mass and the volume of the sample.

 Execute the plan

$$CaC_2O_4 \rightleftharpoons Ca^{2+} + C_2O_4^{2-} \quad K_{sp} = [Ca^{2+}][C_2O_4^{2-}] = ? \quad [Ca^{2+}] = 1 \times 10^{-3}$$

$$.15 \text{ mg } C_2O_4^{2-} \times \frac{1 \text{ g}}{10^3 \text{ mg}} \times \frac{1 \text{ mol}}{88 \text{ g}} \times \frac{1}{.75 \text{ L}} = \sim 2.3 \times 10^{-6} \text{ mol/L } C_2O_4^{2-}$$

$$K_{sp} = [Ca^{2+}][C_2O_4^{2-}] = (2.3 \times 10^{-6})(1 \times 10^{-3}) = 2.3 \times 10^{-9}$$

Answer by matching, eliminating, or guessing

Executing the plan led to a prediction of 2.3×10^{-9}. Fortunately, there is a near match with **(B)**.

Takeaways

Be methodical and organized in your scratchwork.

Things to Watch Out For

Be sure to use the proper data. For instance, mass and molecular weight are commonly mixed up. That is an easy way to arrive at a wrong answer on the MCAT.

Key Concepts

Solubility is an important biological mechanism for nutrient transfer; be familiar with the differences between IP and K_{sp} and how to use them to determine ion concentrations.

5. Olestra ($C_{13}H_{14}O_{11}$), once a popular food additive, has been found to reduce the absorption of certain nutrients. For example, each mole of Olestra effectively removes 8 moles of vitamin K from the digestive tract. How much vitamin K must be ingested to achieve serum levels equivalent to the RDI, if 0.34 g of Olestra is taken concurrently?

A. 3.18 g
B. 3.31 g
C. 3.49 g
D. 3.81 g

 Assess the question

This question asks for the number of *moles* of vitamin K required, but all the numerical information in the passage and question stem deal with *grams*. This is a classic stoichiometry set up, and should tip us off to watch our units. Fortunately for us, the answers are relatively far apart, so approximations shouldn't cause a problem.

 Plan your attack

We'll need the amount of vitamin K that Olestra removes, given in paragraph 4. Then, we'll need to figure out the total amount of vitamin K the bag needs, using the information in Table 1. Finally, we'll need to convert grams to moles.

 Execute the plan

Begin with 0.34 g Olestra and use the periodic table to find the molecular mass (roughly 346 g/mol) and then moles. Simplifying the math: 0.34 g Olestra/340 g/mol = ~0.001 mol Olestra

Then use the conversion factor of 8 to 1: $0.001 \text{ mol Olestra} \times \left(\dfrac{8 \text{ mol vitamin K lost}}{1 \text{ mol Olestra consumed}} \right)$ = 0.008 mol vitamin K —lost. At this point no matter how much vitamin K is required, at least 0.008 moles must be consumed (because that's how much will be lost with Olestra). This corresponds to ($.008 \text{ mol} \times \dfrac{445 \text{ g}}{1 \text{ mol vit K}}$ = 3.56 g); any answers *significantly* less than 3.56 can be eliminated.

The amount desired in the serum (equivalent to the RDI) is 120 μg—a nominal amount (which should allow one to confidently choose an answer). Taking into account the bioavailability, in order to reach serum levels of 120 μg, 120 μg/0.9 = ~133 μg must be available for absorption. Since the first 3.56 grams will be unavailable, the total amount that must be ingested is 3.56 g + 133; since 133 μg is an insignificant amount, a good approximation is 3.56 g.

 Answer by matching, eliminating, or guessing

Our prediction of 5×10^{-7} mol matches **choice (C)**. Note that two of the wrong answers stem from using the wrong number in the stoichiometry calculation. **(A)** comes from *subtracting* 80 μg from the RDI, while **(B)** results from using just the 80 μg removed by Olestra. **(D)** is a classic trap answer in multi-step calculations: we need 200 *micrograms* of vitamin K, not 200 *micromoles*.

Takeaways

Conversion factors may sometimes be given in a passage or question stem; be sure to utilize them appropriately (using labels whenever necessary).

Things to Watch Out For

Rounding error will need to be taken into account at times. It's best to keep notes (mental or on your scratch paper) about the approximations that have been made, so that adjustments can be made quickly and accurately.

Things to Watch Out For

Don't rush through stoichiometry calculations. Make sure that you're using the correct ratios, and that the units cancel out in each step.

11.7 General Chemistry Practice

GENERAL CHEMISTRY PASSAGE III (QUESTIONS 1–6)

The conversion of reactants to products can be mediated by a number of factors. In a reaction that has a high free energy of activation for the conversion of reactants to an intermediate, the observed reaction rate is based on the concentration of the intermediate in solution. Take the following example:

Reactants $\rightleftharpoons$ Intermediate $\rightarrow$ Products

where there is an equilibrium constant, K', for the equilibrium between the reactants and the intermediate. The rate of the overall reaction, V, is dictated by:

$$V = \nu[I]$$

where ν is the rate constant, and $[I]$ is the concentration of the intermediate. The activation energy required to complete this reaction is the difference between the free energy of the reactants and that of the transition state (between the reactants and the intermediate). Depending on the reaction, this free energy of activation may be very large. A large free energy of activation implies that relatively few of the reactants will have sufficient energy to overcome the barrier and [ultimately] become products. The free activation energy and the equilibrium constant (for the reactants and the intermediate) are related by:

$$\Delta G' = -RT \ln K'$$

This equation, combined with the equation for the overall reaction rate, shows that the rate can be affected by changing the activation energy of the system; the lower the activation energy, the quicker the reaction will proceed.

In biological systems, enzymes work to lower activation energies and therefore allow reactions to reach equilibrium more quickly. Reaction rates and enzyme activity alike depend on the temperature of the system. For reaction rates, the temperature affects K_{eq}, thereby establishing a new equilibrium. For optimal enzyme activity, only a certain range of temperatures is suitable. As the enzyme is heated, the enzyme denatures and the conformation of the active site is compromised.

P1.

E1.

E2.

P2.

1. Which of the following equations relates the rate of the reaction to the activation energy?

   A. $v[I]RT\ln K_{eq}$
   B. $v[I]e^{-(\Delta G'/RT)}$
   C. $v[R]e^{(\Delta G'/RT)}$
   D. $v[R]10^{-(\Delta G'/2.3RT)}$

2. A scientist studying the kinetics of a two-substrate reaction observes rates in the ratio 4:1:16. After the first trial, the only change was a reduction in the concentration of A (by a factor of four). For the third trial, the concentration of A was unchanged from the second trial, and the concentration of B was quadrupled. Which of the following best represents the rate law for this reaction?

   A. $k[A][B]$
   B. $k[A]^2[B]$
   C. $k[A][B]^2$
   D. $k[A]^2[B]^2$

3. All of the following quantities do NOT increase after the addition of the appropriate enzyme, EXCEPT:

   A. K_{eq}.
   B. $\Delta G'$.
   C. V.
   D. ΔG°.

4. The interactions between an enzyme and the substrate typically involve multiple, weak and reversible interactions. Which factor is the LEAST abundant between the substrate and enzyme?

   A. Van der Waals forces
   B. Hydrophobic effects
   C. Covalent bonding
   D. Hydrogen bonding

5. If the example reaction described in the passage is exothermic with a rate-limiting first step, which of the following could represent the energy profile for the reaction?

   A.

   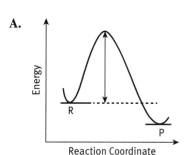

   B.

   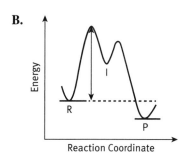

   C.

   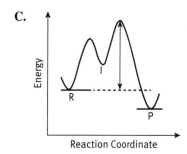

   D.

   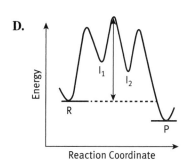

6. Suppose an enzyme is only active when a given carboxylic acid residue is in the carboxylate form. If the K_a of the acid is 4×10^{-5}, which of the following correctly matches the pH of the solution with the ratio of active to inactive enzymes?

A. pH 5.0 and 1:1
B. pH 4.4 and 10:1
C. pH 4.0 and 1:1
D. pH 3.4 and 1:10

This chapter continues on the next page ▶ ▶ ▶

General Chemistry Practice Passage Explanations

P1. Factors mediating reactions

E1. Rate of the overall reaction

E2. Relationship between free energy and equilibrium

P2. Enzymes lower activation energy

1. (D)

The reaction velocity, or rate, is given as $V = v[I]$, which is the jumping-off point for this question. The passage gives K' as the equilibrium constant for the transition between [R] and [I] and looking at the second equation in the passage it can be seen that K' and $\Delta G'$, the activation energy, are related. To get K' and subsequently $\Delta G'$ into the equation, solve for [I] in terms of K'. Since K' is the equilibrium constant, its expression is governed by $K' = \dfrac{[I]}{[R]}$, which can be rearranged to $[I] = [R]K'$. Solving for K' in terms of $\Delta G'$ requires the rearrangement of $\Delta G' = -RTlnK'$ to $lnK' = -\Delta G'/RT$. Solving to get rid of the natural log gives $K' = e^{-\Delta G'/RT}$. Combining that equation with the earlier expression for the rate gives $v[R]e^{-(\Delta G'/RT)}$. But this doesn't match any answers. One more step is then required to solve this. When solving for $lnK' = -\Delta G'/RT$ one can multiply by a factor of 2.3 to change from natural log to log base 10 giving $2.3 \, log \, K' = -\Delta G'/RT$, which yields **choice (D)** or $v[R]10^{-(\Delta G'/2.3RT)}$. Alternatively, using the process of elimination: **(A)** does not relate "rate of the reaction to the activation energy;" **(B)** implies $e^{-(\Delta G'/RT)} = 1$ (in order to satisfy $v[I]e^{-(\Delta G'/RT)} = v[I]$), which means the activation energy is *always* zero, so it cannot be correct; finally, the passage states that the "lower the activation energy, the quicker the reaction" so **(C)** is out, because it shows a direct relationship between the two.

2. (C)

Determining reaction rates requires seeing how reactions react when changing the concentrations of one substrate while keeping the others constant. This question first quarters the concentration of A or multiplies it by $\dfrac{1}{4}$. This produces a drop in the reaction rate that is equivalent to the drop in concentration, so the reaction rate is first order with respect to A. This eliminates **choice (B)** and **choice (D),** as they both have A as a second-order reactant. Determining the order of B as a reactant is a little more complicated. The scientist increases the concentration of B by a factor of 4 and the reaction rate increases to 4 times the original. This means that the reaction rate is 16 times greater, since we have already lowered the reaction rate to $\dfrac{1}{4}$ of the original. This means that B is a second-order reactant and matches **choice (C).**

3. (C)

Eliminate those that are not increased. Choice **(A)** can be eliminated because enzymes do not alter the equilibrium constant; they just allow the reaction to reach equilibrium more quickly. From the passage, it can be seen that $\Delta G'$ is lowered, so eliminate **choice (B)**. Also, enzymes do not change the difference in free energy between the reactants and products, $\Delta G°$, just the free energy of activation—so **choice (D)** is out. Enzymes increase the reaction rate, so V increases, meaning it's the exception to those that do not increase—match **(C)**.

4. (C)

Stabilizing transition states in biological systems involves making sure unstable parts of the molecules, i.e., parts that have charges that they don't want, have something to interact with to stabilize them. The enzyme itself doesn't usually contribute or accept electrons, but rather lets opposite charges interact to lessen the energy of a system. This means forces that are not transferring or sharing electrons will be more abundant than those that actually bond. There are many more instances of the non-covalent forces as these are usually present in numerous places in an enzyme's active site to help stabilize. Enzymes do not usually covalently bond to their substrate, as this would raise the energy required to dissociate the enzyme from the substrate and would slow the reaction down. Covalent bonding or **choice (C)** will be the least prevalent.

5. (B)

The reaction in the passage has a discrete intermediate and is thus a two-step reaction. This means that the correct graph will have two energy activation hills and will have a valley in the middle representing the intermediate. This eliminates **choices (A)** and **(D)**, since they have too few and too many peaks respectively. The next thing to consider is the question stem. It indicates that the first step of the reaction, the conversion of reactant to intermediate, is the rate-limiting step. This means that it will be the slowest step and thus have the largest activation energy, which shows that **choice (B)** is correct.

6. (D)

The pK_a is a function of the K_a, which describes the ratio of concentration of conjugate base to acid at equilibrium. Given the K_a the pK_a can be calculated [precisely] as 4.4 (or more quickly as 4.6). At a certain pH, the actual ratio of conjugate base to acid is described by the Henderson–Hasselbalch equation. The equation $pH = pK_a + \log\left(\dfrac{[conj.base]}{[acid]}\right)$ can be rearranged to yield $\dfrac{[conj.base]}{[acid]} = 10^{pH-pK_a}$. So at a pH = pKa (4.4), the ratio of active to inactive is 1:1, which means we can eliminate **choices (A)**, **(B)**, and **(C)**. According to the HH equation, at a pH one point below the pKa (3.4) the ratio of active to inactive is 1:10, which matches **choice (D)**.

CHAPTER TWELVE

Organic Chemistry

Organic chemistry has long been regarded as a significant hurdle to medical school, full of long hours in the lab and challenging synthesis pathways. Over the years, the AAMC has been placing less significance on organic chemistry on the MCAT, and more emphasis on molecular biology, biochemistry, and genetics. On the MCAT in 2015, 5 percent of the questions in the Biological and Biochemical Foundations of Living Systems section and 15 percent of the questions in the Chemical and Physical Foundations of Biological Systems section will be related to organic chemistry. Regardless of these changes, organic chemistry is still important to achieve a high score. Organic chemistry knowledge is still required to evaluate chemical structures and to predict the behavior of molecules within a biological system. You can expect the MCAT to test organic chemistry within the context of what is needed for further understanding of biochemistry and reactions essential for an understanding of medical testing and pharmacology.

12.1 Reading the Passage

Passages related to organic chemistry may come in the form of a passage that is exclusively related to organic chemistry and its application to a biological system, or a passage that covers multiple subject areas, especially biochemistry. There is a clear relationship between these two sciences in that understanding of organic chemistry structures and reactions is essential to understanding the behavior of biochemical systems. Therefore, success in organic chemistry on the MCAT depends on your ability to apply your knowledge of organic chemistry to biochemical systems.

PASSAGE TYPES

Organic chemistry passages will either present information or an experiment.
- Information passages
  - Often short, and accompanied by diagrams illustrating reactions or mechanisms.
  - May also be integrated with other subject areas, such as biochemistry or biology.
  - May present a new reaction or a series of related reactions, or describe a compound or an experimental technique. However, organic chemistry passages will always be related to a living system.

- Experiment passages
  - Presentation of one or more experiments.
  - Experimental data may be in the form of percentage yield from a synthesis, a written summary of the reaction, or description of the appearance or spectroscopic properties of a product.
  - The product of a synthesis may then be used in a biochemistry experiment, meaning that the synthesis reaction and the biochemistry experiment go hand in hand.

PASSAGE TYPES IN ORGANIC CHEMISTRY

	Information Passages	Experiment Passages
Content	Reads like a textbook; may integrate concepts of organic chemistry and biochemistry.	Reads like a lab report or a journal article that summarizes an experimental procedure. The product of an organic chemistry reaction may be the substrate for a biochemistry experiment.
Questions	Many questions will not require information from the passage. Those that do are likely to be more theoretical.	Will often focus on the hypothesis, procedure, and outcome. If multiple experiments, questions are likely to focus on the relationships between the experiments.

OUTLINING THE PASSAGE

Organic chemistry passages will often feature synthesis pathways or molecular structures. In addition, the passage may be a mixture of organic chemistry and biochemistry, rather than a pure organic chemistry passages. While approaching a passage, be sure to think about how the organic chemistry science applies to a living system, and look for the connections between the sciences presented in the passage.

Scan for Structure

- Start by evaluating the overall structure of the passage. Is the passage entirely text-based? Does the passage contain both text and diagrams? What types of diagrams are present? Charts, graphs, tables, synthesis pathways, or diagrams of an experimental procedure?
- Is this passage one to do now or later? Answer this question, and then move on to either the next passage or start reading the passage.

Read Strategically

- As you read, identify the purpose of each paragraph and how the paragraph fits into the overall structure and argument of the passage.
- Identify any connections between figures and the text.
- Consider how the organic chemistry described fits into a living system.
- Anticipate what other topics might be involved in the passage.
- If the passage describes an experiment, be sure to identify the hypothesis, procedure, and outcome.

Label Each Component

- Write down the purpose of each paragraph and figure.
- If a figure is directly related to some portion of the text, identify those connections.
- Write down what is represented in each figure.
- For experimental passages, note the location of the hypothesis, procedure, and outcome.

Reflect on Your Outline

- Determine the overall purpose of the passage. What is being described in the passage? Why was the experiment conducted?

12.2 Answering the Questions

Questions that are exclusively related to organic chemistry are often very straightforward. However, questions that require integration of organic chemistry with another topic may be more difficult. Once again, the same question types seen in the other sciences apply.

- Discrete questions
  - Questions not associated with a descriptive passage.
  - Often preceded with a warning such as, "Questions 12–15 are NOT associated with a descriptive passage."
  - Likely to test basic principles of organic chemistry, such as structures and reactions.
- Questions that stand alone from the passage
  - One of the most common question types of organic chemistry questions.
  - Often requires analysis of structures.
  - When evaluating structures, many of the wrong answer choices will contain structures that are simply not possible given the basic concepts of organic chemistry.
- Questions that require data from the passage
  - Will often require analysis of data or experimental design.
  - May often require evaluation of a synthesis process with a different substrate, thus requiring application of information from the passage to a new situation.
- Questions that require the goal of the passage
  - The nature of these questions will depend on what else is in the passage.
  - If the passage is exclusively organic chemistry, then the goal of the passage is likely to be the outcome of an experiment or synthetic pathway.
  - If the passage contains organic chemistry integrated with biology or biochemistry, then the goal of the passage will depend on the content of the passage as a whole and the context in which organic chemistry is discussed.

DETERMINING THE PURPOSE OF THE QUESTION

MCAT organic chemistry questions may be related only to organic chemistry or may be organic chemistry in the context of another subject area. In addition, language is often used to disguise simple organic chemistry questions as more difficult ones. Pay special attention to the task of the question to ensure that questions like these are discovered and answered correctly.

1. Assess the Question

- Identify the topic and degree of difficulty of the question.
- Determine the time requirement for the question.
- Decide whether this question is one to be answered now or later.

2. Plan Your Attack

- Read the question critically to aid in identifying the task of the question.
- Identify whether the question is exclusively organic chemistry or requires integration with another subject area.
- Determine whether the passage is required to answer the question.
- Identify where the information is located.
- If data analysis is required, locate the correct data set.
- Identify the task of the question.
- Paraphrase the question, if necessary, to prevent missing simple questions disguised as more complicated ones.

3. Execute Your Plan

- Locate the information and analyze the data to determine a possible answer for the question.

4. Answer the Question by Matching, Eliminating, or Guessing

- Match your answer with the answer choices.
- If your answer does not match, proceed to elimination.
- Wrong answer choices in organic chemistry often contain molecular structures that are simply not possible or do not make sense. Look for incorrect charge distribution, wrong numbers of bonds for atoms within the molecule, double bonds in unusual locations, etc.
- If guessing is required, try to eliminate two answer choices. Then, choose the answer choice that is most likely correct, based on your analysis.

12.3 Getting the Edge in Organic Chemistry

With the addition of biochemistry to the MCAT, many organic chemistry questions will require integration with concepts of biochemistry and biology. In this context, expect questions that assess your understanding of the implications of organic chemistry in biochemistry and biology. Simpler organic chemistry questions are likely to be disguised as more complicated ones. Using the task of the question, paraphrase these questions to a simpler form. Doing so will help you to identify these questions and determine the correct answer. Many test-takers will become overwhelmed by these questions, while a critical thinker who paraphrases questions will see the simpler question and answer it correctly.

Organic chemistry questions often contain structures as answer choices. Many wrong answer choices among these questions will be structures that are not possible given the basic fundamentals of organic chemistry. Applying the basic fundamentals of organic chemistry to these answer choices can allow for quick elimination of wrong answer choices.

12.4 Step-By-Step Guide to Organic Chemistry Passages

OUTLINING THE PASSAGE

- **Scan for structure**
  - Determine whether to do this passage now or later.
  - Identify the structure of the passage, including charts, graphs, chemical equations, and synthesis pathways.
- **Read strategically**
  - Identify the type of passage.
  - Pay special attention to the relationships between concepts.
  - In an experiment passage, determine the hypothesis, procedure, and outcome.
  - In an information passage, identify how the information in each paragraph fits together to present a unified picture.
  - Identify what information is presented in each figure or image.
- **Label each component**
  - Write down the purpose of each paragraph and figure.
  - Identify any connections between concepts within the passage.
  - Determine the goal of any synthesis pathway and how the products of that synthesis fit into the rest of the passage, i.e., the product of the synthesis may be the substrate for a biochemical process.
- **Reflect on your outline**
  - Determine the goal of the passage and write it down.
  - Identify the concepts within the passage in an effort to anticipate questions.

ANSWERING THE QUESTIONS

1. Assess the question

- Determine whether this question should be done now or later.
- Identify the topic and the degree of difficulty.
- Good questions to do now in organic chemistry are ones that stand alone from the passage or do not require extensive data analysis in order to determine the correct answer.

2. Plan your attack

- Identify the task of the question. If necessary, paraphrase the question to make it simpler.
- Determine what you already know, and what information you need.
- Identify where to find the required information: the passage, the question, your outline, or your own knowledge
- If you have to go back to the passage, determine where to find the required information by using your outline.
- If data analysis is required, identify the correct data set, as there may be multiple data representations.

3. Execute your plan

- Analyze the data, go back to the passage, and carry out your plan.
- If you get stuck analyzing data, remember that the trend of the data is often enough to yield a correct answer choice.

4. Answer the question by matching, eliminating, or guessing

- Match your answer to the answer choices.
- If there is not a match, eliminate incorrect answer choices. Some of the answer choices may not make sense; eliminate those first.
- If the answer choices are molecular structures, eliminate by starting with structures that simply do not make sense.
- If elimination does not provide a clear answer, guess between two probable answers.

12.5 Preparing for the MCAT: Organic Chemistry

These are the organic chemistry topics that you are likely to see on Test Day. All of the following topics appear in the Chemical and Physical Foundations of Biological Systems section unless otherwise noted.

AMINO ACIDS

- Descriptions of amino acids in terms of absolute confirmation at the α position and as dipolar ions**
- Classification of amino acids as acidic or basic, hydrophobic or hydrophilic**
- Reactions of amino acids, including sulfur linkages for cysteine, peptide linkages in polypeptides and proteins, and hydrolysis**
- Synthesis of α amino acids including the Strecker synthesis and Gabriel synthesis

CARBOHYDRATES

- Descriptions of carbohydrates, including nomenclature, classification, common names, absolute configuration, cyclic structure, conformations of hexoses, epimers, and anomers**
- Reactions of carbohydrates, including hydrolysis of the glycoside linkage**
- Definitions and characteristics of monosaccharides**
- The concept of keto-enol tautomerism of monosaccharides

MOLECULAR STRUCTURE AND ABSORPTION SPECTRA

- Identification and characteristics of the infrared region, including intramolecular vibrations and rotations; recognition of common characteristics of group absorptions and the fingerprint region
- Identification and characteristics of the visible region, including creation of color by absorption and the effect of structural changes on absorption
- Identification and characteristics of the ultraviolet region, including π-electron and nonbonding electron transitions and conjugated systems
- Fundamental concepts of NMR spectroscopy, including protons in a magnetic field, equivalent protons, and spin-spin splitting

*This concept is only tested on the Biological and Biochemical Foundations of Living Systems section.

**This concept can also be tested on the Biological and Biochemical Foundations of Living Systems section.

SEPARATIONS AND PURIFICATIONS

- Concepts of extraction as a distribution of solute between two immiscible solvents
- Concepts and process of distillation
- Process and basic principles of chromatography, including column chromatography, gas-liquid chromatography, high pressure liquid chromatography, paper chromatography, and thin-layer chromatography
- Definition and characteristics of racemic mixtures, including separation of enantiomers

LIPIDS

- Types of lipids, including those for storage (triacyl glycerols and free fatty acids), structural (phospholipids, phosphatides, sphingolipids, and waxes), and signals/cofactors (fat-soluble vitamins and steroids)**
- The process and outcome of saponification
- Descriptions and structures of steroids, terpenes, and terpenoids*

*This concept is only tested on the Biological and Biochemical Foundations of Living Systems section.

**This concept can also be tested on the Biological and Biochemical Foundations of Living Systems section.

ALDEHYDES AND KETONES

- Descriptions and characteristics of aldehydes and ketones, including nomenclature and physical properties
- Characteristics of nucleophilic addition reactions at the carbonyl bond (C=O), including acetal, hemiacetal, imine, enamine, hydride reagents, and cyanohydrin
- Oxidation of aldehydes
- Characteristics of reactions at adjacent positions (enolate chemistry), including keto-enol tautomerism (α-racemization), aldol condensation, retro-aldol, and kinetic *vs.* thermodynamic enolate
- General principles of aldehyde and ketone chemistry, including effect of substituents on reactivity of C=O, steric hindrance, and acidity of the α-H; carbanions

ALCOHOLS

- Description, nomenclature, and physical properties of alcohols, including acidity and hydrogen bonding
- Important reactions of alcohols, including oxidation, protection of alcohols, preparation of mesylates and tosylates, and substitution reactions (S_N1 and S_N2)

CARBOXYLIC ACIDS

- Description, nomenclature, and physical properties of carboxylic acids
- Important reactions of carboxylic groups, including amides (and lactam), esters (and lactone), anhydride formation, reduction, decarboxylation, and reactions at the α carbon, substitution

ACID DERIVATIVES (ANHYDRIDES, AMIDES, ESTERS)

- Descriptions, nomenclature, and physical properties of acid derivatives
- Important reactions of acid derivatives, including nucleophilic substitution, transesterification, and hydrolysis of amides
- General principles of acid derivatives, including relative reactivity of acid derivatives, steric effects, electronic effects, and strain (β-1 actams)

PHENOLS

- Oxidation and reduction of hydroquinones and ubiquinones; biological $2e^-$ redox centers

POLYCYCLIC AND HETEROCYCLIC AROMATIC COMPOUNDS

- Biological aromatic heterocyclics

12.6 Organic Chemistry Worked Examples

PASSAGE I: REACTION MECHANISMS

Enzymatic catalysis of reactions is multifaceted and highly specific. The mechanisms by which enzymes increase reaction rates are as varied as the reactions themselves. Enzymes can induce bond strain in substrates by favoring the conformation of the transition state over that of the substrate. In this way, the substrates are destabilized, thereby decreasing the potential energy difference between the substrate and the transition state. It is important to recognize that enzymes, via this mechanism, do not directly stabilize the transition state.

Enzymes can also be said to reduce the entropy of the reactants, because in order for a reaction to occur, the reactants must align appropriately, which is highly unlikely in solution. Enzymes therefore facilitate reactions by correctly orientating the substrates. Acidic and basic residues of enzymes can activate nucleophiles or electrophiles through protonation or deprotonation. Leaving groups can be stabilized by these residues as well. Enzymes can form either transient ionic or covalent bonds with the substrate. Partial or complete ionic bonding is usually carried out by acidic or basic residue side chains to stabilize developing charges. Covalent bonds may form between residues and the substrate to lower transition state energy. However, these bonds must be broken to regenerate the enzyme. The hydrolysis of protein requires the presence of proteases to catalyze the process. Generally, there are two pathways by which proteins are hydrolyzed.

Pathway 1: A nucleophilic residue of an enzyme attacks the substrate protein to form an acyl-enzyme intermediate. An activated water molecule attacks causing the release of half of the product and regeneration of the enzyme, as shown in Figure 1.

Pathway 2: An activated water molecule performs nucleophilic attack on the peptide bond to hydrolyze it, as shown in Figure 2.

Figure 1. Mechanism of protein breakdown by a serine protease

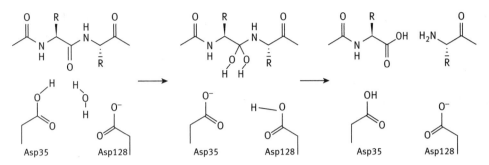

Figure 2. Mechanism of protein breakdown by an aspartic protease

P1.

P2.

F1.

F2.

1. How does aspartate contribute to the first step of the mechanism illustrated in Figure 1?

   A. It directly increases the nucleophilicity of the serine residue through deprotonation.

   B. It functions to maintain an acidic environment for optimal enzymatic activity.

   C. It increases the pK_a of histidine through electrostatic interactions.

   D. It serves to increase the basicity of histidine by protecting its aromaticity.

2. In Figure 1, activated water can perform nucleophilic attack only after half of the substrate has been cleaved off. Which of the following best explains why this is so?

   A. Histidine will preferentially extract a proton from serine before it will activate water.

   B. Steric hindrance prevented water from performing nucleophilic attack.

   C. The carbonyl carbon of the amide was initially not sufficiently electrophilic.

   D. The deprotonated serine is a less effective leaving group than the substrate fragment.

3. Why can aspartic proteases hydrolyze peptide bonds in fewer steps than serine proteases?

   A. Aspartic proteases hydrogen bond with the carbonyl oxygen, while serine proteases do not.

   B. The aspartic acid in serine proteases is located too far from the peptide bond.

   C. Histidine is not a strong enough base to deprotonate water.

   D. Aspartic proteases are able to stabilize tetrahedral intermediates.

4. Based on the mechanism illustrated in Figure 2, what must be true of the active site of aspartic proteases?

   A. It binds to hydrophobic proteins more readily than to hydrophilic proteins.

   B. It binds to bulky proteins more readily than to smaller proteins.

   C. It is kept relatively acidic.

   D. It is kept relatively basic.

5. Why is water necessary to carry out proteolysis instead of simply using an amino acid residue already found on the enzyme?

   A. Water is ubiquitous and therefore maximally increases reaction kinetics.

   B. Water is a small molecule that can easily perform nucleophilic attack without significant steric hindrance.

   C. Water can be activated by basic amino acid residues, making it the most nucleophilic entity in the microenvironment of the active site.

   D. Water allows for the recycling of the enzyme in proteolysis.

6. The amino acid residues of serine proteases, Gly 193 and Ser 195, form an oxyanion hole, which hydrogen bonds to the substrate. When will the oxyanion hole be particularly important?

   A. After the substrate has entered the active site but before hydrolysis has begun

   B. When serine performs nucleophilic attack on the substrate

   C. While the substrate exhibits tetrahedral geometry

   D. While water performs nucleophilic attack on the substrate

This chapter continues on the next page ▶ ▶ ▶

Key Concepts

Carboxylic Acid Derivative mechanism of action

Organic Chemistry Passage I Explanation:

USING THE KAPLAN METHOD

P1. Enzyme functions: bond strain

P2. Enzyme functions: reduce entropy, acid/base, transient bonding

F1. Serine protease–Pathway 1

F2. Aspartic protease–Pathway 2

1. How does aspartate contribute to the first step of the mechanism illustrated in Figure 1?

   A. It directly increases the nucleophilicity of the serine residue through deprotonation.

   B. It functions to maintain an acidic environment for optimal enzymatic activity.

   C. It increases the pK_a of histidine through electrostatic interactions.

   D. It serves to increase the basicity of histidine by protecting its aromaticity.

 Assess the question

The question stem limits the scope of the question to Figure 1. Since the passage does not directly address how serine proteases hydrolyze proteins, it is not necessary to refer to the text. Therefore, it is only the mechanism that must be analyzed.

2 Plan your attack

In order to determine the role of aspartate, it is essential to look at both the reactants and the products following the first step. As is the case with most organic chemistry problems, it is prudent to begin by identifying relevant nucleophiles and electrophiles. To avoid being seduced by wrong answers, making a prediction is a good idea here.

Execute the plan

At a glance, it is clear that the serine is deprotonated and then performs nucleophilic attack on the carbonyl carbon of the substrate. At the same time, histidine appears to be protonated but also deprotonated, and the aspartic acid residue is protonated.

Enzymes are highly specific, so the amino acid residues were not arranged as indicated by coincidence. Each residue will interact with the adjacent residue. With this understanding, it becomes evident that aspartic acid must be stealing a proton from histidine. Removing the proton allows histidine to undergo a rearrangement. One can infer that this rearrangement will help histidine activate the serine residue through deprotonation. Because histidine is extracting a proton from serine, it is behaving as a base. Thus, put together, aspartic acid must be increasing the basicity of histidine. Now it is time to look at the answer choices to find an answer.

4 **Answer by matching, eliminating, or guessing**

Choice (C) states that aspartic acid increases the pK_a of histidine through electro static interactions. This is equivalent to stating that aspartic acid increases the basicity of histidine. As for the electrostatic interactions, before complete deprotonation occurs, aspartic acid hydrogen bonds with histidine. Hence, **choice (C)** is correct.

Aspartic acid does not deprotonate serine *directly* as stated in (**A**); it deprotonates histidine, which deprotonates serine. Histidine contains both protonated and deprotonated nitrogen atoms. If the environment were acidic, as described in (**B**), these nitrogen atoms would both be protonated. **Choice (D)** can be eliminated because although aspartic acid does increase the basicity of histidine, it does not do so by protecting histidine's aromaticity. The aromaticity of histidine is not in jeopardy and if it were, it would not react regardless of aspartic acid's presence.

Key Concepts

Nucleophilic Reaction in Carboxylic Acid Derivatives

2. In Figure 1, activated water can perform nucleophilic attack only after half of the substrate has been cleaved off. Which of the following best explains why this is so?

A. Histidine will preferentially extract a proton from serine before it will activate water.

B. Steric hindrance prevented water from performing nucleophilic attack.

C. The carbonyl carbon of the amide was initially not sufficiently electrophilic.

D. The deprotonated serine is a less effective leaving group than the substrate fragment.

 Assess the question

The question stem specifically asks about Figure 1. It might be a good idea to paraphrase this one. For instance, the question can be paraphrased as, "Why can't water attack the carbonyl carbon initially?" This simplifies the question stem so that it is more manageable.

 Plan your attack

Recognizing the difference between substrate structure originally and substrate structure after half of it is cleaved off is essential. Activation of the water is irrelevant, since water could be activated at any point in the mechanism. To avoid being seduced by wrong answers, making a prediction is a good idea.

 Execute the plan

For water to perform nucleophilic attack, the carbonyl carbon must be sufficiently electrophilic. At the beginning of the mechanism, the carbonyl group is part of an amide, while later it is part of an ester. Because amide groups have greater double-bond character, they are more stable than esters. Therefore, water will not be able to attack the amide, but is able to attack the ester.

Answer by matching, eliminating, or guessing

Choice (C) correctly identifies this reasoning.

There are a couple of ways water could be activated (aspartic acid could do this). Therefore, histidine's preferred target does not explain why activated water cannot perform nucleophilic attack until the substrate is cleaved in **choice (A)**.

Choice (B) can be eliminated because water is a small molecule, so steric hindrance would not be a factor here. Actually, in **(D)**, the deprotonated serine is a better leaving group than the substrate fragment.

Key Concepts

Hydrolysis

> **3.** Why can aspartic proteases hydrolyze peptide bonds in fewer steps than serine proteases?
>
> **A.** Aspartic proteases hydrogen bond with the carbonyl oxygen, while serine proteases do not.
>
> **B.** The aspartic acid in serine proteases is located too far from the peptide bond.
>
> **C.** Histidine is not a strong enough base to deprotonate water.
>
> **D.** Aspartic proteases are able to stabilize tetrahedral intermediates.

 Assess the question

The question stem asks for a comparison between aspartic proteases and serine proteases. Therefore, Figure 1 and Figure 2 must be compared. The written portion of the passage is not necessary to answer this question.

 Plan your attack

The main difference between the mechanism in Figure 1 and the mechanism in Figure 2 is when water performs nucleophilic attack. Therefore, to determine the answer to this question, one must explain this difference.

 Execute the plan

Water can perform nucleophilic attack earlier in the aspartic protease mechanism because the carbonyl carbon is especially electrophilic. The additional aspartic acid residue can hydrogen bond with the carbonyl oxygen. As a result, the carbonyl oxygen becomes relatively more electronegative. The carbonyl oxygen will sap negative charge from the carbonyl carbon so that it becomes relatively electropositive. Water can then attack earlier with aspartic proteases versus serine proteases.

Answer by matching, eliminating, or guessing

Choice (A) must be correct.

Choice (B) is incorrect because the enzymes are folded such that all of the amino acid residues are located within close proximity of each other. Histidine deprotonates water later in the mechanism, so **(C)** is not true. Both serine proteases and aspartic proteases are able to sufficiently stabilize tetrahedral intermediates. If this were not the case, as described in **(D)**, then they would not be able to effectively catalyze proteolysis.

Key Concepts

Amino Acid Chemistry

> 4. Based on the mechanism illustrated in Figure 2, what must be true of the active site of aspartic proteases?
>
> A. It binds to hydrophobic proteins more readily than to hydrophilic proteins.
> B. It binds to bulky proteins more readily than to smaller proteins.
> C. It is kept relatively acidic.
> D. It is kept relatively basic.

1 Assess the question

The question stem asks for a generalization about the aspartic protease's active site.

2 Plan your attack

It is important to recognize that Figure 2 is only a snapshot of a portion of the active site of aspartic proteases. Therefore, a limited number of conclusions can be drawn.

3 Execute the plan

Upon analyzing the mechanism in Figure 2, it is apparent that one of the aspartic acid residues is protonated. Since carboxylic acids are acidic and will lose a proton at a neutral pH, the microenvironment of aspartic proteases must be acidic.

4 Answer by matching, eliminating, or guessing

Choice (C) must be correct.

There are many other amino acids that are not illustrated in Figure 2 that are relevant. Hence, choices **(A)** and **(B)** cannot be drawn with the information that is available. If the microenvironment of the active site were basic, as stated in **(D)**, then the aspartic acid residues would not be protonated.

> **5.** Why is water necessary to carry out proteolysis instead of simply using an amino acid residue already found on the enzyme?
>
> **A.** Water is ubiquitous and therefore maximally increases reaction kinetics.
>
> **B.** Water is a small molecule that can easily perform nucleophilic attack without significant steric hindrance.
>
> **C.** Water can be activated by basic amino acid residues making it the most nucleophilic entity in the microenvironment of the active site.
>
> **D.** Water allows for the recycling of the enzyme in proteolysis.

Key Concepts

Unique Properties of Water

Assess the question

The question is asking for an explanation for the need of a third-party molecule (specifically water) for proteolysis to occur.

Plan your attack

The scope of this question is not limited to Figures 1 and 2, but is extended to include all proteases. Analyzing water's role in proteolysis with aspartic and serine proteases will still be helpful. It will also be useful to recall basic knowledge of enzymes.

Execute the plan

If the amino acid residues of an enzyme were to attack the substrate, then a little piece of the enzyme would be lost during each reaction. Since an enzyme must be regenerated over the course of a reaction, this cannot occur. Therefore, water is necessary for proteolysis.

Answer by matching, eliminating, or guessing

Choice (D) must be correct.

Water is everywhere and thus is a solid option for enzyme catalysis. However, water's viability as an option in **(A)** does not explain why a third-party molecule is essential. There are many amino acid residues with side chains that are potentially much more nucleophilic and would not be dramatically impacted by steric hindrance. Thus, **(B)** cannot be correct. Water is definitely not necessarily the most nucleophilic entity in the microenvironment of the active site, as stated by **(C)**, even after being activated.

Key Concepts

Carboxylic Acid Derivatives

---

6. The amino acid residues of serine proteases, Gly 193 and Ser 195, form an oxyanion hole, which hydrogen bonds to the substrate. When will the oxyanion hole, be particularly important?

   A. After the substrate has entered the active site, but before hydrolysis has begun

   B. When serine performs nucleophilic attack on the substrate

   C. While the substrate exhibits tetrahedral geometry

   D. While water performs nucleophilic attack on the substrate

---

1 Assess the question

The question stem mentions serine proteases, so Figure 1 is key here.

2 Plan your attack

Hydrogen bonding confers stability. Therefore, the answer will be the step in which stability is most needed.

3 Execute the plan

The most unstable steps illustrated in Figure 1 are those that include intermediates. In Figure 1, the intermediates all exhibit tetrahedral geometry. Another way to approach this problem is to use the information in the passage. The passage explains that enzymes catalyze reactions by inducing strain in the substrate by favoring the transition states. "Favoring the transition" essentially means that the enzymes confer stability to them.

4 Answer by matching, eliminating, or guessing

Choice (C) must be correct.

If the substrate were stabilized too much, then the reaction would not proceed forward. In **(A)**, the substrate is held in place by the enzyme, but not much more than that. The amino acid residues of serine proteases work together (in some sense stabilize each other) to facilitate nucleophilic attack on the substrate, as described in **(B)**. However, there is no need to provide extra stability to the substrate. **(D)** can be eliminated because the substrate is relatively stable at this point. It is not carrying any charges and would not require additional stability.

ORGANIC CHEMISTRY PASSAGE II: ALDEHYDES AND KETONES

Amphetamines are a class of potent nervous system stimulants popularized as performance and cognitive enhancers, and in some cases, used recreationally as aphrodisiacs or euphoriants. Amphetamines diffuse across the blood–brain barrier, as well as the placental barrier, making unwanted side-effects a serious concern. In order to mitigate adverse effects, medical dosage and availability is strictly controlled. While debate persists over amphetamine's neurotoxicity in humans, there appears to be evidence that amphetamine metabolism increases the concentration of reactive oxygen species (ROS).

Amphetamines are legally and illicitly synthesized in a variety of ways. Figure 1 outlines the production of racemic amphetamines via two different intermediates.

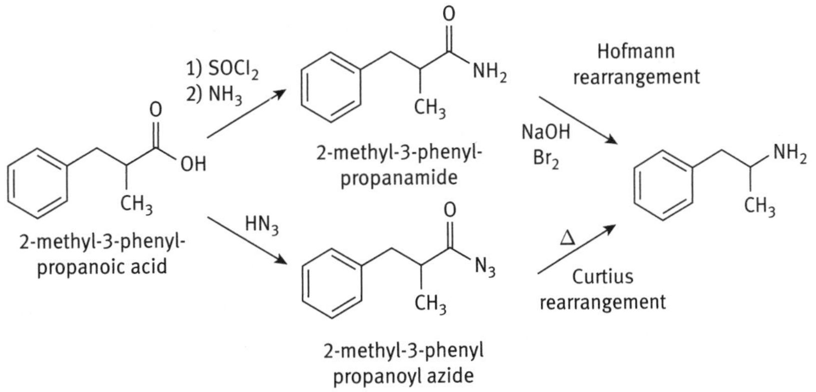

Figure 1. Synthesis of methamphetamine via arrangement

Because the biological activity of amphetamines is stereospecific and amphetamine is often produced as a racemic mixture, it is generally necessary to isolate the biologically active enantiomer. Figure 2 outlines the resolution of racemic amphetamine via hot, basic tartaric acid. In addition, Figure 2 shows a stereospecific synthetic pathway.

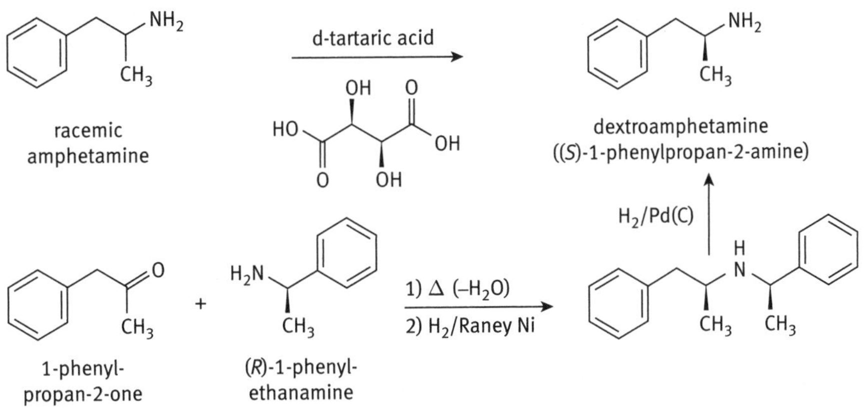

Figure 2. Stereoselective production of D-amphetamine

Amphetamines have biological analogs termed *trace amines*. Trace amines are structurally and metabolically related to traditional monoamine neurotransmitters like dopamine and norepinephrine and are so named because they are only found in trace amounts.

P1.

Fig1.

P2.

Fig2.

P3.

1. Epinephrine, shown below, is not permeable to the blood–brain barrier. Which of the following best explains why amphetamines are permeable and epinephrine is not?

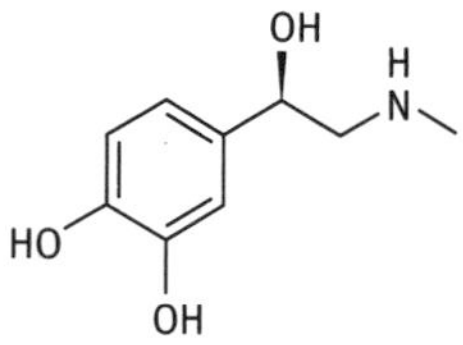

A. Amphetamines are mostly lipid soluble due to the aromatic ring and relative lack of polar protic groups.

B. The methyl group of amphetamines provides stereospecificity for trace amine receptors.

C. ROS species produced by amphetamines facilitate membrane transfer.

D. The polarity of the hydroxyl groups reduces affinity for plasma-membrane transporters.

2. What is the most likely reason why methamphetamine (a secondary amine and amphetamine analog) can elicit sympathetic responses similar to epinephrine despite differences in their chemical makeup?

A. Metabolites of methamphetamine structurally resemble epinephrine receptors.

B. Methamphetamine inhibits epinephrine reuptake mechanisms.

C. Methamphetamine is a configurational isomer of epinephrine and reacts similarly.

D. Epinephrine receptors have a high affinity for the benzene ring of both molecules.

3. What is the primary difficulty in synthetically producing trace amine compounds from ketone intermediates?

A. Carbonyls are prone to ring-closing mechanisms and thus create intermediates unfavorable to amination.

B. Carbonyl compounds, particularly ketones, are relatively unreactive to amines.

C. There are a number of side products possible from carbonyl compounds.

D. Addition to the carbonyl carbon is reversible and synthesis is subject to equilibrium constraints.

4. A student wishing to resolve optically pure amphetamine uses mesotartaric acid, a diastereomer of D-tartaric acid. Is the student likely to be successful?

A. Yes, because mesotartaric acid will combine with each of the enantiomers to form a pair of diastereomers, which can be separated by physical means.

B. Yes, because the enantiomer of D-tartaric acid will react with the racemates to form distinct salts that can be separated by physical means.

C. No, because D-tartaric acid is necessary to form a pair of diastereomers that can be separated.

D. No, because mesotartaric acid will react with the mixture to form distinct salts that are mirror images.

5. Which of the following statements best describes the rearrangements in Figure 1?

A. In the Hofmann rearrangement, primary amides are converted to derivatives by the action of halohydroxides or halogens in alkaline solution. Excess base generates a conjugate acid of the product.

B. In the Curtius rearrangement, an acyl azide is prepared by reaction of an acyl chloride with diazonium followed by treatment with cold nitrous acid. Subsequent heating results in decomposition.

C. Both the Hofmann and Curtius rearrangements involve acyl nitrenes that quickly rearrange to isocyanate isomers, which are isolated or reacted in acidic solvents.

D. Both the Hofmann and Curtius rearrangements involve the addition of water to isocyanates in order to produce an unstable carbamic acid that decomposes to an amine and carbon dioxide.

Key Concepts

When presented with complex molecules or reactions, look for recognizable functional groups or reaction conditions.

Organic Chemistry Passage II Explanation:

USING THE KAPLAN METHODS

P1. Amphetamine uses, permeability and toxicity

Fig1. Synthetic pathways via rearrangements (Hoff/Curtius)

P2. Biological activity is stereospecific

Fig2. Two pathways for optically pure amphetamine

P3. Trace amines described, examples

---

1. Epinephrine, shown below, is not permeable to the blood–brain barrier. Which of the following best explains why amphetamines are permeable and epinephrine is not?

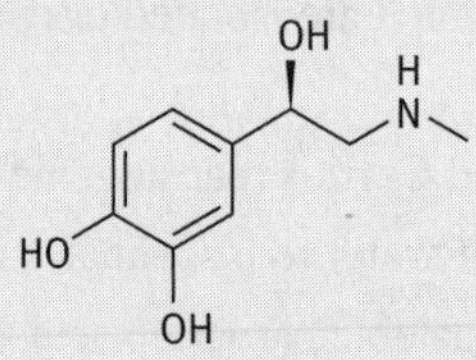

    A. Amphetamines are mostly lipid soluble due to the aromatic ring and relative lack of polar protic groups.

    B. The methyl group of amphetamines provides stereospecificity for trace amine receptors.

    C. ROS species produced by amphetamines facilitate membrane transfer.

    D. The polarity of the hydroxyl groups reduces affinity for plasma-membrane transporters.

---

1 Assess the question

Chemical structure analysis is required to determine the answer, along with a basic understanding of permeability.

Plan your attack

In order to answer this question, it is necessary to focus on the differences between the two molecules. Those differences combined with new information from the passage and required outside knowledge will be enough to find the correct answer. Epinephrine is structurally similar to amphetamines, with the addition of several hydroxyl groups. Look for this to show up in the correct answer.

 Execute the plan

Paragraph 1 indicates that amphetamines can diffuse across the blood–brain barrier. The blood–brain barrier is primarily lipid or small non-polar molecule soluble. Thus, it is possible that the hydrocarbon structure, including the aromatic ring, may allow the molecule to diffuse, while the polar, hydroxyl groups in epinephrine prevent its diffusion.

Choice (A) addresses both components of the prediction and is a strong answer.

Choice (B) is perhaps true, but it does not address why one molecule would be permeable and another would not—so it cannot be the correct answer (to this question).

Choice (C) recalls another fact from the passage, however; even though reactive oxygen species may damage cells and thereby compromise the integrity of the blood–brain barrier, it is not the ROS species that facilitates membrane transfer, it is diffusion—which is a consequence of its structure.

Choice (D) addresses a key difference between the two molecules (the hydroxyl groups), but it neglects the fact that amphetamines *diffuse* across membranes and thus do not require transporters.

Takeaways

When asked to explain a difference in function, look for a difference in structure.

 Answer by matching, eliminating, or guessing

Looking for an answer that addresses the key differences between the molecules led to **(A)** and **(D)**. After careful consideration of the passage information, in conjunction with outside knowledge, it's clear that **(A)** is the best answer.

Things to Watch Out For

Answer choices that bring up unrelated facts about one molecule or another.

Key Concepts

Form dictates function.

2. What is the most likely reason why methamphetamine (a secondary amine and amphetamine analog) can elicit sympathetic responses similar to epinephrine despite differences in their chemical makeup?

   A. Metabolites of methamphetamine structurally resemble epinephrine receptors.

   B. Methamphetamine inhibits epinephrine reuptake mechanisms.

   C. Methamphetamine is a configurational isomer of epinephrine and reacts similarly.

   D. Epinephrine receptors have a high affinity for the benzene ring of both molecules.

 ## Assess the question

Much like the previous question, in order to answer question 2 it will be necessary to explain an observation about two molecules. Unlike its predecessor, the correct answer to this question must address a *similarity* in function despite a difference in form.

 ## Plan your attack

It's best to make a few predictions and then use the process of elimination. There are a few notable differences between the two molecules and one notable similarity. The similarity is a good place to start. In order to elicit a response from the sympathetic nervous system, there must be stimulation of the appropriate receptors. While it's uncertain how methamphetamine works, it's likely one of a few common mechanisms. The molecule could mimic epinephrine and bind to epinephrine receptors. It could also prevent the degradation or reuptake of epinephrine. There are other, more obscure mechanisms, but their validity should be addressed on an individual basis using passage information, outside knowledge, and logic.

 ## Execute the plan

Choice (A) may be tempting, because it provides a possible explanation (that methamphetamine does not itself activate epinephrine receptors), which takes into account structural differences; however, the last portion of this answer is not plausible. The correct answer would indicate that the metabolites are structurally similar to *epinephrine* not the epinephrine *receptor*.

Choice (B) matches a likely mechanism.

Choice (C) states that methamphetamine and epinephrine are configurational isomers—this is incorrect. Furthermore, configurational isomers can react very differently, so this is not the best answer.

Choice (D) provides a possible explanation for the similarity; it focuses on a common element of both molecules. However, given the stereospecificity of amphetamine receptors and the fact that methamphetamine is an analog, it's unlikely that the achiral benzene ring is sufficient to stimulate a sympathetic response.

 Answer by matching, eliminating, or guessing

Executing the plan led to the elimination of **(A)**, **(C)**, and **(D)**, indicating that **(B)** is the correct answer.

Takeaways

Consider what needs to be found in the correct answer, but remain open to unconsidered explanations that are in line with passage information and outside knowledge.

Things to Watch Out For

Commonly, wrong answers will address the question but contradict information from the passage.

Key Concepts

The MCAT will blur the lines between organic chemistry, general chemistry, biochemistry, and biology.

3. What is the primary difficulty in synthetically producing trace amine compounds from ketone intermediates?

   A. Carbonyls are prone to ring-closing mechanisms and thus create intermediates unfavorable to amination.

   B. Carbonyl compounds, particularly ketones, are relatively unreactive to amines.

   C. There are a number of side products possible from carbonyl compounds.

   D. Addition to the carbonyl carbon is reversible and synthesis is subject to equilibrium constraints.

① Assess the question

This question requests the primary difficulty experienced during a synthesis.

② Plan your attack

It's possible to make some predictions based on the compounds in question, but ultimately it will require eliminating those answers that are less problematic.

③ Execute the plan

Carbonyl groups undergo a wide variety of reactions—a preliminary prediction. Further, many of the intermediates are also reactive. There is also an example of amphetamine production from a ketone (the second reaction in Figure 2) that can be used for reference. In the reaction, the amine attacks the carbonyl carbon, forming an alcohol intermediate. There is then dehydration of the alcohol to form the imine intermediate.

Choice (A) may seem reasonable, but it does not even mention ketones and does not answer the question.

Choice (B) indicates that carbonyl groups are unreactive, which is untrue—carbonyl groups, including ketones, undergo a wide variety of reactions.

Choice (C) addresses a fundamental problem when working with reactive species.

Choice (D) must be eliminated because (while true) equilibrium reactions can be coerced via application of Le Châtelier's principle.

 Answer by matching, eliminating, or guessing

Such a question requires elimination. Thorough reasoning will dictate that the best of these choices is **choice (C)**. In fact, synthetic routes for almost all pharmaceuticals suffer from some form of yield issues based on chemical structure.

Takeaways

When presented with multiple answer choices with factual information, eliminate those that are least relevant to the question.

Things to Watch Out For

When asked for a *primary* difficulty, all answer choices should be considered before making a selection.

Key Concepts

The carbonyl is a favorite reaction point on the MCAT; be familiar with its common mechanisms.

4. A student wishing to resolve optically pure amphetamine uses meso-tartaric acid, a diastereomer of D-tartaric acid. Is the student likely to be successful?

   A. Yes, because mesotartaric acid will combine with each of the enantiomers to form a pair of diastereomers, which can be separated by physical means.

   B. Yes, because the enantiomer of D-tartaric acid will react with the racemates to form distinct salts that can be separated by physical means.

   C. No, because D-tartaric acid is necessary to form a pair of diastereomers that can be separated.

   D. No, because mesotartaric acid will react with the mixture to form distinct salts that are mirror images.

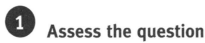

1 Assess the question

This question asks about the reasoning behind the experimental design. The answers are yes/no followed by a brief explanation.

2 Plan your attack

It's best to approach the answers with a prediction in mind. Once a prediction is made, attack the answer. The correct answer will not only answer the question, but also have sound reasoning. If unsure about the content, focus on the reasoning within the answer.

In order to resolve a racemic mixture into optically pure enantiomers, the mixture must be reacted with another optically active reagent. Commonly, acid/base properties are exploited to form salts. The salts thus formed will be diastereomers of each other. Diastereomers have different physical properties and can be separated by physical means (crystallization is common with amines).

Mesotartaric acid is a meso compound and as such is optically inactive. Therefore, it will be incapable of resolving a racemic mixture. It's now time to find the answer that matches the prediction, albeit in other words.

Execute the plan

Choices (A) and **(B)** can be eliminated because the resolution will not work. Further, **(B)** claims that the enantiomer of D-tartaric acid reacts, when the question stem clearly identifies mesotartaric acid as a diastereomer (the two terms are mutually exclusive).

Choice (C) has the first part correct, however, it distorts the second half. D-tartaric acid is useful, but it is not necessary. There many other optically active resolving agents that could be used, including L-tartaric acid.

Choice (D) must be correct and matches the prediction. Distinct molecules that are mirror images are enantiomers, which is what would result from a reaction of a racemic mixture and an optically inactive reagent. Enantiomers cannot be separated by physical means, so the student's procedure would not work.

 Answer by matching, eliminating, or guessing

Executing the plan led to the elimination of **(A)**, **(B)**, and **(C)**, indicating that **(D)** is correct.

Takeaways

In order to resolve a racemic mixture, an optically active reagent must be used.

Things to Watch Out For

Expect to see the same concept mentioned in different terms; the test writers commonly employ synonyms.

Key Concepts

Don't be afraid to make a quick sketch; often times a sketch will elucidate the difference between a reasonable mechanism/ product and an unreasonable one.

5. Which of the following statements best describes the rearrangements in Figure 1?

A. In the Hofmann rearrangement, primary amides are converted to derivatives by the action of halohydroxides or halogens in alkaline solution. Excess base generates a conjugate acid of the product.

B. In the Curtius rearrangement, an acyl azide is prepared by reaction of an acyl chloride with diazonium followed by treatment with cold nitrous acid. Subsequent heating results in decomposition.

C. Both the Hofmann and Curtius rearrangements involve acyl nitrenes that quickly rearrange to isocyanate isomers, which are isolated or reacted in acidic solvents.

D. Both the Hofmann and Curtius rearrangements involve the addition of water to isocyanates in order to produce an unstable carbamic acid that decomposes to an amine and carbon dioxide.

① Assess the question

The question contains functional groups that are not required knowledge for the MCAT. If there is content that appears to beyond the scope of the MCAT, remind yourself that the MCAT is a reasoning test and will often require the high-scoring test-taker to make deductions.

② Plan your attack

This question will require careful analysis of the answer choices. Follow along and look for obviously wrong statements and eliminate.

③ Execute the plan

Starting with **choice (A)** and following the narrative, everything is consistent except the last statement that the conjugate acid is produced—eliminate.

Choice (B) requires careful analysis and deduction regarding the Curtius pathway. The answer mentions a diazonium when in fact the reactant is an azide. This can be deduced either by the names of the reactants (*di*-azonium compounds contain the $R-N_2^+$ functional group) or by looking at the name of the product (an *azide*).

Choice (C) can be eliminated because the Hofmann rearrangement involves a basic workup, so while the workup for the Curtius rearrangement is unknown, the fact that this answer says both, makes it incorrect.

At this point, the process of elimination shows that the correct response is **(D)**. There is no evidence that would directly refute this answer and it must therefore be chosen. Furthermore, based on the reaction in Figure 1, the process described in **(D)** seems plausible.

 Answer by matching, eliminating, or guessing

Executing the plan led to the elimination of **(A)**, **(B)**, and **(C)** in sequence; therefore the correct answer must be **(D)**.

Takeaways

High difficulty problems may require one to deduce unstated steps of a reaction.

Things to Watch Out For

Refer to the passage to double-check for consistency.

Key Concepts

Mechanisms are viable topics for analysis on the MCAT. Be sure to understand the reactants and products of every reaction, but also extend your analysis to side reactions that the intermediates may be involved in.

12.7 Organic Chemistry Practice

ORGANIC CHEMISTRY PASSAGE III (QUESTIONS 1–6)

Humans can only synthesize 11 of the proteogenic amino acids. Nine others are known as *essential amino acids* and must be supplied via diet—although some essential amino acids may be interconverted (the sulfur-containing amino acids are interchangeable in the body, as are the aromatic amino acids).

De novo synthesis of amino acids usually starts with the non-essential amino acid glutamate (the conjugate base of glutamic acid). Glutamate is formed from the molecule α-ketoglutarate, a product of the Krebs cycle. In amino acid synthesis, α-ketoglutarate is aminated by ammonium to form glutamate. Glutamate can then be used to transaminate a number of different precursors into their respective amino acids. The transamination converts glutamate to α-ketoglutarate. For example, pyruvate, shown in Figure 1, can be aminated by glutamate to form alanine.

Pyruvate

Amino acid synthesis in the lab follows a variety of other pathways using molecules not usually found in the human body. *Strecker* synthesis starts with a carefully chosen aldehyde. The aldehyde is reacted with ammonium ions leading to an iminium intermediate. The iminium intermediate is then attacked by a cyanide ion that forms an aminonitrile. Subsequently, this aminonitrile is converted to a carboxylic acid by the addition of water and acid, proceeding through a 1,2-diamino diol intermediate.

Amino acids have unique *isoelectric points* (pI), a pH where the amino acid will have a net neutral charge. The pI is determined by the pK_as of the various functional groups. The isoelectric point can be found for individual amino acids or for a polypeptide chain. In the polypeptide chain, most of the carboxylic acid and amino groups are bound and thus have no charge. Therefore the charge, and subsequently, the pI, is influenced most significantly by the side chains in the polypeptide.

P1.

P2.

F1.

P3.

P4.

1. Which of the following amino acids will be negatively charged at physiological pH?

   A. Glutamic acid
   B. Arginine
   C. Valine
   D. Phenylalanine

2. The figure below shows an ionized form of tyrosine and its pK_a values. Based on this information, what is tyrosine's pI?

   A. 5.64
   B. 6.17
   C. 9.04
   D. 9.57

3. Which of the following is a significant disadvantage of using Strecker amino acid synthesis to create amino acids for the body?

   A. The ammonium ion causes the reaction to proceed too quickly to control.
   B. The nucleophile used can also attack side chains with carbonyls.
   C. The nucleophilic attack on the carbonyl causes racemization.
   D. All amino acids formed from this synthesis are useless biologically.

4. Given the structure of l-alanine and α-ketoglutaric acid, what is the structure of L-glutamic acid?

   A.

   B.

   C.

   D.

5. Suppose a portion of a peptide chain contains a large amount of phenylalanine, alanine, and valine residues. If the peptide is part of an enzyme that is dissolved in the cytoplasm, where on the enzyme is this region likely to be located?

   A. In the active site of the enzyme
   B. In the allosteric site of the enzyme
   C. In the interior of the enzyme
   D. On the exterior of the enzyme

6. Which of the following setups would be most appropriate for isoelectric focusing of protein molecules?

A. a pH gradient (0–14) from left to right, with a positive charge on the left and a negative charge on the right

B. a pH gradient (0–14) from right to left, with a positive charge on the left and a negative charge on the right

C. a pH gradient (0–14) from bottom to top, with a positive charge on the right and a negative charge on the left

D. a pH gradient (0–14) from top to bottom, with a positive charge on the right and a negative charge on the left

This chapter continues on the next page ▶ ▶ ▶

Organic Chemistry Practice Passage Explanations

P1. Essential amino acids

P2. Process of de novo synthesis

F1. Pyruvate structure

P3. *Strecker* synthesis

P4. Role of pI

1. (A)

At physiologic pH, the carboxylic acid and the amino group of an amino acid have a negative charge and positive charge, respectively. This implies that if a molecule is to be negatively charged at physiological pH, then the side chain must carry a negative charge. Based on this prediction, look for an amino acid with an acidic side chain. A match is found with an "acid" in **choice (A)**.

2. (A)

When calculating the pI for an amino acid, the side chain must be considered. In this case the side chain is a relatively unreactive phenol group—which will remain uncharged until it donates a proton (near a pH equal to its pK_a). At a low pH the amine group will be protonated and the carboxylic acid group will be neutral (as shown). At a pH equal to the pK_a of the carboxylic acid, approximately half of the carboxylic acids will be deprotonated and carry a negative charge. This makes the molecule neutral as a whole. As the pH nears the pK_a of the protonated amino group, the molecule will become negatively charged. The pH between these two pK_as is the pI and is calculated as the average.

$$pI = \frac{(2.24 + 9.04)}{2} = 5.64 \text{ or } \textbf{choice (A).}$$

3. (C)

When the ammonium attacks the aldehyde, the carbonyl carbon is sp^2 hybridized. This means the electrophile is planar and the nucleophile can attack from either the top or the bottom. This implies that there will be a racemic mixture of amino acids (for all amino acids except glycine). D-amino acids are not useful biologically as practically all amino acids in the body are of the L form. This means that approximately half of the amino acids produced will not be useful, thus potentiating a disadvantage to Strecker synthesis, or **choice (C)**.

4. (B)

L-amino acids are of the *S* configuration (according to Cahn–Ingold–Prelog rules) except for cysteine and glycine. The correct form of glutamic acid will be similar in chirality to the alanine shown in the question. This means that the configuration at the α-carbon should be *S*. The passage provides a few clues that can elucidate the molecular formula for glutamic acid; it's stated in the second paragraph that pyruvate can be aminated by glutamate to form alanine and that in the process glutamate is deaminated to α-ketoglutarate. (pyruvate + glutamate $\leftrightarrow$ alanine + α-ketoglutarate). Therefore, there must be five carbons in glutamate and its conjugate acid, glutamic acid. This rules out **choice (C)**. **Choice (D)** can be eliminated because it represents glutaric acid, not glutamic acid. Between the remaining answers, **(B)** is correct.

5. (C)

The location of a certain section of a polypeptide chain depends on the types of amino acids contained in that chain. The chain in this question contains nonpolar amino acids, which are also known as hydrophobic amino acids. They do not like to be around water and will group together to avoid it. This means that they are probably not located on any part of the enzyme that is exposed to water and **choice (C)** is the correct answer.

6. (A)

This question is asking how isoelectric focusing works in agar. The idea behind isoelectric focusing is that at a certain pH the molecules are neutral and at other pHs the molecules have charges. Charged particles will abide by Coulomb's Law, experience a force from other charges and accelerate. When there is a positive charge on one end and a negative charge on the other, positive molecules will migrate towards the negative charge and negative molecules will migrate towards the positive charge. Molecules become more positive as the conditions become more acidic. This means the negative charge should be on the opposite side of the acidic side so that when the amino acid is acidic (and positive), it will travel towards the basic side (the negative side). As it moves towards the negative side, the pH increases and the molecule begins to lose its positive charge. Once it has lost its charge, it will no longer experience a force from other charges and it will stop. This matches **choice (A)**.

CHAPTER THIRTEEN

Physics

Many students approach MCAT physics as a series of equations to memorize. However, MCAT physics is not just about the equations, because the MCAT doesn't award points for the simple recollection of equations. In actuality, success on the MCAT with respect to physics requires applying the equations to novel situations. Another important point to note is that the AAMC has eliminated any physics question on the exam that is not applicable to life sciences. What does this mean for you? It means that while you will be spared having to answer questions about a watermelon shot out of a cannon; you *will* have to answer questions about laminar blood flow within the vasculature using your knowledge of basic principles such as fluid dynamics.

It is no mystery that physics is one of the most dreaded content areas tested on the MCAT. However, understanding the fundamental concepts and the ability to apply those concepts can separate the average test-taker from an elite test-taker. MCAT physics is not like an undergraduate course. The MCAT focuses on conceptual understanding as well as the ability to choose the correct mathematical process. All of the questions will involve living systems, and will require outside knowledge. The better prepared you are for what you are going to see, the more confident you will feel on Test Day.

In this chapter, we will explore how MCAT tests physics and what you need to know in order to maximize your score.

13.1 Reading the Passage

One of the worst things you can do as a test-taker is to approach a physics passage with an attitude such as, "I'm going to read this entire passage, memorizing all of the details and data points as I go along, so that I won't need to waste time referring to the passage while I answer the questions." This type of approach results in a tremendous amount of time lost to reading the passage. There are no points for reading and memorizing the passage. In addition, the questions will dictate what you need from the passage. There will always be information in the passage that appears testable, but is simply not tested. Remember that the MCAT is asking you to apply what you know to the topic at hand. For some questions, the topic of the passage won't even be important; you'll simply need to apply what you know.

PASSAGE TYPES

The MCAT features two types of passages in the physics section. Identifying the type of passage you are reading helps you to predict what is going to be important for the questions.

Information passages describe natural or manmade phenomenon, much like a textbook. These passages will often provide definitions of new terms. Test questions are likely to focus on the information presented, and you will be asked to interpret the information in the passage in light of what you already know about the topic.

The second type of physics passage describes an experiment. In **experiment passages**, the experiment conducted usually has a clear goal. Something is varied, something else is measured, and conclusions can be formed. A table or graph with data from the experiment may be presented, and it is likely that you will be asked to interpret the data. When multiple experiments are performed, it is the similarities and differences between the experiments that are likely to be tested: if making a small change to an experiment creates a radically different result, you can bet that there will be a question that requires you to understand why a small change resulted in a different outcome.

As you prepare for the MCAT, remember that your skill at identifying and absorbing what is important within a passage and skimming over what is not important will directly translate into time saved and more points on Test Day. With that in mind, elite test-takers do two things when reading a physics passage: outline the passage and identify the topic.

MCAT Physics–Passage Types

	Information	Experiment
Goal	To present information	To summarize an experiment performed
Contents	Information about some phenomena, presented in a predictable way, a new equation, considerable detail that may or may not be important	A hypothesis, a procedure, data (often in the form of charts and/or tables), a new equation. Some experiment passages will consist of two experiments.
How to Read It	Quickly, identify where the details are located, but no need to memorize. Get the gist of each paragraph, and move on to the next.	Pay attention to the hypothesis behind the experiment, the procedure, and the outcome. If two experiments are conducted with drastically different results, pay attention to the differences between the experiments.
Similar to:	Textbook, journal article	Lab report

OUTLINING THE PASSAGE

As we have already discussed, memorizing the passage is not going to help you maximize your points on Test Day. However, there is another way to make sure that you are able to quickly find required information within the passage. This is known as outlining the passage. By employing your critical reading skills, you should understand the gist of each paragraph. The best way of doing this is by answering this question after each paragraph, "What is this paragraph doing? Why is it here?" Remember, the MCAT is not a haphazard set of passages and questions sloppily thrown together. This is a test that has been crafted by the AAMC as an aptitude test for medical school. Each paragraph, each word, and each answer choice has been placed there for a reason.

Scan for Structure

In this step, take a brief look at the visual aspects of the passage. Is the passage wordy? Does it contain an equation or a diagram? Are there charts and graphs present? After identifying the visual elements, determine a degree of difficulty. The degree of difficulty will vary depending on the test-taker, as each individual has his own strengths and weaknesses. Now, it is time to "triage" the passage. Triage is a way to determine which passages receive priority. The MCAT does not award more points for correct answers on more difficult passages. Since each question is worth the same, the best way to maximize your points is to do the easy passages first. This allows you to take control of the test and make the best of your own strengths. If you determine that a passage is fairly easy for you to do, then do it. If it's more difficult or appears to be very time-consuming, do it later.

Read Strategically

As you start to read the passage, it will become very clear what type of passage you are reading. An experiment passage will describe an experiment, while an information passage will present information. Using this knowledge, you can adapt your critical reading skills such that you are actively pulling out the information that is likely to be important for that passage type. Questions on experiment passages will focus on the hypothesis tested, the details of the experiment procedure, the outcome of the experiment, and data analysis. As you read an experiment passage, paying special attention to these elements of the passage helps you to pick out what is important, and skim through what is less likely to be tested.

On an information passage, the most important thing to pull out of each paragraph is the purpose of the paragraph. Read each paragraph as though it were a stand-alone paragraph, focusing on meaning and the purpose of that paragraph within the passage as a whole. In physics, the passage is likely to focus on a theory or description of natural phenomena that is related to what was presented in your physics courses. It will likely be understandable, but there will be a tremendous number of details. While it is important for you to understand those details, do not waste time trying to analyze each detail and how the information fits into the big picture. Simply notice that the detail is there and move on. You only have to understand enough of the passage to answer the questions.

Label Each Component

In this step, write down a brief description of each paragraph, equation, image, or chart. This should only be a couple of words, or as much as a sentence. If there is a paragraph that describes only variables, make a note of this, as it is likely that you will need this information later. If there is an equation, write down the purpose of that equation. If a paragraph contains only theory, write down the main point of that theory. Be sure to consider the overall function of that paragraph, such as (but not limited to) experiment procedure, variables, experiment outcomes, or expanding on a theory present in previous paragraphs. Each paragraph, equation, graph, table, and image has been placed there for a reason. Identifying "why" can help you to maximize your points when you get to the questions.

Reflect on Your Outline

Every passage has a reason why it was written. In this step, identify the **goal** of the passage. The goal of the passage is the main point or topic of the passage. Did the passage describe an experiment or discuss a theory? What would be the reason why the author sat down to write this passage? In physics, this will tell you the overall topic of the passage. However, for physics, there is an additional step. Many of the theories in physics are interrelated and this poses an opportunity for the testmaker to ask questions regarding any concept that may be related to the topic of the passage. For example, it is likely that a discussion of circuits may be followed by questions regarding electric fields, capacitors, and potential energy. Identifying the concepts helps you to anticipate where the questions might go. This is another method of taking control of the test, and anticipating what is coming next.

THE PROCESS OF OUTLINING

- Scan the passage to determine whether it should be done now or later.
- Read the passage.
- Label each paragraph. Summarize each paragraph, including the meanings of new terms or equations. Each paragraph label should be very short, at least a word or two, but no longer than a sentence.
- Reflect on the passage. At the end of the passage, identify the goal of the passage.
- Then, only in physics, identify the concepts that could be tested with the passage in question.

13.2 Answering the Questions

Physics questions on the MCAT all demand the same thing: that the test-taker must have a solid foundation in physics. There are a few "plug and chug" or graph-interpretation questions in MCAT physics, but most of the questions will require a higher level of conceptual thinking. Therefore, well-developed critical thinking skills are an essential requirement for attaining a high score on Test Day, especially with regard to physics. Historically, MCAT questions have taken two forms: questions that require the test-taker to recall a specific piece of information and questions that require the test-taker to apply previous knowledge to a new situation in order to determine the answer. However, with the recent changes to the MCAT in 2015, two new question forms have been added. These questions will require the test-taker to analyze raw data as well as critique study designs. You will need to understand the fundamentals of study design as well as the requirements of a study in order to produce statistically significant outcomes. In addition, these questions will require the ability to draw conclusions from raw data, such as that presented in a chart or graph.

As discussed previously, there are four types of questions that appear in the science sections of the MCAT. Let's see how these four types of questions connect to MCAT physics.

Discrete Questions

- Do not accompany a passage
- Always preceded by a warning such as, "Questions 12–15 are NOT based on a descriptive passage."
- Will invariably require a thorough understanding of the science behind the question.
- With a solid foundation in physics, these questions can be easy points on Test Day.
- All of the information required will be in the question stem, the answer choices, or your own outside knowledge.

Questions that Stand Alone from the Passage

- Will follow a passage, but the passage will not be required to determine the correct answer.
- These are really discrete questions hidden within the passage-based questions.
- May be thematically related to the passage, but require no further information from the passage.
- In physics, these questions are very common.

Questions that Require Data from the Passage

- Will require data from the passage, but an understanding of the passage as a whole is not required.
- In order to answer the question, you will have to find the information in the passage and apply it to determine the answer.
- You will have to know how to apply this information from the passage to arrive at the correct answer.
- The information in the passage is usually in the form of a variable or known quantity that must be used in order to find the answer.

Questions that Require the Goal of the Passage

- This question type is most likely to appear following an experiment passage.
- Cannot be answered solely by outside knowledge; an understanding of at least a portion of the passage will be necessary.
- A methodical approach and critical reading skills, such as the Kaplan way, will be essential for these questions.

DETERMINING THE PURPOSE OF THE QUESTION

Many test-takers regularly misread questions or miss an important detail that drastically changes an answer. Furthermore, many test-takers misinterpret the answer choices or miss a correct answer choice. The best way to avoid these mistakes is to adopt a systematic method for answering questions and use this method on every single question. As a reminder, the Kaplan Method consists of four steps (see Figure 13.1):

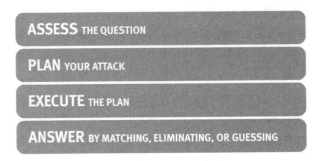

ASSESS THE QUESTION

PLAN YOUR ATTACK

EXECUTE THE PLAN

ANSWER BY MATCHING, ELIMINATING, OR GUESSING

Figure 13.1. The Kaplan Method for questions

1. Assess the Question

Read the question, but avoid reading the answers. Determine the type of question and the level of difficulty. Is this question going to be more difficult for you? Is this question a good use of time? Does the question require a long calculation? Now it is time to make a decision. Is this a question that you want to do now or later? Good questions to do now in physics are questions that require a simple calculation or involve a topic with which you feel very comfortable. Questions that are quick and easy to answer are worth just as much as the more difficult questions.

2. Plan Your Attack

This portion of the Kaplan method for physics involves determining what you have to do to reach the answer. This is known as the **task**. Do you know what information you already have? What are the known variables? Given what you already know about the question, which equation is likely to yield the correct answer? Or is the question more theoretical? Is the information in the passage, your outline, the question stem, or in your fund of knowledge? The task of the question can be simple—not all MCAT physics questions are going to be particularly difficult. Do not waste time, energy, or points on thoughts of "It can't be this easy." Sometimes, it really will be easy.

3. Execute Your Plan

Now that you have determined a plan of attack, it is time to carry out that plan. This is known as executing your plan. Go back and find the information or the equation. Do the calculation. Apply what you know to the question and passage to determine the answer.

4. Answer the Question by Matching, Eliminating, or Guessing

When you have reached an answer from the execution of the plan, now you can read the answer choices. The idea here is to find the answer choice that is closest to your answer. If you do not seen answer that is close to your answer, then you have to revise your answer. The process of elimination can also be used to determine the correct answer. This is especially effective after you've carried out the steps in the Kaplan Method because, by this point, you have also considered possibilities that will NOT answer the question correctly. Finally, if the process of elimination does not narrow down the answer, then take an educated guess. If you are down to two choices, use your reasoning skills to determine which one is most likely to be correct. For physics, if you have to use the process of elimination or guessing, these methods can be enhanced by identifying answer choice(s) contain the correct units or signs. Even if you can't remember the correct equation, chances are that you do know if the answer should be positive or negative, or what units the correct answer will have. Use this information to aid in your selection of an answer. Finally, there may be some answer choices that are simply NOT possible. Eliminate these answer choices, and you will increase your odds of selecting the correct answer.

13.3 Getting the Edge in Physics

Obtaining an elite score on Test Day requires you to not only understand the fundamental concepts of physics but also have the ability to apply these concepts and perform the required mathematical operations. This ability starts with your foundation in physics. It is not enough to memorize the equations and hope that it will all be "plug and chug." Yes, you need to know the equations, but you also need to have a conceptual understanding of the physics behind the equations.

On Test Day, there will be two types of physics passages: information and experiment passages. On an information passage, the questions will mostly focus on the information in the passage. You are likely to see many questions that will not require information from the passage. On experiment passages, a complete understanding of the experiment is required; this includes the hypothesis tested by the experiment, the details of how the experiment was done, and how to interpret the data obtained from the experiment. The questions accompanying an experiment passage will likely require you to use information found in the passage, as well as draw conclusions and make predictions based on the data provided.

A methodical, systematic method for answering questions is required to maximize your points on Test Day. In physics, the Kaplan Method helps you to avoid making unnecessary mistakes, while also maximizing your potential. Remember, that correct answer choices will match the appropriate sign and units for that particular vector or scalar quantity.

13.4 Step-By-Step Guide to the Physics Passage and Questions

READING THE PASSAGE

- Identify the type of passage
  - This should be evident in the first couple of sentences or by glancing at the passage.
  - If the paragraph is mostly words, with no charts or graphs, it is likely to be an information passage. If there are graphs and tables with data, it is likely to be an experiment passage. If you find that there is a lot of theory with multiple points of view, then it is a persuasive information passage (but it will probably look like an information passage at first).

- Read critically through the passage, outlining each paragraph.
  - The outline of the paragraph should answer the question, "What is this paragraph doing in the passage?"
  - Identify if a paragraph is mostly explanations of an equation, or if it is mainly defining variables.
  - If there are charts and graphs, note what is summarized by each chart and graph. No need to analyze, just identify what is represented there.
  - If there is an equation, note what the equation is for without analyzing it.

- Identify the goal of the passage
  - Determine the goal of the passage by answering the question, "What is the author trying to do with this passage?"
  - Identify the physics concepts within the passage by answering the question, "What concepts are represented here?"

ANSWERING THE QUESTIONS

1. Assess the question
- Identify the question type.
- Determine the purpose of the question as well as the difficulty level of the question.
- Triage: is this question worth the time? Does it involve a lengthy calculation? Am I likely to get this question correct in a timely manner?
- Make a decision: is this question a good one to do now or to come back to?
- If it is a good one to do now, then proceed.

2. Plan your attack
- Determine what must be done in order to answer the question carefully.
- Identify where to find the information to answer the question. Is it in the passage, your outline, the question stem, or your own knowledge?
- If the question requires a calculation, determine the known variables and the unknown variables. Then, select the correct equation.
- If the question requires you to apply your knowledge to a new situation, identify what you already know about the situation.

3. Execute your plan
- Find the required information. Perform the calculation. Answer the question by applying your knowledge.

4. Answer by matching, eliminating, or guessing
- Read the question and the answer choices.
- Find a match for your answer.
- If a calculation was required, be sure that your answer choice has the correct sign and units.
- If there is no match, then proceed to the process of elimination.
- If you find that the process of elimination is not providing you with a solid answer, then make an educated guess and move on to the next question.

13.5 Preparing for the MCAT: Physics

As you prepare for the Chemical and Physical Foundations of Biological Systems section of the MCAT, these are the topics that you are likely to see on Test Day.

TRANSLATIONAL MOTION

- The SI units used to measure dimensions
- The components of a vector (magnitude and direction)
- How vectors can be added to determine displacement
- The difference between speed and velocity
- The use and application of quantities such as average and instantaneous velocity
- The units of acceleration and how the value of acceleration can be used to identify a final velocity or distance traveled

EQUILIBRIUM

- The concept of force and the SI units used to describe a force
- The concept of torque and how motion on a lever arm results in torque

FORCE

- The concept of force and the SI units used to describe a force

WORK

- Units used to describe work
- The work done by a constant force is given by $W = Fd \cos \theta$
- Work Kinetic Energy Theorem and its implications
- The pressure–volume diagram and how work can be calculated from this diagram by determining the area under the curve
- The concept of conservative forces such as gravity
- Mechanical advantage and the trade-off of force for voltage

ENERGY

- The definition of kinetic energy and the units of kinetic energy
- Equation used to describe kinetic energy: $KE = \frac{1}{2} mv^2$
- Potential energy and its relationship to gravity, position, and springs
- The equations used to describe potential energy in different situations, including $PE = mgh$ (gravity and position), $PE = \frac{1}{2} kx^2$ (spring)
- The conservation of energy
- The units of power and the relationships between power, work, and time

THERMODYNAMICS

- The pressure-volume diagram and how work can be calculated from this diagram by determining the area under the curve
- The modes of heat transfer—conduction, convection, and radiation
- The concept of expansion of solids as they heat, and the coefficient of expansion

FLUIDS

- The definition of density and its relationship to specific gravity
- The definition of buoyancy and its relationship to Archimedes' Principle
- Pascal's law and hydrostatic pressure, including how hydrostatic pressure varies with depth; $P = \rho g h$
- Viscosity and how it affects the flow of a fluid; Poiseuille's Law
- The relationship between cross-sectional area and velocity of a fluid; continuity equation; $Av = $ constant
- Understand the relationship between turbulence and velocity of a fluid
- How Bernoulli's equation applies to nonviscous fluids, and its common applications
- The definition of the Venturi effect and the use of a pitot tube to measure fluid velocity
- The definition of surface tension, and how surface tension affects the behavior of a fluid

GAS PHASE

- The definition of the Kinetic Molecular Theory of Gases
- The definition and application of Boltzmann's constant
- Definition of heat capacity, and the behavior of gases at a constant volume and constant pressure

ELECTROSTATICS

- The definition of a charge, how charges are conducted and conserved
- The definition of an insulator and how insulators are used
- The definition of an electric field (E) and how an electric field can be defined by field lines and charge distribution
- Identification and understanding of potential differences, including the absolute potential at a point in space

CIRCUIT ELEMENTS

- The definition of current, including the equation for current ($I = \Delta Q / \Delta t$)
- The concept of a conductor
- Understanding and application of sign conventions and units to circuits
- The definition of the electromotive force and its relationship to voltage
- The definition of resistance and its application to circuits
- Calculations and conceptual understanding of resistors in parallel and in series
- The definition and equation for resistivity ($\rho = R * A / L$)
- The definition of capacitance and its application to parallel plate capacitors and energy of charged capacitors

- Calculations and conceptual understanding of capacitors in parallel and in series
- The definition and application of dielectrics
- Conductivity of metallic and electrolytic substances
- How meters are used to measure potential differences and currents

MAGNETISM

- Definition of a magnetic field **B**
- Motion of charged particles in magnetic fields; Lorentz Force

PERIODIC MOTION

- The definitions of amplitude, frequency, and phase, and how they are calculated given a wave
- The differences between transverse and longitudinal waves
- Measurements of wavelength and propagation speed

SOUND

- How sound is produced
- The differences between the speeds of sound within various mediums including solids, liquids, and gases
- Application of the decibel as a log scale to describe the intensity of sound
- The use of damping or attenuation
- Changes in the perceived frequency from the emitted frequency as a result of a moving source or observer; the Doppler effect
- The definition of pitch
- Understanding the resonance of sound within different structures, including pipes and strings
- The definition and application of ultrasound
- The definition of shock waves

LIGHT AND ELECTROMAGNETIC RADIATION

- Conceptual understanding of interference and the implications of Young's double-slit experiment
- The definition of diffraction as related to thin films, diffraction grating, and single-slit diffraction
- Identification and understanding of other diffraction phenomena, including X-ray diffraction
- The definitions of polarization of light and circular polarization
- Understanding and application of the properties of electromagnetic radiation, including constant velocity c *in vacuo*
- Understanding of electromagnetic radiation as consisting of perpendicularly oscillating electric and magnetic fields, and that the movement of electromagnetic radiation is perpendicular to both
- How the electromagnetic spectrum is classified, including the visual spectrum and color
- The definition of a photon and that the energy of the photon is $E = hf$

GEOMETRICAL OPTICS

- The nature of reflection from a plane surface, including the concept that the angle of incidence = angle of reflection
- The definition of refraction and refractive index n
- Application of Snell's law: $n_1 \sin \theta_1 = n_2 \sin \theta_2$
- The definition of dispersion and how it relates to a change of index of refraction with wavelength
- The definition of total internal reflection and the conditions required
- Identification of the center of curvature, focal length, and real or virtual images in spherical mirrors
- Understanding converging and diverging lenses
- Application of the lensmaker's formula to lens systems; $1/p + 1/q = 1/f$ with sign conventions
- Performing calculations and demonstration of conceptual understanding of combinations of lenses
- The definition of lens aberration
- General function of optical instruments, including the human eye

This chapter continues on the next page ▶ ▶ ▶

13.6 Physics Worked Examples

PHYSICS PASSAGE I: FLUID DYNAMICS

Cardiovascular disease is the leading cause of death in the world. It is primarily caused by atherosclerosis, which is characterized by thickening and hardening of arterial walls due to the deposition of cholesterol, triglycerides, and other substances. The accumulation of cholesterol plaques within arteries causes stenosis, or narrowing, which in severe cases can drastically reduce the blood supply to downstream tissues and result in ischemia.

At low levels of stenosis, increasing stenosis causes the dilation of the arteries to preserve flow up to the point where the vascular bed is maximally dilated. Further stenosis increases impedance to blood flow to the point where the blood flow starts to drop and becomes dependent on vascular pressure. Thus, at high levels of stenosis, increasing stenosis causes an increase in vascular pressure, but a decrease in flow.

An experiment was performed to determine the relationship between the severity of stenosis, vascular blood pressure, and the volumetric flow rate of blood. Controlled, artificial stenoses were induced in the femoral artery of a dog using an external balloon catheter. Vascular pressure and flow rate were measured simultaneously just proximal to the stenosis. The resulting pressure waves were plotted against the flow waves in the form of pressure-flow loop areas (PFLAs) as shown below in Figure 1. Each loop in the figure is the sum of ten cardiac cycles and corresponds to a specific degree of stenosis. PFLA is sometimes expressed as *normalized PFLA,* the ratio of PFLA at a given degree of stenosis to the maximum PFLA observed at any degree of stenosis. The *loop slope,* which can be defined as the slope of the line passing through the lowest and highest points on the loop, corresponds to the relative increase in pressure required to increase the flow rate.

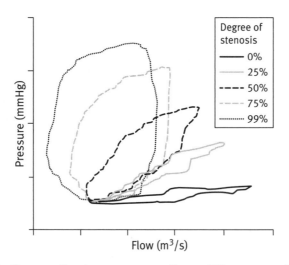

Figure 1. Pressure-flow loops corresponding to different stenosis levels.

P1.

P2.

P3.

Fig1.

1. Based on the results of the experiment, which of the following graphs correctly depicts the relationship between normalized PFLA and the degree of stenosis?

A.

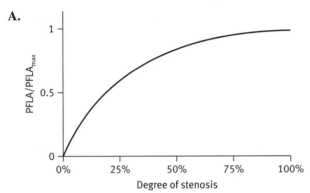

B.

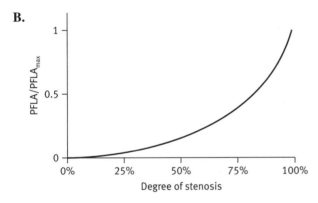

C.

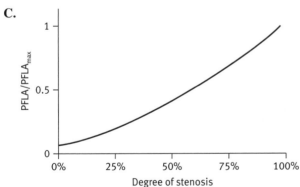

D.

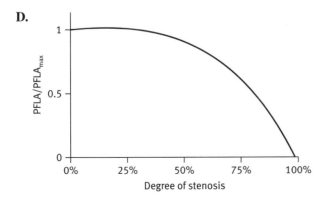

2. Which of the following statements about the variables described in the experiment is correct?

   A. Pressure and flow are independent variables, while degree of stenosis is the dependent variable.

   B. Degree of stenosis is the independent variable, while pressure and flow are dependent variables.

   C. Degree of stenosis, pressure, and flow are all independent variables.

   D. Degree of stenosis, pressure, and flow are all dependent variables.

3. The velocity of blood in a supine patient is 40 cm/s immediately proximal to a stenosis, and 80 cm/s immediately distal to it. Assuming that the density of blood equals the density of water, how would the vascular pressures compare at those two points?

   A. The pressure at the proximal point is 240 Pa greater than the pressure at the distal point.

   B. The pressure at the distal point is 240 Pa greater than the pressure at the proximal point.

   C. The pressure at the proximal point is 480 Pa greater than the pressure at the distal point.

   D. Additional information is required to answer this question.

4. Assuming a fixed rate of blood flow, which of the following statements about the volumetric rate of blood flow in the body is FALSE?

   A. At a fixed rate of blood flow, the cross-sectional area of the blood vessel is inversely proportional to the velocity of blood flow.

   B. Flow rate is directly proportional to the pressure drop along a blood vessel.

   C. Flow rate is inversely proportional to the viscosity of blood.

   D. Flow rate is directly proportional to the length of the blood vessel.

5. Based on information in the passage, when the degree of stenosis increases:

    A. PFLA increases and the loop slope increases.

    B. PFLA increases and the loop slope decreases.

    C. PFLA decreases and the loop slope increases.

    D. PFLA decreases and the loop slope decreases.

This chapter continues on the next page ▶ ▶ ▶

Physics Passage I Explanation:

USING THE KAPLAN METHODS

P1. Introduction to stenosis

P2. Effect of stenoses on vascular pressure and blood flow rate

P3. Experiment to determine relationship between stenotic severity, pressure and flow.

Fig1. Pressure-flow loops at varying degrees of stenosis.

1. Based on the results of the experiment, which of the following graphs correctly depicts the relationship between normalized PFLA and the degree of stenosis?

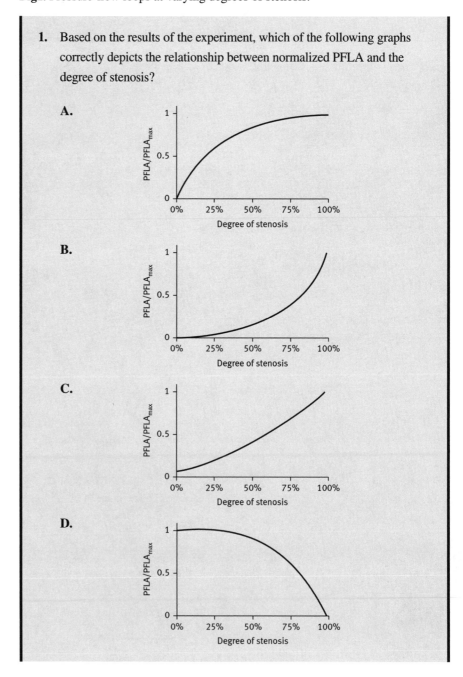

Assess the question

This Skill 4 question tests the information presented in Figure 1. The correct choice will be a graph consistent with the data in Figure 1.

2 Plan your attack

We need the definition of normalized PFLA, which is given in paragraph 3. Then we'll look at the graph in Figure 1 to determine the relationship between PFLA and the degree of stenosis.

3 Execute the plan

Paragraph 3 states that normalized PFLA (the variable plotted on the y-axis in the answers) is the ratio of PFLA at that degree of stenosis to the maximum possible PFLA at any degree of stenosis, so it's a number between 0 and 1. Figure 1 shows that as the degree of stenosis increases, the PFLA increases. As a result, the normalized PFLA increases as well. This means we can eliminate any answer choice that shows a negative correlation between the variables on the x- and y-axes in the answer choices, namely **choice (D)**.

Since the remaining answer choices show a positive correlation between the variables on the axes, analyze Figure 1 further. With zero stenosis, the loop area is nonzero, which means the correct answer should have a positive y-intercept.

4 Answer the question

Looking at the remaining three answer choices, **(A)** and **(B)** have their y-intercepts at zero, so we can eliminate them. That leaves **choice (C)** as the correct answer: the graph in **choice (C)** shows a positive, almost linear correlation between normalized PFLA and degree of stenosis, which matches the data in Figure 1.

2. Which of the following statements about the variables described in the experiment in the passage is correct?

   A. Pressure and flow are independent variables, while degree of stenosis is the dependent variable.
   B. Degree of stenosis is the independent variable, while pressure and flow are dependent variables.
   C. Degree of stenosis, pressure, and flow are all independent variables.
   D. Degree of stenosis, pressure, and flow are all dependent variables.

1 Assess the question

This is a Skill 3 question that requires an understanding of the concept of independent and dependent variables. A close look at the answer choices shows that pressure and flow are always listed together, so we only need to consider one of the two.

2 Plan your attack

An independent variable is a causative factor in an experiment—a variable we manipulate. The dependent variable is an output or effect of the experiment—a variable we measure. To answer this question, we need to determine the role of pressure, flow, and degree of stenosis.

3 Execute the plan

Paragraph 3 states that controlled, artificial stenoses are produced by a catheter. This degree of stenosis influences the vascular pressure and rate of blood flow, which are measured just proximal to the stenosis. Thus, degree of stenosis is a causative factor, and hence an independent variable, while pressure and flow are effects of the causative factor, and hence dependent variables.

4 Answer the question

Our prediction matches **choice (B)**.

This chapter continues on the next page ▶ ▶ ▶

3. The velocity of blood in a supine patient is 40 cm/s immediately proximal to a stenosis, and 80 cm/s immediately distal to it. Assuming that the density of blood equals the density of water, how would the vascular pressures compare at those two points?

    A. The pressure at the proximal point is 240 Pa greater than the pressure at the distal point.

    B. The pressure at the distal point is 240 Pa greater than the pressure at the proximal point.

    C. The pressure at the proximal point is 480 Pa greater than the pressure at the distal point.

    D. Additional information is required to answer this question.

① Assess the question

This is a Skill 2 question that requires the application of Bernoulli's principle. No information from the passage is required to answer this question.

② Plan your attack

Write the expression for Bernoulli's principle at the two points of interest. For this problem, the two points are the locations immediately proximal and distal to the stenosis. Hence, Bernoulli's equation for this problem can be written as:

$$P_p + \frac{1}{2}\rho v_p^2 + \rho g h_p = P_d + \frac{1}{2}\rho v_d^2 + \rho g h_d$$

Since the question stem states that the patient is supine, we can assume that $h_p \approx h_d$ This cancels out the third term on both sides of the equation to give:

$$P_p + \frac{1}{2}\rho v_p^2 = P_d + \frac{1}{2}\rho v_d^2$$

Execute the plan

The question stem provides the proximal and distal velocities, and states that we should use the density of water, $1000 \frac{\text{kg}}{\text{m}^3}$, for the density of blood. Plugging these values into the equation from the "Plan" step, we can determine the difference between the two pressures, $P_p - P_d$.

$$P_p + \frac{1}{2}\left(1000 \frac{\text{kg}}{\text{m}^3}\right)\left(0.4 \frac{\text{m}}{\text{s}}\right)^2 = P_d + \frac{1}{2}\left(1000 \frac{\text{kg}}{\text{m}^3}\right)\left(0.8 \frac{\text{m}}{\text{s}}\right)^2$$

$$P_p - P_d = 500\left(0.8^2 - 0.4^2\right) \text{Pa} = 500\left(0.64 - 0.16\right) \text{Pa} = 500\left(0.48\right) \text{Pa}$$

$$P_p - P_d = 240 \text{ Pa}$$

Answer the question

Since $P_p - P_d$ is positive, the proximal vascular pressure exceeds the distal vascular pressure by 240 Pa. This matches **choice (A)**.

4. Assuming a fixed rate of blood flow, which of the following statements about the volumetric rate of blood flow in the body is FALSE?

A. Flow rate is inversely proportional to the cross-sectional area of the blood vessel.

B. Flow rate is directly proportional to the pressure drop along a blood vessel.

C. Flow rate is inversely proportional to the viscosity of blood.

D. Flow rate is directly proportional to the length of the blood vessel.

① Assess the question

This is a Skill 1 question testing the relationship between blood flow and other parameters; specifically, we need an answer that is false.

② Plan your attack

To answer this question, we need to think about what equations connect flow rate to the parameters in the answer choices (cross-sectional area, pressure drop, viscosity, and length). Those variables are found in two equations: the continuity equation and Poiseuille's law. We won't need any information from the passage.

③ Execute the plan

The continuity equation states that for a closed system, the product Av (cross-sectional area times velocity), is a constant. Poiseuille's law holds that

$$\text{flow rate} = \frac{\pi(\Delta P)r^4}{8L\eta}$$

where ΔP is the pressure drop across the vessel, r is the radius of the vessel, L is the length of the vessel, and η is the viscosity of the fluid.

Now that we have the equations, we can look at the answer choices, and find the one that contradicts one of these equations.

Answer the question

(**A**) is a restatement of the continuity equation, so it is true and can be eliminated. Similarly, both (**B**) and (**C**) are consistent with Poiseuille's law: flow rate is directly proportional to ΔP and inversely proportional to η. Therefore we can eliminate them as well, leaving **choice (D)** as the answer we seek; according to Poiseuille's law, flow rate is *inversely* proportional to length, not directly proportional.

5. Based on information in the passage, when the degree of stenosis increases:

   A. PFLA increases and the loop slope decreases.
   B. PFLA increases and the loop slope increases.
   C. PFLA decreases and the loop slope increases.
   D. PFLA decreases and the loop slope decreases.

① Assess the question

This is another Skill 4 question that tests the information presented in Figure 1. To answer this question, we need to know how the degree of stenosis influences PFLA and loop slope.

② Plan your attack

Look at the graph in Figure 1 to determine the relationship between PFLA, loop slope (which is defined in paragraph 3), and the degree of stenosis. Since the loops change incrementally from one extreme to another, we can use the loops at the two extremes to determine the effects of the degree of stenosis.

③ Execute the plan

With zero stenosis, the loop area is the smallest, and the line between the lowest and highest points is nearly horizontal (that is, close to zero). At the other extreme, 99 percent stenosis, the loop area gets larger and larger, so PFLA increases. The loop slope is much higher as well, since the line between the lowest and highest points is nearly vertical. So both PFLA and loop slope should increase.

④ Answer the question

Once we know that PFLA increases, we can eliminate (C) and (D). Knowing that loop slope also increases makes **choice (A)** the correct answer.

This chapter continues on the next page ▶ ▶ ▶

PHYSICS PASSAGE II: THERMODYNAMICS

Normal respiratory function is an autonomic nervous system process regulated by the pons and medulla oblongata. However, injury or disease may impact this function such that a patient's own system cannot sustain itself with adequate respiration. Patients in these circumstances must receive outside assistance through mechanical ventilation. This assistance, meant to supplement or replace normal spontaneous breathing, can be accomplished through either a negative pressure system or a positive pressure system.

Several early ventilators, including the "iron lung," used *negative pressure* ventilation. This mechanism simulates the normal function of the respiratory system. In an iron lung, the patient's entire body, except the head and neck, is enclosed within a large chamber. To simulate inhalation, the iron lung removes air from the chamber, decreasing the pressure below that within the lungs, creating a pressure gradient. As a result, the lungs expand, which causes air from the environment to be sucked into the lungs. A typical iron lung might create a pressure gradient of –3 mm Hg between the lungs and the outside air to generate an inspiration of 0.5 liters.

Most modern ventilators, however, rely on *positive pressure* ventilation. Such a machine pressurizes the air slightly before delivering it to the patient, who is often intubated. In both mechanisms, expiration is facilitated when the ventilator ceases its pressure generation. This allows the thoracic cavity to return to initial pressure and volume, as the natural elasticity of the chest wall pushes air out. The expiration happens quickly enough that it can be considered an adiabatic process.

P1.

P2.

P3.

1. For a patient on positive pressure mechanical ventilation, which of the following must necessarily be true regarding the air expired during one breath?

   A. No work is done.
   B. No overall change in internal energy takes place.
   C. The magnitude of work done is equal to the overall change in internal energy that takes place.
   D. The heat energy transferred is equal to the overall change in internal energy that takes place.

2. For the iron lung described in the passage, how much work does air do in inflating the patient's lungs? (Note: 1 mm Hg = 133 Pa; 1 L = 10^{-3} m^3; $R =$ 0.0821 $\dfrac{\text{L·atm}}{\text{mol·K}}$ or 8.31 $\dfrac{\text{J}}{\text{mol·K}}$.)

   A. 50.46 J
   B. 0.49 J
   C. −0.49 J
   D. −50.46 J

3. A pulmonologist wants to conduct an experiment to determine if inspiration is an adiabatic process. To answer this question, which of these sets of quantities would he need to be able to measure?

   I. Pressure changes within the lung
   II. Temperature changes within the lung
   III. Volume changes within the lung

   A. I only
   B. II only
   C. II and III only
   D. I, II, and III only

4. Suppose a mechanical ventilator existed that used the stepwise process illustrated below.

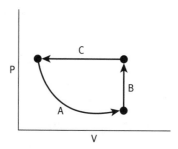

   Which of the following must be FALSE for this process?

   A. The temperature increases during step C.
   B. The internal energy increases during step B.
   C. No work is done during step B.
   D. The temperature remains constant during step A.

5. For a patient on negative pressure ventilation, the process of inhalation, with respect to the gas within the lungs, can best be described as:

   A. spontaneous, with entropy increasing.
   B. spontaneous, with entropy decreasing.
   C. non-spontaneous, with entropy increasing.
   D. non-spontaneous, with entropy decreasing.

Key Concepts

First law of thermodynamics, Gas laws

Physics Passage II Explanation:

USING THE KAPLAN METHODS

P1. Mechanical ventilation
P2. Negative pressure ventilation
P3. Positive pressure ventilation

> 1. For a patient on positive pressure mechanical ventilation, which of the following must necessarily be true regarding the air expired during one breath?
>
>   **A.** No work is done.
>   **B.** No overall change in internal energy takes place.
>   **C.** The magnitude of work done is equal to the overall change in internal energy that takes place.
>   **D.** The heat energy transferred is equal to the overall change in internal energy that takes place.

 Assess the question

Here, we're asked to find a true statement about positive pressure ventilation. Looking at the answer choices, our answer will involve work and internal energy.

 Plan your attack

Positive pressure ventilation is described in paragraph 3. We'll need to use the details provided there, combined with our knowledge of work and internal energy in thermodynamic processes. In particular, we're likely to need the first law of thermodynamics, $\Delta U = Q_{in} - W_{out}$.

 Execute the plan

The last sentence of paragraph 3 is critical here. It tells us that we can assume that expiration can be considered an *adiabatic* process. By definition, the heat exchanged in an adiabatic process is zero. Since no heat is transferred, $Q = 0$ and, according to the first law of thermodynamics, $\Delta U = -W$.

Answer by matching, eliminating, or guessing

Looking at the answer choices one at a time, we can eliminate (**A**) because work is done. Similarly, since work is done, there is a change in internal energy, so (**B**) is false. **Choice (C)**, though, matches our conclusion exactly, so it must be the correct answer. (**D**) is incorrect because no heat is transferred in an adiabatic process.

Key Concepts

Work, Gas laws

---

2. For the iron lung described in the passage, how much work does air do in inflating the patient's lungs? (Note: 1 mm Hg = 133 Pa; 1 L = 10^{-3} m^3; $R = 0.0821\ \dfrac{L \cdot atm}{mol \cdot K}$ or $8.31\ \dfrac{J}{mol \cdot K}$.)

   A. 50.46 J

   B. 0.49 J

   C. −0.49 J

   D. −50.46 J

 Assess the question

The question stem tells us that we're going to calculate the work done in inflating the lungs. A quick look at the answer choices tells us that the magnitude and sign of the answer are more important than the exact value.

 Plan your attack

To answer this question, we'll need the data from paragraph 2 on the iron lung, as well as the formula for work. Given the information in the question stem, we'll probably also need to do some unit conversions.

 Execute the plan

Since paragraph 2 gives us information on pressure and volume, the work formula we'll need is $W = P\Delta V$. The key question here is what value to use for P. The −3 mm Hg in paragraph 2 is the *gradient* formed, not the actual pressure involved. Since 1 atm ≈ 760 mm Hg, 3 mm Hg is a small enough number that we can ignore it, and assume the actual pressure is 1 atm.

Now we can use our work formula:

$$W = P\Delta V = \left(1\,\text{atm}\right)\left(0.5\,\text{L}\right) = 0.5\,\text{L} \cdot \text{atm}$$

This gives us a work value in L·atm, but the answer choices are all in joules. We can use the two values of R provided, though, to make this conversion. Since the denominators are the same, it follows that 8.314 J = 0.0821 L·atm. The R constant can help us make this unit conversion. Notice for the two values of R, the denominators of the units are the same. Thus, we can then use that ratio to convert the work to joules:

$$0.5\,\text{L}\cdot\text{atm} \times \frac{8.31\,\text{J}}{0.0821\,\text{L}\cdot\text{atm}} \approx 0.5\,\text{L}\cdot\text{atm} \times 100\,\frac{\text{J}}{\text{L}\cdot\text{atm}} = 50\,\text{J}$$

Now we have our answer and all we have to do is match it to an answer choice. Both **choice (A)** and **choice (D)** have a magnitude of work close to what we calculated, but which is correct? The question asked for work done BY the air that causes expansion, so since the air is doing work on the lungs we know that it should be a positive value. **Choice (A)** is our answer.

 ## 4   Answer by matching, eliminating, or guessing

Based on the magnitude of our estimate, we can eliminate **(B)** and **(C)**. But is the sign positive or negative? Here, the lungs have work done *on* them, their internal energy should increase, and the work done should be positive. Thus the correct answer is **(A)**.

Things To Watch Out For

If you recognize that a problem is going to involve a multistep calculation, consider triaging it for later.

---

3. A pulmonologist wants to conduct an experiment to determine if inspiration is an adiabatic process. To answer this question, which of these quantities would need to be monitored during the experiment?

I. Pressure within the lung
II. Temperature within the lung
III. Volume within the lung

A. I only
B. II only
C. II and III only
D. I, II, and III only

 Assess the question

This question is a Roman numeral question asking which quantities—out of pressure, temperature, and/or volume—would need to be measured to determine if a process is adiabatic.

 Plan your attack

This question doesn't require any information out of the passage. It will require, however, our knowledge of adiabatic processes.

 Execute the plan

By definition, in an adiabatic process, $Q = 0$, as no heat flows in or out of the system. Therefore, the change in internal energy equals the work done: $\Delta U = -W_{out}$. So, to determine whether the process is adiabatic or not, we need to be able to calculate the work done and the internal energy, and determine if the two quantities are equal. So the "real" question being asked here is *What quantities do we need to know to measure ΔU and $-W_{out}$?*

Answer by matching, eliminating, or guessing

Looking at our answer choices, item II, temperature, comes up in three choices; if it's wrong, we're done. But internal energy is $U = \frac{3}{2}nRT$, so we need temperature to measure it. So item II is correct, and we can eliminate **(A)**.

We can eliminate the two remaining wrong answers by considering the definition of thermodynamic work, $W = P\Delta V$, so measuring the work would require knowing both temperature and volume. Thus, the correct answer is **choice (D)**; we need all three quantities.

Things to Watch Out For

Sometimes trap answers are answers that would be correct for a slightly different question. For example, in this question, **(B)** would be correct if the question were asking about an *isothermal* process.

Key Concepts

First law of thermodynamics, PV
diagram, Work

4. Suppose a mechanical ventilator existed that used the stepwise process illustrated below.

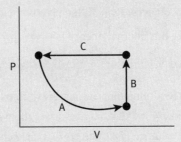

Which of the following must be FALSE for this process?

A. The temperature increases during step C.

B. The internal energy increases during step B.

C. No work is done during step B.

D. The temperature remains constant during step A.

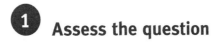

Assess the question

This question is asking for a false statement about the process shown in the diagram.

Plan your attack

Since this question gives us a new diagram to study, it's unlikely we'll need any information in the passage. We will, however, need our knowledge of thermodynamics, especially the types of processes depicted in the diagram. Two of the choices deal with step B, so that may be a good place to start.

Execute the plan

Step B is isovolumetric (or isochoric): the pressure increases while volume remains constant. Since pressure–volume work is given by $P\Delta V$, no work is done. From the ideal gas law, $PV = nRT$, we can also conclude that if V is constant, temperature is proportional to pressure, so the temperature will increase as well. (**B**) and (**C**) both agree with these statements, so neither of them is the answer we seek.

In step C, pressure is constant while volume changes. Using $PV = nRT$ once more, we can conclude that if pressure is constant and volume decreases, T will decrease as well.

 Answer by matching, eliminating, or guessing

Choice (A) says that temperature *increases* during step C, when it should decrease; since it is a false statement, it's the answer we're looking for.

As for step A, since we don't have enough information to determine whether PV remains constant or changes, we can't definitively conclude whether **(D)** is true or false. The question stem keeps us from worrying about that, however: it asks for a statement that *must* be false; *could* be false isn't good enough here.

Key Concepts

Second law of thermodynamics, Entropy

5. For a patient on negative pressure ventilation, the process of inhalation, with respect to the gas within the lungs, can best be described as:

   A. spontaneous, with entropy increasing.
   B. spontaneous, with entropy decreasing.
   C. non-spontaneous, with entropy increasing.
   D. non-spontaneous, with entropy decreasing.

1 Assess the question

This question asks us to consider inhalation in negative pressure ventilation, and determine whether it is a spontaneous process or not, and whether we would expect entropy to increase or decrease.

2 Plan your attack

To answer this question, we'll need the description from paragraph 2 of how negative pressure ventilation works. We'll also need our knowledge of spontaneous processes and entropy.

3 Execute the plan

Paragraph 2 tells us that in negative pressure ventilation, *the iron lung removes air from the chamber, decreasing the pressure below that within the lungs, creating a pressure gradient.* The movement of gas from areas of higher pressure to areas of lower pressure occurs naturally, and should proceed without any outside forces. So the expansion should be considered spontaneous.

But what happens to the entropy? Entropy is a measure of randomness or disorder, and, in part, is proportional to the number of gas particles in a system. Since air enters the lungs during inhalation, the number of moles of gas in the lungs tends to increase, and therefore, the entropy should increase as well.

4 Answer by matching, eliminating, or guessing

Once we know the process is spontaneous, we can eliminate (**C**) and (**D**). Determining that the entropy in the lungs must increase allows us to eliminate (**B**) and select **choice (A)** as the correct answer.

This chapter continues on the next page ▶ ▶ ▶

13.7 Physics Practice

PHYSICS PASSAGE (QUESTIONS 1–5)

The rhythmic contraction of the heart is initiated by the firing of myogenic electrical impulses at the sinoatrial node located in the wall of the right atrium. Any deviation from the normal range of 60–100 rhythmic heartbeats/min in adults is classified as cardiac dysrhythmia, a potentially fatal condition. Defibrillators can "reset" the heart and reestablish the normal functioning of the sinoatrial node by delivering therapeutic doses of electrical energy to the heart. A circuit diagram of a defibrillator is shown in Figure 1.

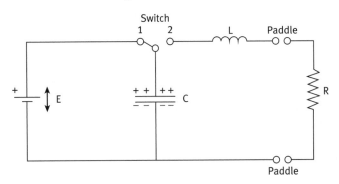

Figure 1. Circuit diagram of a defibrillator with paddle electrodes

A typical defibrillator consists of a capacitor (C), inductor (L), and a power supply. When the switch is in position 1, the defibrillator is in charging mode, and the power supply E is used to store charges across the plates of the capacitor. The work done to charge the capacitor is stored as potential energy U in the capacitor, and can be calculated using the equation below:

$$U = \frac{1}{2} A\kappa\varepsilon_0 E^2 d$$

where A is the area of the capacitor plates, κ is the dielectric constant, ε_0 is the permittivity of free space, and d is the distance between the capacitor plates.

When the switch is in position 2, the defibrillator is in discharging mode and the circuit is completed by the patient, who is represented as a resistor R in the circuit diagram. Metal paddles with insulated handles are held on the patient's skin with about 25 lbs of force to deliver the stored electrical energy of the capacitor to the patient. To prevent the capacitor from discharging and delivering its stored energy too quickly, the inductor is used to prolong the duration of current flow.

P1.

F1.

P2.

E1.

P3.

1. A defibrillator consisting of a 5-mF capacitor with a distance of 10 mm between its plates is powered by a step-up transformer that supplies peak voltages of 10,000 V. What is the maximum electrical energy that can be delivered by this capacitor to a patient?

   A. 25×10^{-3} J
   B. 0.5 J
   C. 25 J
   D. 50 J

2. Many standard defibrillators exhibit a type of defibrillation waveform known as a *biphasic waveform*, as depicted below.

   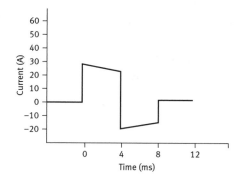

   What is the magnitude of the total charge delivered in a single biphasic current pulse of such a defibrillator?

   A. 85 μC
   B. 170 μC
   C. 85 mC
   D. 170 mC

3. The figure below shows the raw ECG data of a person with a healthy heart. The graph shows superimposed noise from the 60 Hz power supply and motion artifacts from breathing. Given the standard EKG wave to the left, what are the heart rate and respiratory rate, respectively, for this individual?

   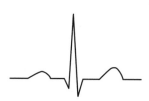

   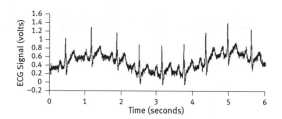

   A. 1.5 Hz, 0.25 Hz
   B. 25 Hz, 5 Hz
   C. 60 Hz, 12 Hz
   D. 80 Hz, 20 Hz

4. A defibrillator is used to deliver 50 J of energy to a patient over a period of 20 ms. If the current flowing through the inductor component of the defibrillator is 2 A, what is the effective resistance of the electrical pathway through the patient?

   A. 250 Ω
   B. 625 Ω
   C. 850 Ω
   D. 1,250 Ω

5. Gel is applied to the skin where the electrodes of a defibrillator will be placed. This is most likely done in order to:

   A. minimize electrical conductance of the body and reduce the possibility of serious burns to the skin.
   B. maximize electrical conductance of the body and reduce the possibility of serious burns to the skin.
   C. minimize electrical conductance of the body and ensure that a sufficiently high amount of electrical energy is delivered to the myocardial tissue.
   D. maximize electrical conductance of the body and ensure that a sufficiently high amount of electrical energy is delivered to the myocardial tissue.

Physics Practice Passage Explanations

USING THE KAPLAN METHODS

P1. Introduction to defibrillators

Fig1. Circuit diagram of defibrillator

P2. Charging phase of defibrillator

E1. Equation for potential energy stored by capacitor

P3. Discharging phase of defibrillator

1. (C)

The first step is to set up an equation for energy stored by a capacitor. The maximum electrical energy that can be delivered by a capacitor is equal to the energy stored by the capacitor, which, according to the passage, is given by:

$$U = \frac{1}{2}A\kappa\varepsilon_0 E^2 d$$

However, since the question stem only provides us with the values for E, C, and d, we need to rewrite the equation in terms of those variables. We know that $C = \frac{A\kappa\varepsilon_0}{d}$, which rearranges to give $A\kappa\varepsilon_0 = Cd$. Hence, the equation for potential energy can be written as:

$$U = \frac{1}{2}CE^2 d^2$$

The second step is to plug in the values for E, C, and d:

$$U = \frac{1}{2}\left(5\times 10^{-3}\ \text{F}\right)\left(10\times 10^{-3}\ \text{m}\right)^2\left(10^4\ \text{V}\right)^2 = 25\ \text{J}$$

Hence, the correct answer is **choice (C)**, 25 J.

2. (D)

The first step is to calculate the area under the pulse from 0 to 4 ms. That portion of the graph can be divided into a triangle and rectangle. The triangular portion has a height of about 5 A, and hence the area of the triangle is $\frac{1}{2}(5\ \text{A})(4\ \text{ms}) = \frac{1}{2} \times 5\ \text{A} \times 4\ \text{ms} = 10$ millicoulombs. The rectangular portion has a height of about 25 A, and hence the area of the rectangle is 25 A × 4 ms = 100 millicou-

lombs. Hence the total charge delivered by this portion of the biphasic waveform is 110 millicoulombs.

The next step is to calculate the area under the pulse from 4 to 8 ms. The triangular portion in this area of the graph has a height of 5 A, and hence the area of the triangle is 10 millicoulombs, like in step 1. However, the rectangular portion here has a height of about 15 A (remember to only consider magnitude), and hence the area of the rectangle is 15 A × 4 ms = 60 millicoulombs. Thus, the total charge delivered by this portion of the biphasic waveform is 70 millicoulombs.

The final step is to calculate the total charge delivered by the biphasic pulse. The total charge delivered by a single biphasic current pulse is simply the sum of the two calculations: 110 mC + 70 mC = 180 millicoulombs.

This is closest to **choice (D)**, which is the correct answer.

3. (A)

The first step is to calculate the heart rate. A single heartbeat translates into an ECG signal that looks like the waveform below—known as the PQRST signal.

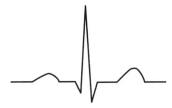

The ECG data in the question stem shows that the time period of one PQRST signal cycle is about 0.7 s. The frequency of a heartbeat is hence 1/0.7 = 1.43 Hz.

Next, we need to calculate the respiratory rate. The PQRST signal looks like it is superimposed on a slower wave in the ECG data shown in the question stem. The slower wave must be the motion artifact from breathing, since the power supply line has a relatively high frequency of 60 Hz. The time period of this slower signal is about 4 s, which means its frequency is ¼ = 0.25 Hz.

This is closest to **choice (A)**, which is the correct answer.

(B) is off by about a magnitude of ten for each rate. **(C)** is the lower end of the range for the heart rate and respiratory rate when measuring the beats and breaths per *minute*.

(D) is the upper end of the range for the heart rate and respiratory rate when measuring the beats and breaths per *minute*.

4. (B)

The question describes the defibrillator in the discharging mode—that is, the switch is in position 2. First, calculate the power delivered by the defibrillator:

$$P = \frac{\Delta E}{\Delta t} = \frac{50 \text{ J}}{20 \times 10^{-3} \text{ s}} = 2500 \text{ W}$$

Next, calculate the resistance offered by the patient. Since the inductor and the effective resistance of the patient are in series, the current flowing through the inductor is the same as that flowing through the resistance. The power of this effective resistance is given by $P = I^2R$, which can be rearranged to solve for R. Plugging in the values for I and P, we get:

$$R = \frac{P}{I^2} = \frac{2500 \text{ W}}{\left(2 \text{ A}\right)^2} = \frac{2500}{4} \,\Omega = 625 \,\Omega$$

Hence, the resistance of the electrical pathway through the patient is $625 \,\Omega$, **choice (B)**.

5. (B)

Gel acts as a conductor and ensures a better connection between the paddles and skin. This reduces the electrical resistance, and thus increases the conductance offered by the patient to the discharging defibrillator. If the resistance offered by the skin were too high, the power delivered to the patient by the defibrillator would be too high, since $P = I^2R$. This would transfer dangerously high amounts of energy to the skin, which could result in skin burns. **Choice (B)** is the correct answer.

(A) is the opposite of the correct answer choice. Per **choice (C)**, application of gel *maximizes* electrical conductance of the body.

While application of gel does maximize conductance of the body as stated by **(D)**, it would decrease the power and the total energy delivered to the myocardial tissue.

Critical Analysis and Reasoning Skills

CHAPTER FOURTEEN

Arguments and Formal Logic

The MCAT is ultimately a test of critical thinking, and as such, the ability to characterize, understand and assess arguments plays an important role, and the use of formal logic is an important tool in working with arguments as they appear on the MCAT. Mastery of arguments and understanding formal logic allow for deeper understanding of the stated information, and will be essential to obtaining a high score on Test Day. Of all CARS questions, 30 percent involve *Reasoning Within the Text* and 40 percent require *Reasoning Beyond the Text*. You can expect more than three-quarters of your points on CARS to benefit from clear logical thinking. In order to provide a solid foundation for your mastery of arguments and formal logic, we'll start by examining arguments, then move on to using formal logic in arguments.

14.1 What Is an Argument?

In its most basic form, an argument is simply a statement composed of two stated parts, the evidence and conclusion, and one or more unstated, but implied parts, the assumption(s) or inference(s). Arguments as they appear on the MCAT have nothing to do with heated debates but are simply conclusions the author makes (regardless of whether or not they are actually true or false), the evidence the author uses to back up his conclusion, and the unstated assumptions or inferences implied in the argument to provide further evidence that will make the conclusion more likely to be true, at least from the author's point of view. There are three levels of arguments that we call the **domains of discourse**: the basic difference between the three is very simply things *vs.* words *vs.* ideas. Though the domains can never be entirely separated from one another, each has distinctive parts and relationships that must not be confused.

Key Concepts

Logic is the formal study of arguments. It falls into the conceptual domain of discourse.

Key Concepts

A concept has a meaning or definition, but is not by itself true or false. Ideas should be distinguished both from the **terms** used to represent them, on the one hand, and from the natural objects or events that might be given as **examples** of them.

- **Concepts** are ideas that have meanings (definitions or connotations).
- Ideas can be related in various ways, often indicated with Relation keywords in a passage. **Relation keywords** are tools for recognizing the organization within texts.
  - Similarity and Difference are very common relation keywords.
  - Opposition, Sequence, and Comparison keywords are less common, but significant in a passage.
  - The relation between the whole and its parts can be important in some CARS passages.

Key Concepts

Claims are the middlemen in the logical hierarchy, composed themselves of concepts and their relationships, and, in turn, composing arguments. Claims consist of at least a subject and a predicate, and have both meaning and truth value (the capacity to be true or false).

DOMAINS OF DISCOURSE

- The **natural domain** corresponds to object, events, and experiences—everything that can be found in the world around us.
- The **textual domain** corresponds to words, sentences, and paragraphs—everything that directly faces you in an MCAT passage.
- The **conceptual domain** corresponds to concepts, claims, and arguments—everything that underlies logic.

14.2 What Are the Elements of Arguments?

CONCEPTS

It might seem obvious but the fundamental element of a logical argument is an idea, called a **concept**. Concepts have **meanings**, but are not necessarily true or false. Note, though, that questions in CARS can employ synonyms and paraphrases of ideas in different wording than is used in the passage. In short, it will be essential on Test Day to look for concept-for-concept correspondences, not exact word-for-word matches.

CLAIMS

What distinguishes a **claim** from a mere concept is **truth value**, the capacity to be *either true or false*. While claims may be quite complex (potentially consisting of numerous concepts related together in diverse ways), having a truth value requires only two parts at minimum: a **subject** and a **predicate**, such as *the yeti is ten feet tall*.

- **Claims** can also be called assertions, statements, propositions, beliefs, or contentions.
- Claims are made up of combinations of concepts and relations of ideas.
- They possess truth value, and can thus be true or false.
- Claims can also be related through various relationships.
  - If two claims are **consistent** (compatible or in agreement) with one another, then both can be true simultaneously.
  - If two claims are **inconsistent** (contradictory or conflicting) with one another, then it is impossible for both to be true simultaneously.
  - If one claim **supports** another, then this claim being true would make the other claim more likely to be true as well.
  - If one claim **challenges** (refutes or objects to) another, then this claim being true would make the other claim more likely to be false.

INFERENCES, ASSUMPTION AND IMPLICATIONS

While concepts and claims fall under the stated parts of arguments, the unstated parts require you to bridge the gap between the stated evidence and conclusion or to identify the conclusion based on the stated evidence. You will likely see an abundance of questions that require you to identify inference, assumption, or conclusion.

- **Inferences** are unstated parts of arguments. One way to recognize an inference is by the negative effect it would have on the argument if it were denied
- **Assumptions** are unstated pieces of evidence.
- **Implications** are unstated conclusions.
- Inferences are claims that must be true or—at the very least—must be highly probable.

COUNTERARGUMENTS

The **counterargument** is an argument made against a conclusion. While some writers will *only* offer counterarguments, their purpose being to argue against some claim, many authors raise counterarguments merely for the sake of refuting them, which is an indirect way to support their conclusion.

Key Concept

Unstated claims in arguments are known as inferences. Inferences are either assumptions (unstated evidence) or implications (unstated conclusions).

Key Concept

Counterarguments, also called refutations, objections, or challenges, are the opposite of evidence because they go against the conclusion.

14. 3 How Will Arguments Be Tested?

INFERENCE AND ASSUMPTION QUESTIONS

Your skill in parsing arguments is mostly commonly tested on the MCAT by inference and assumption questions, often asking what would weaken or strengthen them.

- There are three main ways of strengthening an argument:
  - One could provide a new piece of evidence that supports the conclusion.
  - One could support evidence that already exists to support the conclusion.
  - One could challenge refutations against the conclusion.
- There are three main ways of weakening an argument:
  - One could provide a new refutation that goes against the conclusion.
  - One could support refutations that already exist.
  - One could challenge evidence for the conclusion.

ANALOGICAL REASONING QUESTIONS

The MCAT will also pose questions based on analogies, using the similarities between two things to argue for an additional commonality between them. The **known** entity is the one with characteristics that have already been established. The **unknown** entity is the one that is only partially understood. In some cases, the passage provides the known term, with its various characteristics, and the question gives the new context that establishes the unknown. In such questions, you are being asked to extrapolate, extend, or apply the ideas from the passage to a new situation, so you can take the information from the passage as a given.

- An analogy can be strengthened by greater similarity between the known and unknown.
  - The more points of similarity between the two, the stronger the analogy.
  - The more relevant (structural as opposed to superficial) the similarities between the two, the stronger the analogy.
  - The fewer relevant differences between the two, the stronger the analogy.

14.4 What Is Formal Logic?

The most abstract application of logic, formal logic, examines patterns of reasoning to determine which ones necessarily result in valid conclusions. Formal logic consists of a conditional statement, such as *if I am in Pennsylvania* and a necessary result, *then I am in the United States*. As you see, the conditional statement is sufficient to necessarily bring about the result. On the MCAT, arguments made using conditional claims, with conditional relationships, are featured in some form in every passage and play some role in most CARS questions.

MCAT Expertise

The MCAT will *not* directly test your understanding of formal logic. For example, no question will directly ask you to form a contrapositive. Many questions, however, will *implicitly* test your understanding.

14.5 What Are the Elements of Formal Logic?

CONDITIONALS

A **conditional** is a unidirectional relationship that exists between two terms.

- Conditionals can be represented with language (*if X, then Y*), or symbols: **X → Y**.
- The **antecedent** (**X**) can also be called a **sufficient condition**, **evidence** (in cases of justification), or **cause** (in cases of causation).
- The **consequent** (**Y**) can also be called a **necessary condition**, **conclusion** (in cases of justification), or **effect** (in cases of causation).
- A **conditional claim** is true if it is impossible to have a true antecedent and a false consequent simultaneously.
- Operations of formal logic can be represented in a **truth table** (Table 14.1).

Key Concept

In Table 14.1, all four possible combinations of the truth of X and Y are presented, as well as the resultant truth of the conditional claim in the final column:

X	Y	X → Y
true	true	true
true	false	false
false	true	true
false	false	true

Table 14.1. Truth table for conditional claims

APPLICATIONS FOR CONDITIONALS

Conditionals can function in several different ways in CARS passages and questions. Of the list below, justification and causation are the most common ways that conditionals will be used.

- **Justification** is the relationship of logical support between a piece of evidence and its conclusion.
- **Causation** is the one-way relationship of the antecedent leading to the consequent (cause and effect).
- **Correlation** is the relationship of two events accompanying one another.
- **Whole–parts relationship**.
  - ○ One concept can be a part of another concept (the whole) in the conceptual domain.
  - ○ One component or characteristic can be part of an object in the natural domain.

SUFFICIENT *VS.* NECESSARY

Sufficient and necessary refer to the one-way relationship between the antecedent (X) and the consequent (Y) and the impossibility of having an antecedent without its consequent. If the consequent is not true, then the antecedent is also not true. Revisiting the previous example, to be in the United States it is sufficient to be in Pennsylvania. However, it is not necessary to be in Pennsylvania in order to be in the United States; any state will do.

CONTRAPOSITIVE

The contrapositive is logically equivalent to the original conditional, but carries a different connotation. Whenever an author makes any kind of conditional claim, it is always possible to translate the conditional claim into other relationships, most notably, the contrapositive. By definition, the contrapositive of if X, then Y is if not Y, then not X. Note that in the contrapositive, the X and Y terms switch positions, with the Y term now first. The contrapositive can be represented using a tilde (~) to stand for negation (~X thus means not X or the negation of X):

Conditional: $X \rightarrow Y$

Contrapositive: $\sim Y \rightarrow \sim X$

One of the most useful reasons for forming the contrapositive is that it's a guaranteed inference, a logical equivalent for any conditional claim made in a passage.

14.6 How Will Formal Logic Be Tested?

The MCAT will not provide you with a formal logic statement and require you to form the contrapositive, but formal logic will allow you to dig deeper into claims. If, for example, the condition is that all lions are mammals, and you form the contrapositive that if it's not a mammal, it's not a lion, you have the information you need to answer a question about mammals and lions. Appreciating the general characteristics of formal logic will clarify your thinking and garner you many additional points.

14.7 Getting the Edge Using Arguments and Formal Logic

As we said in the beginning, the MCAT is ultimately a test of critical thinking, and that skill is manifest in your ability to recognize an argument, take it apart (sometimes using formal logic), and answer questions based on it. While academic texts can be vague and subject to interpretation, every question you face on the CARS section will have only one defensible answer. The value of logic is precisely in its ability to clarify your thinking, allowing you to mirror the cognitive processes the testmakers use, and hone in on correct responses.

But the abstract knowledge of arguments is not enough. The only way to be successful with CARS is to practice questions and passages. Every question that you get wrong on a practice passage or question is an opportunity to review how you approached the question. Systematically reviewing questions to determine weaknesses in your critical thinking skills will help you to identify and address those weaknesses. If you find that you are stuck at a score plateau on practice tests, then it is essential to take an honest look at your critical thinking skills to break through that plateau.

CHAPTER FIFTEEN

CARS Question Types

The MCAT is fundamentally a test of critical thinking, and this becomes very evident in the CARS section. Here you are not reading for its own sake but thinking about what you read in order to answer a range of question types. It's important to be able to identify each type since different question types are more efficiently answered with different approaches. As you go through the question types you'll see in this chapter, remember that there are no MCAT points to be had in reading a passage; all your points are in the questions. The more efficiently you can identify and attack a question, the greater your opportunity to get it right.

15.1 What Kinds of Questions Will You Be Asked?

Questions accompanying CARS passages will range from ones that can be answered simply by referring to the passage text, to those that require thinking about what is not stated, but implied in the text. Thus, question types require different approaches, involve different levels of difficulty, and ask you to think in different ways. You will have questions that require you to simply use the information in the text, called Foundation of Comprehension questions; questions that require deeper reasoning about the information in the text; and questions that require reasoning beyond the text. Regardless of the complexity of question type, all correct answers result in the same number of points. Think clearly and carefully about each one.

15.2 Foundation of Comprehension Questions

Though there are a variety Foundation of Comprehension question types, they have in common the fact that the answer is in the text and does not require you to manipulate the text in any way.

MAIN IDEA

Main Idea questions ask for the author's primary goal and often contain words like *central thesis*, *primary purpose*, or *main idea*. Less commonly, these questions may ask for a different aspect of the rhetorical situation such as the *audience* or the *medium*.

- Plan: Look at what you wrote in your outline for the Goal.
- Execute: Reread the Goal in your outline, taking note of the charge and degree of the verb (positive versus negative, extreme versus moderate).
- Answer: Match your expectations for the right answer. If there is no clear match, or if you cannot perform any of the earlier steps of the Kaplan Method for CARS Questions, use the process of elimination.
  - Wrong answer choices may be too narrow (Faulty Use of Detail) or too broad (Out of Scope).
  - Wrong answer choices may have the wrong tone (positive, negative, ambivalent, or impartial) or degree (too extreme or too moderate).

DETAIL

Detail questions ask about what is stated explicitly in the passage and tend to use words like *the author states* or *according to the passage*, with declarative language like *is* and *are*. Detail questions are the most likely to use the **Scattered** format, which uses Roman numeral options or words like *EXCEPT*, *NOT*, or *LEAST*.

- Plan: Look for content buzzwords in the question stem and your outline to determine where the relevant information will be found.
- Execute: Reread the relevant sentence, as well as the sentences before and after. Create your prediction by putting the answer in your own words.
  - Make the prediction brief so you can repeat it to yourself between answer choices.
  - For Scattered Detail questions, locate all three of the wrong answers in the passage to be able to eliminate them from the options.
- Answer: Match your expectations for the right answer. If there is no clear match, or if you cannot perform any of the earlier steps of the Kaplan Method for CARS Questions, use the process of elimination.

FUNCTION

Function questions ask about what the author is trying to *do* during the passage. These questions are similar to Main Idea questions, although they focus on the purpose of only one portion of the passage (usually one sentence or one paragraph). Function questions tend to use words like *purpose*, *motive*, or *intention*, or completions like *in order to* or *because*.

- Plan: Use your outline to locate the relevant paragraph.
- Execute: Look at your Label for the relevant paragraph and the Goal at the bottom of your outline. If buzzwords in the question stem direct to specific sentences, reread those portions, thinking about how they fit into the purpose of the paragraph and the overall passage.
- Answer: Match your expectations for the right answer. If there is no clear match, or if you cannot perform any of the earlier steps of the Kaplan Method for CARS Questions, use the process of elimination, removing any answer that conflicts with the author's main argument or the paragraph's purpose.

Key Concept

Both Main Idea and Function questions can often be answered solely by looking at your passage outline. The answers to Main Idea questions should reflect the author's Goal, whereas the answers to Function questions should usually reflect the Label you've assigned for a given paragraph.

DEFINITION-IN-CONTEXT

Definition-in-Context questions ask you to define a word or phrase as it is used in the passage. These questions often call attention to the term to be defined using quotation marks or italics, but not always.

Definition-in-Context questions always reference a word, phrase, or an entire claim from the passage.
- Plan: Use your outline to locate the relevant paragraph.
- Execute: Reread the sentence with the word or phrase, and perhaps the surrounding context. Rephrase the author's definition of the term in your own words.
- Answer: Match your expectations for the right answer. If there is no clear match, or if you cannot perform any of the earlier steps of the Kaplan Method for CARS Questions, use the process of elimination.

15.3 Reasoning Within the Text Questions

Unlike Foundation of Comprehension questions, which direct you primarily to the explicit ideas in the text, **Reasoning Within the Text** questions require you to think about what is implicit, but not stated, in the text. The two most common types of these questions are Inference and Strengthen–Weaken. Reasoning Within the Text questions account for 30 percent of what you'll encounter on Test Day, according to the AAMC's official statements.

INFERENCE

Inference questions look for the unstated parts of arguments. The answers *must* be true given what is claimed in the passage.
- Unstated parts of arguments
  - **Assumptions** are unstated evidence.
  - **Implications** are unstated conclusions.
  - These questions often contain words like *assume*, *because*, *conclude*, *imply*, *infer*, *justify*, *reasonable*, or *suggest*.
- Plan: Determine whether you are looking for an assumption (evidence) or implication (conclusion). Then determine which claim the answer is supposed to support (assumptions) or be supported by (implications).
- Execute: Reread the relevant sentence, noting the explicit evidence or conclusions given.
  - For assumption questions, the answer is either similar to the evidence given or links the evidence to the conclusions.
  - For implication questions, the answer is either similar to the conclusions given or is another logical conclusion one could draw from the evidence.

- Answer: Match your expectations for the right answer. If there is no clear match, or if you cannot perform any of the earlier steps of the Kaplan Method for CARS Questions, use a special form of the process of elimination called the Denial Test:
  - ○ Negate each answer choice.
  - ○ Whichever answer choice—when negated—has the most detrimental effect on the argument made in the passage is the correct answer choice.

MCAT Expertise

While the Denial Test will always reveal the correct answer in an Inference question, it's very time-consuming. If you cannot set good expectations for the right answer during the Execute step, triage the question and return to it later with the Denial Test.

STRENGTHEN–WEAKEN

Strengthen–Weaken questions concern the logical relationship between conclusions and evidence that strengthens them or refutations that weaken them. There are two subtypes of these: strengthen–weaken within the passage, and strengthen–weaken outside the passage. Those using information outside the passage will be discussed later in this chapter.

- These questions often contain words like *relate*, *support*, *challenge*, *relevance*, *significance*, or *impact*.
- These questions bring in a new piece of information rather than using information directly from the passage.
- Plan: Determine the two claims and the connection between them; you will usually be given at least one of these elements and will have to find the other(s).
  - Identify where each piece of the argument can be found: in the question stem, in the passage, or in the answer choices.
  - If no claims are given in the question stem, plan to triage it and answer it by the process of elimination later.
  - If one claim is given in the question stem, determine whether it is a conclusion, piece of evidence, or a refutation.
  - If two claims are given in the question stem, identify the relationship between them.
- Execute: Research the relevant text to determine the missing claim or the connection between them. Use Logic keywords to help assemble the argument.
- Answer: Match your expectations for the right answer. If there is no clear match, or if you cannot perform any of the earlier steps of the Kaplan Method for CARS Questions, use the process of elimination.

OTHER REASONING WITHIN THE TEXT QUESTIONS

While you will mostly see inference and assumption questions on CARS passages, there are three more types of questions that you should be able to identify in order to approach them most efficiently.

- **Clarification questions** ask for statements that are roughly synonymous, but the clarifying statement tends to be supporting evidence for the conclusion because it is more specific or exact.
  - These questions often contain words like *clarify*, *explain*, or *reflect*.
  - Approach these questions like Strengthen–Weaken (Within) questions, except that the meanings of the two claims should be roughly synonymous.
- **Weakness questions** ask for implicit refutations to arguments discussed in the passage.
  - These questions often contain words like *implicit weaknesses* or *reasonable objections*.
  - Approach these questions like the Denial Test for Inference questions, except that the correct answer will be the most detrimental to the argument made in the passage *without* being negated.
- **Paradox questions** ask for the resolution of an apparent logical contradiction.
  - These questions often contain words like *paradox*, *dilemma*, or *discrepancy*.
  - Approach these questions with the process of elimination, crossing out any answer choice that is inconsistent with one or both of the claims of the paradox, or with the passage as a whole.

Key Concept

Answering a Weakness question is just like using the Denial Test for Inference questions. The difference is that the correct answer choice will be detrimental to the arguments in the passage *without* being negated.

Key Concept

A paradox is a set of two claims that appear to be inconsistent on the surface. The correct answer in a Paradox question will be consistent with both of the claims, and will usually attempt to explain the surface inconsistencies between the two claims.

15.4 Reasoning Beyond the Text Questions

Questions that fall into the broad category of **Reasoning Beyond the Text** are easy to identify because they always involve novel information (in the question stem, set of answer choices, or both) that is not stated or even suggested by the passage, and which may not even seem to be related at first. There are two main categories of these questions: Apply and Strengthen–Weaken (Beyond). The fundamental difference is one of direction: apply questions go from passage to new situation, while (Beyond) questions go from new situation to passage.

APPLY

Apply questions require you to take the information given in the passage and extrapolate it to a new context. Apply questions may ask for one of three tasks.

- They may ask for the author's **response** to a situation, using words like *response, reply, most likely to agree with*, or *least consistent with*.
- They may ask for the most probable **outcome** in a situation, using words like *outcome, result, expectation*, or *consequence*.
- They may ask for an example of an idea discussed in the passage, using words like *example* or *instance*.
- These questions often begin with words like *Suppose, Consider*, or *Imagine*.
- Plan: If the question stem is long, jump to the end to determine what it's asking. Read any information given in the question stem closely, looking for hints that connect it to the passage.
- Execute: Reread the relevant text, keeping in mind the specific type of Apply question involved.
  - For Response questions, determine the author's key beliefs, which are generally reflected in the passage using Author keywords.
  - For Outcome questions, pay attention to cause–effect relationships in the passage, which are generally reflected in the passage using Logic keywords.
  - For Example questions, look for text that provides definitions, explanations, or the author's own example, noting any necessary or sufficient conditions.
- Answer: Match your expectations for the right answer. If there is no clear match, or if you cannot perform any of the earlier steps of the Kaplan Method for CARS Questions, use the process of elimination.
  - Eliminate any answer choices that are inconsistent with the author's views, especially for Response questions.
  - Eliminate any answer choice that does not contain necessary conditions (which must occur in all instances of a concept), especially for Example questions.

STRENGTHEN–WEAKEN (BEYOND THE PASSAGE)

Like Strengthen–Weaken Within the Text questions, Strengthen–Weaken (Beyond the Passage) questions concern the logical relationship between conclusions and evidence that strengthens them or refutations that weaken them. However, unlike the other type of Strengthen–Weaken question, at least one of the claims involved will not be from the passage, but will be unique to the question stem or answer choices. Strengthen–Weaken (Beyond) questions are also distinct in that they treat the passage as flexible, subject to modification by outside forces.

- These questions often contain words like *relate*, *support*, *challenge*, *relevance*, *significance*, or *impact*. In contrast to Strengthen–Weaken (Within the Passage) questions, they often contain words like *could* or *would*.
- Read the question stem closely, looking for hints of analogy to parts of the passage.
- Plan: Determine the two claims and the connection between them; you will usually be given at least one of these elements and will have to find the other(s).
  - Identify where each piece of the argument can be found: in the question stem, in the passage, or in the answer choices.
  - If no claims are given in the question stem, plan to triage it and answer it by using the process of elimination later.
  - If one claim is given in the question stem, determine whether it is a conclusion, piece of evidence, or refutation.
  - If two claims are given in the question stem, identify the relationship between them.
- Execute: Research the relevant text to determine the missing claim or the connection between them. Use Logic keywords to help assemble the argument.
- Answer: Match your expectations for the right answer. If there is no clear match, or if you cannot perform any of the earlier steps of the Kaplan Method for CARS Questions, use the process of elimination.

OTHER REASONING BEYOND THE TEXT QUESTIONS

Though not the most common type of Reasoning Beyond the Text questions, Probable Hypothesis, Alternative Explanation, and Passage Alteration questions do occasionally appear. They can be identified by the words in the questions themselves.

- **Probable Hypothesis questions** ask for causes of new situations presented in the question stem.
  - ○ These questions often contain words like *probable hypothesis*, *likely cause*, or *most reasonable explanation*.
  - ○ Approach these questions like Apply questions, except that you are looking for analogous cause–effect relationships in the passage.
- **Alternative Explanation questions** ask for causes that differ from the ones given in the passage, but which still provide an explanation for a phenomenon.
  - ○ These questions often contain words like *alternative explanation*, *other cause*, or *different reason*.
  - ○ Approach these questions by eliminating any answer choice that would not lead to the effect in the question stem. If stuck between multiple answers, eliminate those that conflict most significantly with the passage.
- **Passage Alteration questions** ask for changes the author could make to the passage to make it consistent with new information.
  - ○ These questions often contain words like *alter*, *change*, or *update*.
  - ○ Approach these questions by looking for the answer that produces the desired effect with the least amount of modification to the ideas in the passage.

15.5 How Will CARS Question Types Appear on the Exam?

As you see in the review of all question types, questions can be worded in different ways, ask for different types of answers, and require different types of thinking and reasoning. However, all CARS questions have one thing in common: they do not ask for any information outside the stated or implicit information in the passage, question, or answers. Everything you need to answer a question correctly can be extrapolated from one of these three parts, even when the question asks you to reason an implicit conclusion or apply information to a new situation. Bringing in outside information will set you on the wrong track, just as using an irrelevant formula in science will deflect you from the correct answer. You can be sure, then, that regardless of the question type or complexity, the MCAT testmaker has given you everything you need to answer the question correctly.

15.6 Getting the Edge Using CARS Question Types

Remember what you read in the beginning of this chapter: there are no points in the passage; all points are in the questions. So use your time wisely. Don't focus and spend most of your time reading and understanding everything in the passage, and don't even try to memorize anything. Just make your outline and refer to it to determine what part of the passage you need to review in order to answer the question. Let the questions be your guide to what is important in the passage. If there is no question about a part of the passage you read slowly and carefully, you have wasted your time in the reading. Furthermore, when you can identify the question type, you can also identify the most efficient and effective way to attack the question. As with all parts of the MCAT, the best way to improve your performance with CARS questions is to practice and then effectively review. Systematic review of how you answer questions will help you determine weaknesses and formulate a study plan to ameliorate them. If you find that you are not improving steadily, take an honest look at your critical thinking skills to determine what you need to do to improve your score.

CHAPTER SIXTEEN

Reasoning Within Passages

In this chapter of the Critical Analysis and Reasoning Skills Unit, students will:

- Witness the utilization of the Kaplan Method for passages, questions, and arguments in the context of a couple of exceptionally challenging passages
- Practice the application of the Kaplan Method for passages, questions, and arguments with some practice passages.

16.1 CARS Worked Example I

A PHILOSOPHY PASSAGE

Every student of the sciences is taught to be wary of mistaking correlation for causation, but few fully appreciate the difference. Among the first to give an account of this distinction was David Hume (1711–76) in his early masterpiece *A Treatise of Human Nature*, the composition of which commenced at the prodigious age of 15, when Hume was himself but a student. Though often thought to be surpassed by his treatment of cause and effect in the more mature *An Enquiry Concerning Human Understanding*, the discussion in the *Treatise* is remarkable for situating causation squarely within the context of human psychology.

Hume's analysis begins from a simple principle, "that all our ideas are copy'd from our impressions," by which he means that all knowledge ultimately derives from sense experience—an axiom he shares with fellow empiricists Locke and Berkeley. Causation is no different, and thus Hume sets out to determine the original impressions (today more commonly called *perceptions* or *sensations*) whence this idea derives. According to his analysis, causation is nothing that is intrinsic to any particular object but rather only emerges in the relations between two objects, namely, a cause and an effect. He notes three specific relations that are "essential" to the idea of causation: contiguity (spatial proximity), temporal priority of cause before effect, and an additional "necessary connexion" between the two. This last is what distinguishes causation from mere coincidence, so Hume devotes several sections to uncovering what it is.

His conclusion may shock those unaccustomed to skeptical thinking. Hume argues that this necessary connection that makes one entity the cause of another is purely a creation of the mind: "necessity is nothing but that determination of the thought to pass from causes to effects and from effects to causes, according to their experienc'd union." Such behavior is the product of *custom*, a mental habit established after we repeatedly perceive similar sequences of cause and effect, such as when a moving billiard ball transfers momentum to a resting one after they collide—one of parlor gamesman Hume's favorite examples. Logic does not dictate that momentum should be transferred in a collision, for we could easily imagine one ball colliding into another and producing any number of other results; only experience shows us it is so.

Hume's inquiries lead him to formulate the following definition: "A cause is an object precedent and contiguous to another, and so united with it, that the idea of the one determines the mind to form the idea of the other, and the impression of the one to form a more lively idea of the other." He can remain confident that this determination of the mind is a customary connection, not a logical one, with his astute observation that all causal reasoning presupposes "that the future resembles the past," a claim which need not be true. In fact, such a claim could only ever be taken on faith—for how could it be proved? If one were to argue that, *in the past*, what would become the future at that point has always turned out to resemble the prior past, so we can expect the same *in the future*, one would be begging the question. How do we know the laws of nature won't change tomorrow?

If Hume is right, there is naught but the quirks of the psyche that properly distinguishes causation from what he designates "constant conjunction" (correlation). Later thinkers would come to call this the "problem of induction," for it demonstrates how all inductive reasoning—which moves from particular pieces of evidence to a universal conclusion—is ultimately uncertain.

P1.

P2.

P3.

P4.

P5.

1. Which of the following statements is assumed without support in paragraph 3?

    A. Hume says that the necessary connection between cause and effect is simply a mental custom.

    B. Momentum is transferred if an object in motion collides with an object at rest.

    C. The mind infers a necessary connection after experiencing one instance of a cause and its effect.

    D. The truth of a claim is not logically determined if it can be imagined otherwise.

2. According to the discussion in the final paragraph, one example of "inductive reasoning" would be concluding that an automobile tire will never go flat on the basis of:

    A. repeated daily observations of the tire staying intact.

    B. the logical necessity of all tires being incapable of going flat.

    C. a customary habit of jumping to faulty conclusions.

    D. knowledge that the tire is made of an indestructible material.

3. Based on the passage, what best explains how "all causal reasoning presupposes 'that the future resembles the past'" (paragraph 4)?

    A. Reasoning about causality is ultimately founded on an assumption established by custom rather than by logic.

    B. The laws of nature must be unchanging from past to future.

    C. It is not necessarily the case that the past and future resemble one another.

    D. Past conjunctions of cause and effect would yield no causal knowledge if the future operated by new laws of nature.

4. The claim "causation is nothing that is intrinsic to any particular object" most nearly means that objects:

    A. can never be adequately comprehended by the human mind.

    B. are by nature effects rather than causes.

    C. can be understood as causes only relative to other entities.

    D. cannot be the cause of other objects.

5. Which of the following, if true, would most UNDERMINE Hume's conclusions about cause and effect?

    A. There is no reason to believe that the laws of nature will change tomorrow.

    B. Some knowledge is attainable completely independent of experience.

    C. Most students of science fully appreciate the difference between correlation and causation.

    D. Claims about causal relations can always be doubted.

Key Concepts

Question Types II: Reasoning Within the Text

Inference Questions–Assumption Subtype

---

1. Which of the following statements is assumed without support in paragraph 3?

   A. Hume says that the necessary connection between cause and effect is simply a mental custom.

   B. Momentum is transferred if an object in motion collides with an object at rest.

   C. The mind infers a necessary connection after experiencing one instance of a cause and its effect.

   D. The truth of a claim is not logically determined if it can be imagined otherwise.

 Assess the question

In addition to the reference to the third paragraph, the most important words in the question stem are "assumed without support." The phrasing suggests an Inference question, most likely an Assumption. The correct choice will be a statement that must be true, given what is said in that paragraph, but that is not backed up with its own reasoning. Given that the scope is limited to only one paragraph, a question like this is probably worth doing as soon as encountered.

 Plan your attack

The reference does not specify what part of paragraph 3 to look at, so it may be worth doing a quick reread of the paragraph, or at least the label for P3 in the passage outline constructed while first reading. After this preparation, the process of elimination is the way to go. Read each choice, and then find the relevant text in paragraph 3. If a choice is *not* assumed by the author, then it can be eliminated. But that's not all: the wording in the stem suggests another way an answer can be ruled out; namely, if a choice is a claim that the author would endorse but that *is* supported elsewhere in paragraph 3.

 Execute the plan

Start with **choice (A)**, "Hume says that the necessary connection between cause and effect is simply a mental custom." The relevant text is the following:

"Hume argues that this necessary connection that makes one entity the cause of another is purely a creation of the mind: 'necessity is nothing but that determination of the thought to pass from causes to effects and from effects to causes, according to their experienc'd union.' Such behavior is the product of *custom*, a mental habit established after we repeatedly perceive similar sequences of cause and effect ..."

Clearly the language in this choice is cobbled together from the sentence that surrounds the quotation, so it must be something the author would endorse. However, this is ultimately a claim about what Hume *says*, and the best way to strengthen claims that offer interpretations of a writer is to quote the writer directly. Because the author does quote Hume directly, this is not "assumed without support," and so can be eliminated.

For **choice (B)**, "Momentum is transferred if an object in motion collides with an object at rest," look to this part of the paragraph:

"Logic does not dictate that momentum should be transferred in a collision, for we could easily imagine one ball colliding into another and producing any number of other results; only experience shows us it is so."

Though the first part of this sentence states that the claim cannot be supported logically, the clause following the semicolon notes that this claim is demonstrated by experience. That reference to support rules out this choice as well.

With **choice (C)**, "The mind infers a necessary connection after experiencing one instance of a cause and its effect," there is actually an inconsistency with the passage. This is found when the author notes that custom is "a mental habit established after we *repeatedly* perceive similar sequences of cause and effect" (emphasis added). There's no reason to believe that the mind does this after only one experience, so cross off this option too.

At this point, process of elimination shows that the correct response is **choice (D)**, "The truth of a claim is not logically determined if it can be imagined otherwise."

 ## Answer by matching, eliminating, or guessing

Executing the plan led to the elimination of (A), (B), and (C), indicating that choice (D) is correct. This is confirmed with the first part of the last sentence in P3: "Logic does not dictate that momentum should be transferred in a collision, for we could easily imagine one ball colliding into another and producing any number of other results." The Evidence keyword *for* suggests the author takes the ability to imagine

Takeaways

When a question asks for a statement "assumed without support," the correct answer may be directly stated or only implied in the passage. Regardless, the author will write nothing else about why to believe such a statement.

Things to Watch Out For

Watch out for when a question stem presents multiple ways of eliminating incorrect responses.

something to be otherwise as evidence that it is not dictated, or determined, by logic. But why should the imagination be any guide about what is logically determined? The author offers no reasons, so this assumption is unsupported.

SIMILAR QUESTIONS

1. What would the author most likely consider to fall under the category of "any number of other results," as described at the end of paragraph 3?

2. In the third paragraph, the author uses the example of colliding billiard balls in order to:

3. Recent psychological evidence shows that people sometimes assume a causal connection after seeing only one example of a cause and its effect. What relevance does this have to Hume's argument?

This chapter continues on the next page ▶ ▶ ▶

SOLUTIONS TO SIMILAR QUESTIONS

1. The context of the phrase is, "Logic does not dictate that momentum should be transferred in a collision, for we could easily imagine one ball colliding into another and producing any number of other results." In short, any answer that indicated some consequence other than the transfer of momentum—such as the first ball passing through the second, the balls being annihilated, or the first ball lifting off the ground and hovering in mid-air while the second ball bores a hole into the ground—would work.

2. The purpose of the billiard balls example is to provide a more concrete basis for the abstract claims made in P3. The correct answer to a question like this would either say something along those lines or simply stress how it functions to support Hume's account of causation.

3. The relevance to Hume's argument is relatively minimal. Though the passage notes that causal connections are made after repeated instances of seeing a cause and its effect, it never suggests that this always has to happen. Since the question stem only says "sometimes," there is not a significant challenge. The correct choice will say something to the effect that this evidence neither strengthens nor weakens the argument considerably.

This chapter continues on the next page ▶ ▶ ▶

Key Concepts

Question Types III: Reasoning Beyond the Text

Apply Questions–Example Subtype

> 2. According to the discussion in the final paragraph, one example of "inductive reasoning" would be concluding that an automobile tire will never go flat on the basis of:
>
> A. repeated daily observations of the tire staying intact.
> B. the logical necessity of all tires being incapable of going flat.
> C. a customary habit of jumping to faulty conclusions.
> D. knowledge that the tire is made of an indestructible material.

1 Assess the question

The paragraph reference, quotation, and use of the term "example" help to identify this question as one of the subtypes of Apply questions. The stem provides a lot of clues, so this one is worth attempting now.

2 Plan your attack

In order to furnish an example of a concept from a passage, it is essential to be clear on the meaning of that concept. Go back to the passage and learn as much as possible about the cited term: "all inductive reasoning—which moves from particular pieces of evidence to a universal conclusion—is ultimately uncertain." The dashes set apart a definition for the term, recognizing two key components that make up induction. The question stem provides half of this, the "conclu[sion] that an automobile tire will never go flat." This is a universal claim (one that applies in every case), as suggested by the word "never," which admits no exceptions. The words "on the basis of" confirm that the correct answer will be the evidence that supports this conclusion.

3 Execute the plan

The correct choice must exemplify "particular pieces of evidence," but what does this really mean? The final paragraph notes how the problem that Hume identified with causation was later called the "problem of induction," suggesting that causal reasoning and inductive reasoning are closely related (although the author does not specify precisely what this relation is). Because of this connection, it is possible to use the examples that the passage provides of causal reasoning as a basis for predicting what will count as inductive reasoning.

The third paragraph offers a crucial hint, with its reference to the formation of customary casual associations "after we repeatedly perceive similar sequences of cause and effect." These repeated perceptions are the "particular pieces of evidence" mentioned in P5. Putting it all together now, the correct answer should make reference to multiple cases in which the tire does not go flat.

 Answer by matching, eliminating, or guessing

Choice (A) presents an immediate match for these expectations. The general conclusion, "this tire will never go flat" could be inductively supported by "repeated daily observations of the tire staying intact."

Takeaways

Anything that appears in a question stem should be taken for granted, regardless of how peculiar it may seem. The claim that a tire will never go flat is clearly false—the physical world provides ample evidence that everything eventually succumbs to entropy. However, what matters for this question is the reasoning behind the conclusion, not its truth value.

Things to Watch Out For

While every choice provides some basis for making that conclusion, the most tempting is **(C)**, which echoes a lot of the language from the passage. The problem with it, though, is that there is no indication in the passage that inductive conclusions must be "faulty" or wrong, but only that they are "uncertain," which is far less negative.

SIMILAR QUESTIONS

1. Which of the following comes closest in meaning to "quirks of the psyche" (paragraph 5)?

2. What is one implication that the "problem of induction" poses for knowledge in the sciences?

3. Judging on the basis of the passage as a whole, what constitutes the difference between correlation and causation that the author asserts "few fully appreciate" (paragraph 1)?

SOLUTIONS TO SIMILAR QUESTIONS

1. As noted in the earlier discussion in the two preceding paragraphs, it's the customary association made by the mind between a cause and its effect that constitutes the relationship of causation, according to Hume. The answer could simply be the word "custom" or an elaboration in more words upon that concept.

2. Though "knowledge in the sciences" is never explicitly mentioned in the passage, the discussion in P1 directly connected "student[s] of the sciences" to the distinction between correlation and causation. Thus, the correct choice might point out that it undermines that distinction by making it a product of the mind, not of the physical objects themselves. Alternatively, the right answer might simply reflect the ideas at the end of P5 and note how the problem makes scientific conclusions, derived from inductive reasoning that uses experiments (scientifically controlled experiences) as evidence, uncertain.

3. The answer to this question will most likely be found in the last paragraph, when the author returns to the issue as it was framed in the introduction. Expect a trap answer to discuss the difference between causation and *coincidence*, discussed in P2. A correlation or "constant conjunction" has to involve repeated instances, making it more than a mere coincidence. What differentiates constant conjunction (repeated examples of B following A) from causation (A being the cause of B) is simply custom, according to Hume, so the correct response will say as much.

This chapter continues on the next page ▶ ▶ ▶

Key Concepts

Question Types II: Reasoning Within the Text

Other Reasoning Within the Text Questions

3. Based on the passage, what best explains how "all causal reasoning presupposes 'that the future resembles the past'" (paragraph 4)?

  A. Reasoning about causality is ultimately founded on an assumption established by custom rather than by logic.

  B. The laws of nature must be unchanging from past to future.

  C. It is not necessarily the case that the past and future resemble one another.

  D. Past conjunctions of cause and effect would yield no causal knowledge if the future operated by new laws of nature.

 Assess the question

Questions that ask for explanations will often fall into one of the two "Other" types. Since no new situation is suggested, this is Other Reasoning Within the Text, rather than Other Reasoning Beyond the Text. Since Other questions are often difficult, this may be worth saving for the last question of the passage, though the direct quotation will make research a bit easier.

 Plan your attack

Put the phrase into context:

"[Hume] can remain confident that this determination of the mind is a customary connection, not a logical one, with his astute observation that all causal reasoning presupposes 'that the future resembles the past,' a claim that need not be true. In fact, such a claim could only ever be taken on faith—for how could it be proved? If one were to argue that, *in the past*, what would become the future at that point has always turned out to resemble the prior past, so we can expect the same *in the future*, one would be begging the question. How do we know the laws of nature won't change tomorrow?"

This is the most intricate idea in the entire passage, though it's given a relatively brief formulation. The author (echoing Hume) is saying that the claim "the future resembles the past" is an assumption in any argument made with a conclusion about cause and effect. So, to rely upon an example the passage itself furnishes, throughout human history there have been repeated observations that a collision causes momentum to be transferred from a moving object to a static (but not immobile) one, such as seen with a rolling ball hitting a standing ball in games like billiards or croquet. In physics, a change in momentum is known as an impulse, so abbreviate this idea as, "a collision causes an impulse" or **C → I**.

Past observations have always confirmed **C → I**, but to be able to claim that this statement is universally or generally true, one must also say **C → I** is equally true for the future. Since the future is something that, by definition, has not yet been observed, there can be no experience to draw on to support **C → I**. To argue that **C → I** is true, one must assume that what has not been experienced (the future) will produce the same results (more examples of **C → I**) as what has been experienced (the past).

This claim, "the future resembles the past," could otherwise be thought of as the idea that the laws of nature (such as **C → I**) are unchanging. Of course, it can receive the same treatment as **C → I** in the previous paragraph. Back in the 18th century, when Hume was writing, there were many observations that suggested the laws of nature were uniform, that the future resembled the past. Since that time, in what would be the future relative to the 18th century, there have been yet more observations supporting this uniformity. Thus, it is safe to conclude that, in the past, the laws of nature have remained uniform (the future has resembled the past). But now, once again, there are no observations of the future (relative to the present) to rely upon to confirm that this uniformity would hold tomorrow and beyond. So, to prove that the future always resembles the past, one has to assume that in this respect *the future will resemble the past*, which is known as "begging the question" or "circular reasoning." This type of reasoning is fallacious because it takes for granted what it purports to demonstrate with evidence.

Execute the plan

Having unpacked the claim, now it's time to find the answer choice that actually provides the explanation requested. Begin with **(A)**, "Reasoning about causality is ultimately founded on an assumption established by custom rather than by logic." The last part is simply a reference to the claim that the future resembles the past, which means that altogether this choice is simply a restatement of the quoted line from the question stem. This provides at most a minimal explanation, so it is unlikely to be the correct answer, particularly since the question asks for "what best explains."

The statement in **choice (B)** ("The laws of nature must be unchanging from past to future") is, as was noted in the Plan step, simply another way of saying the future resembles the past. This is another restatement, this time of only part of the quotation in the question stem, so it's even less helpful than the previous choice. It can safely be ruled out.

While **(C)**, "It is not necessarily the case that the past and future resemble one another," does not rehash the quoted claim, it is effectively a reiteration of something said in P4, that the claim that the future resembles the past "need not be true." This is another way of saying the claim is not logically or necessarily true, but it does not explain how the claim is presupposed in causal reasoning. Thus, this choice can also be eliminated.

The process of elimination would suggest the answer must be **choice (D)**, "Past conjunctions of cause and effect would yield no causal knowledge if the future operated by new laws of nature." Be sure to evaluate it first to ensure that it is superior to the minimal explanation given by **(A)**.

Takeaways

When asked to provide an explanation for a claim, the correct answer will do more than just make the same assertion in slightly different language, but will offer an account of why or how it is true.

Things to Watch Out For

Question stems that use superlative language (*most, best,* and other *-est* words) will occasionally feature choices that seem to provide minimal answers to the question, but which will pale in comparison to the correct response.

 ## Answer by matching, eliminating, or guessing

Upon examination, **(D)** provides by far the best explanation, going beyond the mere repetition of claims to some of the underlying ideas in the text. "Causal knowledge" must be referring to the knowledge gained from causal reasoning, that is, the conclusions, which are backed by observation. Now, these observations ("past conjunctions of cause and effect") would be worthless if the future stopped resembling the past, because that past knowledge would no longer apply. The author's rhetorical question at the end of P4 ("How do we know the laws of nature won't change tomorrow?") is hinting at this same idea, but this choice spells it out explicitly.

SIMILAR QUESTIONS

1. What provides support for the author's contention that the claim considered in P4 "could only ever be taken on faith"?

2. How would the author most likely explain the suggestion made in the fourth paragraph that it "need not be true" that the past and future resemble each other?

3. Which of the following would Hume most likely characterize as an instance of "the impression of the one [determining the mind] to form a more lively idea of the other"?

SOLUTIONS TO SIMILAR QUESTIONS

1. The author notes that the proof offered for this claim begs the question, that is, that the supposed demonstration of the claim requires assuming the claim is true to begin with. A statement cannot support itself any more than a house could serve as its own foundation. This demonstration that the reasoning is circular in turn serves as support for the contention from the question stem. A claim taken on faith is one believed without sufficient evidence, and circular reasoning is definitely not sufficient evidence. The exact form of the correct choice will be tough to predict, but it should generally reflect this line of thinking.

2. The discussion in P3 would actually be helpful in reaching an answer for this question. A statement that needs to be true (is necessarily true) is one the truth of which is dictated by logic alone. Recall that the example in P3 suggested a claim was not logically true because other outcomes could be imagined: "Logic does not dictate that momentum should be transferred in a collision, for we could easily imagine one ball colliding into another and producing any number of other results." Thus, the author would likely say something similar for the claim that the future resembles the past, asserting perhaps that one could imagine the laws of nature changing. If it can be imagined that the future does not resemble the past, using the same reasoning from P3, then it need not be true that the future resembles the past. The correct answer should be consistent with this analysis.

3. This question requires unpacking the archaic language that Hume uses in his definition of cause. In P2, the author equates *impressions* with "*perceptions* or *sensations*," while it's clear from the examples used in P3, that the term *ideas* could be used to refer to images, such as colliding billiard balls. Consequently, the correct response will probably suggest a perception of one entity (either a cause or an effect) leading the mind to imagine the appropriate counterpart.

This chapter continues on the next page ▶ ▶ ▶

Key Concepts

Question Types I: Foundations of Comprehension

Definition-in-Context Questions

4. The claim "causation is nothing that is intrinsic to any particular object" most nearly means that objects:

   A. can never be adequately comprehended by the human mind.
   B. are by nature effects rather than causes.
   C. can be understood as causes only relative to other entities.
   D. cannot be the cause of other objects.

 Assess the question

Phrases like "most nearly means" almost always indicates a Definition-in-Context question, which carries the task of identifying the meaning of a term, statement, or other segment of the text. These tend to be more straightforward, so even though the paragraph reference is not given, this kind of question is worth attempting when first encountered.

 Plan your attack

As the name of the question type suggests, going back to the passage for context will be essential. The relevant part of the passage is located in P2: "According to [Hume's] analysis, causation is nothing that is intrinsic to any particular object but rather only emerges in the relations between two objects, namely, a cause and an effect." The part left out of the question stem provides a useful contrast, suggesting a distinction between a property that can be found in a single object (say, mass or volume) and one that can only be found when multiple objects are related together. The context suggests that causation is of the latter sort: it is wrong to label something as a *cause* unless it produces some *effect*; nor should something be labeled *effect* without having a corresponding *cause*.

 Execute the plan

After locating and analyzing the relevant text, it's helpful to make a prediction about how to complete the sentence after the colon. For instance, the equivalent claim could be that "objects cannot be causes by themselves" (which stresses the first half of the sentence from P2) or something like "objects are not causes unless they have effects" (which stresses the second half).

Answer by matching, eliminating, or guessing

Choice (C) presents a match for the latter prediction, saying "objects can be understood as causes only relative to other entities."

SIMILAR QUESTIONS

1. Which of the following, according to the author's account of Hume, is NOT an essential aspect of causal relationships?

2. According to the Newtonian account of gravity widely accepted when Hume wrote the *Treatise*, bodies exert gravitational forces on one another, even when separated at a great distance. What impact does this have on Hume's account of causation?

3. In the second paragraph, the author states that "Hume sets out to determine the original impressions…whence this idea [of causation] derives." What does the author most likely mean by this?

SOLUTIONS TO SIMILAR QUESTIONS

1. The reference to *essential* (though left out of quotes in the stem) suggests the list offered in P2: "contiguity (spatial proximity), temporal priority of cause before effect, and an additional "necessary connexion" between the two." The wrong answers are likely to be variants of each of those three items, while the correct response will be another idea, quite possibly lifted from another portion of the passage to seem more plausible, such as "having a universal conclusion" (which applies to inductive reasoning, not the concept of a cause-and-effect relationship).

2. One of the requirements of Hume's understanding of causation noted in P2 is "contiguity (spatial proximity)," that is, nearness in space. If one object causes another object at a great distance away to be attracted, then this would suggest that Hume's requirement is not being satisfied. Consequently, the correct response would have to say that Hume's account was in some way weakened.

3. The correct response to this Definition-in-Context question will reflect the following concerns. The passage notes in a parenthesis how the term *impressions* is equivalent to "*perceptions* or *sensations*," that is, the components of sense experience. Thus, if Hume is right in saying that all knowledge is derived from experience, the idea of causation should be derived from experience as well. The author is simply describing how Hume uses that "simple principle" to direct his analysis.

This chapter continues on the next page ▶ ▶ ▶

Key Concepts

Question Types III: Reasoning Beyond the Text

Strengthen–Weaken (Beyond Passage) Questions–Weaken Subtype

---

5. Which of the following, if true, would most UNDERMINE Hume's conclusions about cause and effect?

   A. There is no reason to believe that the laws of nature will change tomorrow.

   B. Some knowledge is attainable completely independent of experience.

   C. Most students of science fully appreciate the difference between correlation and causation.

   D. Claims about causal relations can always be doubted.

 Assess the question

The phrase "if true" typically indicates a Strengthen–Weaken (Beyond Passage) question, and *undermine* is just a synonym of *weaken*. The vaguely worded "Hume's conclusions about cause and effect" could refer to just about any part of the passage. This question will likely require some process of elimination (especially given the word *most*) and may also require research in multiple paragraphs, so it's one best reserved for later, after several other questions have been successfully tackled and the passage is more familiar.

 Plan your attack

Evaluate the impact that each choice's truth would have on arguments made in the passage. It does not matter how strong the language is or how implausible the situation described may be—the question stem asks only for the most powerful negative effect on Hume's ideas in particular. Plan to check every choice and be wary if the challenge is barely significant (such a choice would only be true if all the alternatives were completely off the mark, which is relatively rare).

The answer choices may contain language similar to the passage, they may be quite novel, or there may even be a mix. Regardless of how close the choices mirror the original text, locate the relevant portions of the passage for each one, and look out for outright contradictions and other types of challenges. Because Hume is the target, limit this search to quotations, paraphrases, and explanations of Hume's ideas—not the author's own opinions.

Execute the plan

For **(A)**, "There is no reason to believe that the laws of nature will change tomorrow," the relevant text is in P4, at the end of an analysis of a direct quote from Hume, the rhetorical question, "How do we know the laws of nature won't change tomorrow?" As a rhetorical question, it has one answer the author immediately expects readers to jump to: "We don't know." In short, this rhetorical question amounts to the claim that it's not possible to know whether the laws of nature will remain the same in the future.

Even if it were true that there is no reason at all to expect those laws to change tomorrow, the absence of evidence is not equivalent to the evidence of absence. In other words, just because there is no reason to believe that some event *will* happen does not by itself give an affirmative reason to believe that it *won't* happen. What this means is that the truth of **(A)** does not significantly challenge the truth of the statement that the laws of nature will change tomorrow—yet the actual assertion attributed by the author to Hume is not that this will definitely happen, but only that it's not possible to *know*, one way or another, whether it will. **Choice (A)** certainly does not undermine *that* idea, since it also amounts to a claim of ignorance.

Choice (B) directly pertains to the discussion at the start of P2:

"Hume's analysis begins from a simple principle, 'that all our ideas are copy'd from our impressions,' by which he means that all knowledge ultimately derives from sense experience—an axiom he shares with fellow empiricists Locke and Berkeley."

The language of *begins*, *simple principle*, and *axiom* (another name for a foundational assumption) all indicate that this is a claim that Hume takes for granted, while the colorful quotation shows that it's an acknowledged assumption, one that Hume deliberately calls attention to. As an axiom, it serves as a necessary condition for the conclusions that Hume reaches. Thus, if it's not true that "all knowledge ultimately derives from sense experience," then Hume's argument is in considerable trouble.

Given that **(B)** states that "Some knowledge is attainable completely independent of experience," it poses a direct contradiction to Hume's foundational principle. It would be difficult to offer a more substantial challenge than attacking a grounding assumption, so this is almost certainly the correct choice. If running low on time on Test Day, select this and move on. If timing is not an issue, it would be fine to continue checking the other choices to ensure that this one has the most negative impact.

Although **(C)**, "Most students of science fully appreciate the difference between correlation and causation," directly conflicts with the opening sentence, "Every student of the sciences is taught to be wary of mistaking correlation for causation,

Takeaways

It's always possible to revise a Plan as it is being Executed, if the answer choices lead in such a direction. Just because you begin the process of elimination does not mean that you have to finish it when you come across a choice that perfectly answers the question. Save the time reading the remaining wrong options for working on another question.

Things to Watch Out For

In passages with multiple viewpoints, such as the author and another writer who the author discusses, watch out for choices in questions of all types that reflect the wrong views.

but few fully appreciate the difference," this claim constitutes the author's lead-in to the discussion of Hume. It undermines the *author's* framing of the issue, but it is not relevant to any idea tied to Hume himself.

As expected, **choice (D)** also fails to have a negative impact. In fact, the statement "Claims about causal relations can always be doubted," is completely consistent with the author's concluding thought in P5, that "all inductive reasoning ... is ultimately uncertain." Since it supports the author, and the author is never critical of Hume, there is no way this choice could undermine Hume.

 Answer by matching, eliminating, or guessing

After checking the other answers, it's clear that only **choice (B)** had a significantly negative impact on anything that can be connected immediately to Hume. In fact, its impact was so detrimental (analogous to demolishing a house's foundation) that such an answer can safely be taken as correct without consulting the remaining options.

SIMILAR QUESTIONS

1. Which of the following observations, if valid, would most bolster the Humean account of causality considered in the passage?

2. What role does the quoted claim "that all our ideas are copy'd from our impressions" play in the passage?

3. What is the author's primary argument about causation?

This chapter continues on the next page ▶ ▶ ▶

SOLUTIONS TO SIMILAR QUESTIONS

1. This is essentially the Strengthen counterpart to the question originally posed. Like the original, it also poses some difficulty in setting expectations. The correct choice may simply mimic a piece of supporting evidence from the passage, or instead offer something that's only analogous. Even with Reasoning Beyond the Text, there will always be some connection to the actual evidence presented in the passage.

2. As noted above, this is a principle that serves as a prerequisite (necessary condition) for Hume's treatment of cause and effect. The correct choice might call it an assumption or some equivalent phrase.

3. The correct response to this question will either simply present the conclusion to the argument, namely that only custom separates causation from correlation, or it will present the conclusion along with some evidence. In the latter case, be sure the evidence is consistent with what is presented in the passage, because two answer choices could have the same conclusion (the language may vary only slightly or even be identical) and differ only with respect to the evidence cited.

This chapter continues on the next page ▶ ▶ ▶

16.2 CARS Worked Example II

A SOCIAL SCIENCE PASSAGE

According to a 2014 report by Oxfam International, the world's richest 85 people possess as much as the poorest 3.5 billion, and nearly half of all wealth is owned by just 1 percent of the global populace. Many measures of inequality, when plotted annually, adopt a potentially disconcerting U-shape: declining after the reforms implemented by many industrialized populations in the wake of the Great Depression, inequality is now returning to levels not seen since the 1920s—and on the verge of surpassing them. With statistics like these, elite figures, from the President of the United States to the Pope of the Catholic Church, have had to admit that inequality has become a prominent issue.

The truly interesting question concerns neither the existence of economic inequality nor the fact of its continuing growth, but its origin. What has caused—and even more crucially, what is perpetuating—this polarization in wealth? After weighing the evidence, my contention is that this development is ultimately a *political* outcome, not an *economic* one. By this I mean it is the product of deliberate decisions by political leaders (elected, appointed, or otherwise) and other influential socioeconomic elites, rather than the natural result of market forces, as many other scholars have suggested.

At issue are the differing political fortunes of two factions, the centrality of which have been recognized by economists from Karl Marx to Thomas Piketty, laborers and capitalists, the class of workers and the owners who employ them. When labor was politically ascendant (for instance, in the aftermath of FDR's New Deal), inequality decreased. However, with the rise of the political ideology of neoliberalism (embraced by leaders on both ends of the accepted political spectrum, like the United Kingdom's Margaret Thatcher and Tony Blair and the United States's Ronald Reagan and Bill Clinton), inequality began to rebound.

Neoliberalism purports to promote "free markets," but perhaps a better characterization of it is the promotion of the free movement of capital. Capital tends to have its own law of gravity, except that it seems to fall upwards, accumulating in floating paradises known as tax havens that contain the coffers of the planet's wealthiest. Few people would vote explicitly for this program, yet most governments in democratic nations throughout the world are filled with officials who act in ways that further the polarization of wealth, whether knowingly or unwittingly.

Much of the ascendance of neoliberal ideology stems from a discrepancy in organization. The United States presents a clear-cut example of one side of this phenomenon. From 1940 to 1980, between about one-fifth and one-quarter of all employed workers in the United States were members of labor unions. According to Piketty et al., 1940–80 is also the bottom of the inequality U-curve. Subsequently, there was a precipitous decline in union participation in the 1980s, followed by continuing erosion, so that now only about one-ninth of all US workers are union members—all the while, inequality has steadily climbed upwards.

On the other side, the capitalists have only become better organized. In fact, their mobilization—not coincidentally—shortly precedes the extensive disempowerment of unions in and around the 1980s. For example, the infamous yet influential Powell Memorandum (written in 1971 by a man who would become a US Supreme Court Associate Justice) explicitly advocated coordinated action among capitalists: "Strength lies in organization, in careful long-range planning and implementation, in consistency of action over an indefinite period of years, in the scale of financing available only through joint effort, and in the political power available only through united action and national organizations." That "careful long-range planning" has paid serious dividends.

P1.

P2.

P3.

P4.

P5.

P6.

1. Which of the following would specifically bolster the author's primary line of argumentation?

   I. Evidence that coordination among capitalists in the 1970s directly contributed to the decline of labor unions in the 1980s

   II. Findings demonstrating that current levels of inequality have eclipsed the historical records set in the 1920s

   III. A study showing that the rate of polarization of wealth has increased since the global financial crisis of 2007–8

   A. I only
   B. I and II only
   C. II and III only
   D. I, II, and III

2. Based on the passage, what is the author's most likely reason for regarding a U-shaped curve as "potentially disconcerting" (paragraph 1)?

   A. Inequality has returned to a level not seen since before the Great Depression.
   B. Deliberate choices by political leaders have led to an increase in inequality.
   C. The extreme polarization of wealth has detrimental consequences for society.
   D. The growth in inequality shows how capitalists are motivated solely by greed.

3. Which of the following, when taken in conjunction with the information presented by the passage, would best explain the author's use of "not coincidentally" (paragraph 6)?

   A. The ascendance of neoliberalism in democratic politics is largely responsible for the rise in inequality.
   B. The capitalists began coordinating their efforts immediately after recognizing unions were losing their power.
   C. A majority of citizens decided to relinquish membership in the working class and become capitalists instead.
   D. The democratically elected politicians financed by neoliberal organizations enacted anti-labor policies.

4. The author suggests a correlation between each of the following pairs of phenomena EXCEPT:

   A. more coordination among capitalists and less coordination among laborers.
   B. higher participation in labor unions and lower levels of equality.
   C. strength of organization and political success in democratic nations.
   D. the rise of neoliberalism and a widening of the gap between rich and poor.

5. In Citizens United *v*. Federal Election Commission (2010), the US Supreme Court ruled that restrictions on political advocacy spending by capitalist corporations, labor unions, and other associations were prohibited by the First Amendment. Assuming that such spending is effective, the most reasonable expectation based on the passage is that inequality in the United States will:

A. stop increasing because the ruling eliminates regulations that were promoting the polarization of wealth.

B. continue increasing because corporations will be able to outspend unions, resulting in more pro-capitalist policies.

C. begin decreasing because unions will be able to outspend corporations, resulting in more pro-labor policies.

D. remain at its present level because corporations and labor unions are treated equally under the ruling.

This chapter continues on the next page ▶ ▶ ▶

Key Concepts

Question Types III: Reasoning Beyond the Text

Strengthen–Weaken (Beyond Passage)
Questions–Strengthen Subtype
Roman Numeral Questions

1. Which of the following would specifically bolster the author's primary line of argumentation?

    I. Evidence that coordination among capitalists in the 1970s directly contributed to the decline of labor unions in the 1980s
    II. Findings demonstrating that current levels of inequality have eclipsed the historical records set in the 1920s
    III. A study showing that the rate of polarization of wealth has increased since the global financial crisis of 2007–8

    A. I only
    B. I and II only
    C. II and III only
    D. I, II, and III

 Assess the question

The word *bolster* indicates a Strengthen question of some kind, with the subjunctive *would* suggesting Reasoning Beyond the Text. The fact that the stem is looking *specifically* for an effect on *the author's primary line of argumentation* suggests that the Roman numeral options may include evidence that bolsters related arguments that are only incidental to the author's real concerns. Given the lack of references to particular parts of the text and the fact that there are multiple pieces of evidence to consider, this question might be better saved for later.

2 **Plan your attack**

With a Roman numeral question, a divide and conquer strategy is the best approach. Before doing a close reading of the Roman numerals, look at the answer choices to see if any of them appear in exactly **two** of the four options. This is the one you'll want to test first: if it's true, then you can eliminate the two choices in which it does not appear; if it's false, you can eliminate the two choices in which it appears. Then, with the two remaining options, you'll only have to evaluate one numeral that differs between them. (If more than one numeral appears twice, then start with whichever one seems easier for you. If no numeral appears twice, you may have to test all of them, so just begin with the easiest.)

With this question, numeral III appears in two choices, **(C)** and **(D)**. If III is true, then **(A)** and **(B)** could be eliminated, and only numeral I would have to be tested, because it appears in **(D)** but not **(C)**. If III is false, then **(C)** and **(D)** could be eliminated, and only numeral II would have to be tested in **(B)** but not **(A)**. You'll definitely want to evaluate III first.

One more piece of preparation is essential before beginning the attack: clarifying the author's primary argument. The key lines are found in paragraph 2:

"The truly interesting question concerns neither the existence of economic inequality nor the fact of its continuing growth, but its origin. What has caused—and even more crucially, what is perpetuating—this polarization in wealth? After weighing the evidence, my contention is that this development is ultimately a *political* outcome, not an *economic* one. By this I mean it is the product of deliberate decisions by political leaders (elected, appointed, or otherwise) and other influential socioeconomic elites..."

This makes it clear that the author's argument concerns a cause-and-effect relationship, so supporting evidence would have to indicate causality. Moreover, the suggestion that *neither the existence of economic inequality nor the fact of its continuing growth* are *interesting* is worth noting, because this can help set expectations for the wrong kind of support.

 Execute the plan

Following the Plan outlined previously, start with numeral III, *A study showing that the rate of polarization of wealth has increased since the global financial crisis of 2007–8*. While such evidence would support the claim that inequality is continuing to grow, this is precisely what the author suggested was uninteresting, definitely not *the author's primary line of argument*. To support the main argument, this item would need to offer some indication that decisions by socioeconomic elites caused this accelerating growth, but the mere mention of the financial crisis is insufficient to establish that.

Given that numeral III is false, both **(C)** and **(D)** are ruled out, and it can be inferred that I is true. Looking at II, *Findings demonstrating that current levels of inequality have eclipsed the historical records set in the 1920s*, it is readily apparent that this is more support for inequality's existence and growth, not for the cause proposed by the author. Numeral II is thus false for roughly the same reason that III is, and **choice (B)** can also be eliminated.

Takeaways

With Roman numeral questions, use a divide and conquer strategy: evaluate a numeral that appears in the answer choices exactly twice to cut the possibilities in half after one test.

Things to Watch Out For

When a question stem stresses strengthening or weakening a particular argument, be wary of options that affect separate claims, even ones that may seem related.

 ### 4 Answer by matching, eliminating, or guessing

The divide and conquer approach revealed that **choice (A)** is correct after evaluating only two of the numerals. Though you would want to select **(A)** on Test Day without further delay, we can confirm that only I is true by considering the impact of the sentence *Evidence that coordination among capitalists in the 1970s directly contributed to the decline of labor unions in the 1980s.* This points to another paragraph, P6, where the author states that capitalist *mobilization—not coincidentally—shortly precedes the extensive disempowerment of unions in and around the 1980s* and cites the Powell Memorandum. Numeral I would definitely help to support the author's account of how inequality was caused to increase in the 1980s, and would thus bolster the primary argument.

SIMILAR QUESTIONS

1. The author of the passage is especially concerned about:

2. Who would the author most likely consider to be an example of "other influential socioeconomic elites" (paragraph 2)?

3. The author's apparent intention with paragraph 2 is to:

This chapter continues on the next page ▶ ▶ ▶

SOLUTIONS TO SIMILAR QUESTIONS

1. Main Idea questions often take an abbreviated form, such as with this example. The correct response would have to note specifically the author's argument that deliberate actions by economic and political elites caused inequality to increase.

2. Although the reference in this Apply question is to P2, understanding the author's intent requires paying attention to the details that emerge subsequently. In P3, the author introduces the distinction between laborers and capitalists, then makes it clear that the latter group has become ascendant (an idea further elaborated in P6). The answer might use the words *capitalist*, *owner*, *employer*, *wealthy*, or *rich* to indicate members of that class. Incorrect choices could include elected or appointed political officials, who were mentioned separately from this *other* category.

3. This is just a Function question about P2. Use the Label in your outline to make a prediction. The correct answer might be general, such as *articulate the thesis of the passage*, or it might be quite specific, like *contend that inequality is caused by political choices rather than natural economic forces*.

This chapter continues on the next page ▶ ▶ ▶

Key Concepts

Question Types II: Reasoning Within the Text

Inference Questions–Assumption Subtype

---

2. Based on the passage, what is the author's most likely reason for regarding a U-shaped curve as "potentially disconcerting" (paragraph 1)?

   A. Inequality has returned to a level not seen since before the Great Depression.

   B. Deliberate choices by political leaders have led to an increase in inequality.

   C. The extreme polarization of wealth has detrimental consequences for society.

   D. The growth in inequality shows how capitalists are motivated solely by greed.

 Assess the question

The question stem asks for the *most likely reason* behind a judgment the author makes, which is another way of asking for an assumption. There's a direct reference to paragraph 1, which might make this question a bit more workable and worth trying now, when you first encounter it, even though it concerns implicit parts of an argument.

 Plan your attack

Start by returning to the context of the quoted words: *Many measures of inequality, when plotted annually, adopt a potentially disconcerting U-shape: declining after the reforms implemented by many industrialized populations in the wake of the Great Depression, inequality is now returning to levels not seen since the 1920s—and on the verge of surpassing them.* The clauses following the colon explain the U-shape, but do not really get at the reason for it being *potentially disconcerting*, that is, why it might be alarming or troubling. The correct answer will have to do more, explaining why the return to high levels of inequality is a negative outcome. Evaluate each answer choice to assess whether it accomplishes this.

 Execute the plan

Choice (A), *Inequality has returned to a level not seen since before the Great Depression*, may seem tempting because it mentions the Great Depression, but it simply restates the author's description of the U-curve without explaining it, a typical Faulty Use of Detail trap.

The issue with **choice (B)**, *Deliberate choices by political leaders have led to an increase in inequality*, is different: it offers an explanation, but the wrong one. It may be true that the author's primary argument concerns the causes of this increase in inequality, but this question asks specifically about the evaluation the author makes of this increase. Asking for the reason that an outcome is good or bad is conceptually distinct from asking for the cause of that outcome.

Although **(C)**, *The extreme polarization of wealth has detrimental consequences for society*, does not employ the word *inequality* like the other options, it does use a synonymous phrase. Moreover, unlike the previous choices, this actually gives a reason for why this trend could be disturbing: it carries negative social consequences. The author does suggest that the wealth inequality of the 1920s was responsible for an event so negative that it came to be known as the *Great Depression*, so this is precisely what we were looking for.

 Answer by matching, eliminating, or guessing

Choice (C) matched the prediction made in the Plan step. It can be confirmed as the correct option by a brief consideration of the final contender, **(D)**, *The growth in inequality shows how capitalists are motivated solely by greed*. While greed may not be an emotion that most people applaud, **choice (D)** is similar to **(B)** insofar as it addresses the cause of the outcome rather than an appraisal of its value. Thus, we can be confident that **(C)** is right.

Takeaways

Sometimes Inference questions will ask for very specific assumptions or implications, such as pieces of information that explain a normative (value) judgment.

Things to Watch Out For

A valid inference from the passage could still be an incorrect answer if it fails to meet the requirements of the question stem. Use the clues the stem provides to make a more thorough prediction, and such traps will be much less tempting.

SIMILAR QUESTIONS

1. What is the primary purpose of paragraph 1?

2. What role does the U-curve play in the author's argument?

3. Many prominent politicians and corporate executives deny that inequality is a serious problem. What impact does this fact have on the claims made in the first paragraph?

SOLUTIONS TO SIMILAR QUESTIONS

1. This straightforward Function question is best approached by making a prediction with your Label for P1. It serves the purpose of establishing some background on the problem, offering evidence that inequality is a significant issue, one that is only becoming worse. Wrong options might suggest that it's part of the main argument, when really it's only incidental to the author's concerns, as noted by the beginning of P2.

2. The curve is mentioned in both P1 and P5, so the correct response to this Strengthen–Weaken (Within Passage) question could indicate the role it plays in either or both. In the first paragraph, it is used to establish the existence and growth of inequality, while in P5 it is used to show a connection between the organization of labor and levels of inequality.

3. This is a Strengthen–Weaken (Beyond Passage) question with a scope limited to P1. The fact that many people deny a claim for which there is independent evidence has little impact on the truth of that claim, so it would not significantly challenge the author's suggestion that inequality is serious. The only feasible impact it might have is with respect to the mention of the President, the Pope, and other elite figures: it would explain why the author uses the phrase *have had to admit*, which suggests a kind of reluctant acceptance.

This chapter continues on the next page ▶ ▶ ▶

Key Concepts

Question Types III: Reasoning Beyond the Text

Other Reasoning Beyond the Text Questions

---

3. Which of the following, when taken in conjunction with the information presented by the passage, would best explain the author's use of "not coincidentally" (paragraph 6)?

   A. The ascendance of neoliberalism in democratic politics is largely responsible for the rise in inequality.

   B. The capitalists began coordinating their efforts immediately after recognizing unions were losing their power.

   C. A majority of citizens decided to relinquish membership in the working class and become capitalists instead.

   D. The democratically elected politicians financed by neoliberal organizations enacted anti-labor policies.

 Assess the question

The line *in conjunction with the information presented by the passage* suggests the answer choices will present new ideas, meaning that this is Reasoning Beyond the Text. Since it asks for an explanation of the author's use of a term, this would not exactly fall into either the Apply or Strengthen–Weaken (Beyond Passage) types, but falls under the Other heading. There's a specific reference to the text, which may make this question more manageable, but Other questions can often be challenging, so you may want to triage this one.

 Plan your attack

A question that asks for the best explanation, especially one that seems likely to bring in new information, is one that will likely require examining every answer choice. A good explanation will make the author's intention with the phrase clear, so begin your preparation by returning to the relevant part of the text. After establishing in P5 that labor has become less organized, the author writes:

On the other side, the capitalists have only become better organized. In fact, their mobilization—not coincidentally—shortly precedes the extensive disempowerment of unions in and around the 1980s. For example, the infamous yet influential Powell Memorandum (written in 1971 by a man who would become a US Supreme Court Associate Justice) explicitly advocated coordinated action among capitalists ...

The suggestion is that the improved organization of the capitalists is directly connected (is not a coincidence) to the diminution of organized labor. Given that the author stresses that the one event *shortly precedes* the other, there is the hint that the two are causally connected (because a cause typically comes immediately before its effect). Thus, the correct response should account for how better organization among capitalists could lead to worse organization among laborers.

 Execute the plan

While (**A**) (*The ascendance of neoliberalism in democratic politics is largely responsible for the rise in inequality*) mimics the language of the passage, even echoing the author's thesis, it fails to account for the use of this particular phrase. It is too general to account for the specific phenomenon referenced in P6. Eliminate it.

Choice (B) seems a bit more promising, because it connects the activities of the two classes. However, *The capitalists began coordinating their efforts immediately after recognizing unions were losing their power* gets the timing backwards. The author says that the capitalist coordination came first, and then the decline of the unions, so (**B**) is also wrong.

It may seem like (**C**) (*A majority of citizens decided to relinquish membership in the working class and become capitalists instead*) provides a possible explanation, but it fails for a number of reasons. The very first line of the passage notes the huge discrepancy in numbers between the wealthy class of owners and the poor class of laborers. Though the author mentions that deliberate decisions are important in P2, these are the decisions of political leaders and other elites, not the decisions of the majority of people—it's not clear from the passage that laborers have the power simply to switch roles from employee to employer. Even if some employees could become employers (for instance, entrepreneurs and the self-employed), it seems highly unlikely that a majority of citizens could do so. Finally, this choice does not take care to distinguish between membership in organized labor unions and membership in the class of laborers (employees). The previous paragraph discussed a decline in union membership, not a decline in membership in the working class. Thus, **choice (C)** clashes with the passage too much to be a plausible answer.

The Plan was to check all four answers, so (**D**) should also be evaluated, though we now expect it's correct. The statement *The democratically elected politicians financed by neoliberal organizations enacted anti-labor policies* would indeed provide the necessary explanation, one that is consistent with the discussion in the passage. The quote from the Powell Memorandum even mentions *financing* as a means of attaining political power, a number of neoliberal politicians are noted in P3, and P4 cites the actions of democratic officials who promote the polarization of wealth (in other words, anti-labor policies), so the agreement between this choice and the passage is resounding.

Takeaways

Questions that ask for possible explanations can often be tricky. Be clear on exactly what it is that must be explained.

Things to Watch Out For

Answer choices in Reasoning Beyond the Text questions can present entirely new situations completely unaddressed by the passage without such choices automatically being wrong. However, watch out for situations that directly conflict with the passage—these will most likely be incorrect.

 Answer by matching, eliminating, or guessing

Executing the Plan led to the elimination of the wrong options, revealing **choice (D)** as correct.

SIMILAR QUESTIONS

1. What does the author most likely intend to suggest by the phrase "serious dividends" in the last sentence of the passage?

2. Which of the following can most reasonably be inferred if the author is correct that neoliberalism is "embraced by leaders on both ends of the accepted political spectrum" (paragraph 3)?

3. The author cites the Powell Memorandum to support the claim that:

This chapter continues on the next page ▶ ▶ ▶

SOLUTIONS TO SIMILAR QUESTIONS

1. The phrase is used to suggest that the capitalists were extremely successful in their efforts at coordinated action, so the answer to this Definition-in-Context question would suggest something like political success, or even the economic success that came as a result of policies that promoted the upward flow of capital.

2. This Inference question has a number of possible responses, since there are multiple implications to be drawn from that line and the surrounding context. For instance, one conclusion that can be drawn is that the accepted political spectrum only allows pro-capitalist views, while another is that the options given to voters in contemporary democracies are actually quite limited.

3. This is a Strengthen–Weaken (Within Passage) question, simply asking for how the quotation in the last paragraph is used as evidence. Specifically, this is intended to support the idea that the capitalists were working together to advance their political and economic fortunes.

This chapter continues on the next page ▶ ▶ ▶

Key Concepts

Question Types II: Reasoning Within the Text

Inference Questions–Implication Subtype Scattered Questions

4. The author suggests a correlation between each of the following pairs of phenomena EXCEPT:

   A. more coordination among capitalists and less coordination among laborers.
   B. higher participation in labor unions and lower levels of equality.
   C. strength of organization and political success in democratic nations.
   D. the rise of neoliberalism and a widening of the gap between rich and poor.

 Assess the question

The prominent *EXCEPT* calls attention to the fact this is a Scattered variant of either a Detail question or an Inference question—the word *suggests* is regularly used in both types. However, since it asks for something as complex as a correlation, this question will most likely require deducing some implications from the text. Given the amount of time that is potentially involved in answering a Scattered Implication question (a lot of searching through the passage for ideas that might not be explicitly stated, only implied), this would best be saved for later in a question set.

 Plan your attack

Scattered questions (featuring words like *EXCEPT*, *NOT*, and *LEAST*) typically require the process of elimination to answer. However, it's still worthwhile to set some expectations. The correct answer will either be something that the text fails to mention or—more likely—it will be a twisted version of information contained in the passage. Any choice that contradicted the passage or otherwise distorted its content would have to be right, and could potentially be selected without testing the remaining options.

On the other hand, wrong answer choices will be pairs of phenomena for which the author states or implies a correlation. Keep in mind that cause-and-effect relationships always entail a correlation between the cause and the effect, so any indication by the author of causation would thereby be a suggestion of correlation as well.

 Execute the plan

For (**A**) (*more coordination among capitalists and less coordination among laborers*), the relevant text is at the start of P6: *On the other side, the capitalists have only*

become better organized. In fact, their mobilization—not coincidentally—shortly precedes the extensive disempowerment of unions in and around the 1980s. The fact that the author stresses this is not a coincidence reinforces that the relationship is intended to be more significant, potentially cause and effect. That there is at least a correlation is clear, so **choice (A)** should be ruled out.

With **choice (B)** (*higher participation in labor unions and lower levels of equality*), however, there is an issue when returning to the relevant text, this time from P5: *From 1940 to 1980, between about one-fifth and one-quarter of all employed workers in the United States were members of labor unions. According to Piketty et al., 1940–80 is also the bottom of the inequality U-curve.* There's definitely a correlation being highlighted, but it's between high union participation and low *inequality*, not low *equality*. If inequality is low, then equality must be relatively high, so this choice is the opposite of what the passage suggests. Thus, without further ado, it's safe to conclude that **(B)** is correct.

 ### Answer by matching, eliminating, or guessing

After finding a contradiction in **(B)**, it should be chosen as the correct answer. This could be double-checked by finding the other choices in the text. The correlation in **choice (C)** (*strength of organization and political success in democratic nations*) is implied in the discussion beginning with *Much of the ascendance of neoliberal ideology stems from a discrepancy in organization*, and continuing throughout the final two paragraphs. For **(D)** (*the rise of neoliberalism and a widening of the gap between rich and poor*), the relevant text is from P3: *with the rise of the political ideology of neoliberalism ... inequality began to rebound.* An increase in inequality entails a widening of the gap between rich and poor.

Takeaways

On occasion, Scattered questions can be answered without actually hunting down information for every choice. If you find a direct contradiction (or another obvious distortion), you've likely found your answer.

Things to Watch Out For

When you find an answer choice that perfectly answers the question, don't waste any more time reading wrong answers. Get the point and use that extra time where it could gain you even more!

SIMILAR QUESTIONS

1. Which of the following would the author be most likely to regard as an example of neoliberal ideology?

2. By "free markets" (paragraph 4), the author is most likely referring to:

3. What is the greatest flaw in the author's attempt to explain why inequality began to increase again in the 1980s?

SOLUTIONS TO SIMILAR QUESTIONS

1. For this Apply question, the answer will have to be some idea that promotes the interests of wealthy capitalists over laborers. For example, the idea that *people are poor only because they deserve it* would definitely qualify, since this suggests that rich people are morally justified in hoarding all their wealth while others struggle to survive.

2. For this Definition-in-Context, the correct response will likely reflect the contrast that the author draws: *Neoliberalism purports to promote "free markets," but perhaps a better characterization of it is the promotion of the free movement of capital.* In other words, the term "free markets" is a bit of public relations, the attempt to put a more positive spin on an idea that would not be so popular if described more accurately.

3. While rare, the MCAT will include questions that require you to evaluate the reasoning in the passage, a type of Other Reasoning Within the Text. There are a number of possibilities, but the answer likely has something to do with how weakly established a number of the causal links are. The author offers many correlations, but suggests causal connections without sufficient evidence. There's no concrete evidence provided, for example, that the capitalists colluding together led to the downfall of the unions.

This chapter continues on the next page ▶ ▶ ▶

Key Concepts

Question Types III: Reasoning Beyond the Text

Apply Questions–Outcome Subtype

5. In Citizens United *v.* Federal Election Commission (2010), the US Supreme Court ruled that restrictions on political advocacy spending by capitalist corporations, labor unions, and other associations were prohibited by the First Amendment. Assuming that such spending is effective, the most reasonable expectation based on the passage is that inequality in the United States will:

    A. stop increasing because the ruling eliminates regulations that were promoting the polarization of wealth.

    B. continue increasing because corporations will be able to outspend unions, resulting in more pro-capitalist policies.

    C. begin decreasing because unions will be able to outspend corporations, resulting in more pro-labor policies.

    D. remain at its present level because corporations and labor unions are treated equally under the ruling.

① Assess the question

The lengthy question stem, chock full of new information, immediately reveals Reasoning Beyond the Text, while the language of *most reasonable expectation* tells us that this is an Apply question, specifically one that asks for an Outcome. These kinds of questions can take a while (especially with long answer choices), so saving them for *later*, after working on some easier ones, is not a bad idea.

② Plan your attack

With a new scenario, the key will be finding the points of connection (or analogy) with the passage. The stem says that *restrictions on political advocacy spending* were judged to be *prohibited*, and that this affected corporations, unions, and other groups. In short, that means these organizations gained additional freedom to spend money on political issues at their discretion. The question stem goes on to say explicitly *Assuming that such spending is effective*, which tells you to take it for granted that this spending can have an impact on who gets elected and what policies get enacted. The actual question is a completion (with a colon), but it amounts to the following: given the new freedom of these groups to spend money and assuming it works, what will likely happen to inequality in the United States? Answering this is the task presented.

Execute the plan

Before tackling those wordy answer choices, it's worthwhile to make a prediction for the correct one. Start by clarifying the nature of the trend in inequality leading up to the Supreme Court ruling. The first paragraph mentions the more recent date of 2014, within only a few years of the date from the question stem, so it offers a good reference point. There, we're told that *inequality is now returning to levels not seen since the 1920s—and on the verge of surpassing them.* This is hardly an isolated statement, since the idea that inequality is increasing is noted throughout the passage, which largely seeks to answer the question of why this occurs.

Now the question becomes: how will this upward trend be affected? The third paragraph offers some guidance on this question: *When labor was politically ascendant ... inequality decreased. However, with the rise of the political ideology of neoliberalism ... inequality began to rebound.* Thus, if the ruling benefits labor more, we should expect to see inequality decrease, or at least see the rate of its increase slow or stop. However, if the ruling benefits the capitalists more, then inequality should continue its rise or even accelerate.

So, who benefits more? Even though the ruling applies to both capitalist corporations and labor unions, the discussion in the last two paragraphs suggests that capitalists are in a much stronger position to take advantage of the ruling. In P5, the author notes that about half as many US workers belong to unions as once did (one-ninth versus one-fourth or one-fifth), while P6 is explicit about the success of capitalists in working together even hinting that their coordinated efforts may have caused the decline in organization among laborers. Since the capitalists have the advantage, the ruling will likely only exacerbate the discrepancy between rich and poor, leading to even greater inequality.

 Answer by matching, eliminating, or guessing

More thorough preparation means a quicker match when you finally look at the answer choices. Only **choice (B)** (*continue increasing because corporations will be able to outspend unions, resulting in more pro-capitalist policies*) is consistent with the prediction made.

Choices (A) (*stop increasing because the ruling eliminates regulations that were promoting the polarization of wealth*) and **(C)** (*begin decreasing because unions will be able to outspend corporations, resulting in more pro-labor policies*) can both immediately be discounted, since they indicate a downward trend. Moreover, there's

Takeaways

While a lengthy question stem takes longer to read, it also gives you more material to work with. Be sure to use that to your advantage and formulate a more thorough prediction for the correct answer.

Things to Watch out For

Some wrong answer choices may be completely consistent logically but are incorrect because they neglect vital information from the passage.

no reason to suppose that the restrictions prohibited by the ruling were promoting the polarization of wealth, nor to suspect that unions would have the ability to out-spend corporations.

Choice (D) (*remain at its present level because corporations and labor unions are treated equally under the ruling*) comes closer to the truth, but fails to take into account the realities described in the passage. If corporations and unions began on equal footing, then it would be true that this ruling would help neither, because it grants the same freedom to both. However, the passage makes it abundantly clear that the two groups are not at all on equal footing, that the capitalists were ascendant when this ruling was handed down. To suggest that inequality remains at its present levels would also be to ignore the fact that it continues to increase: if the ruling truly had no effect on the status quo, then presumably inequality would just keep following the upward trend described in the passage.

SIMILAR QUESTIONS

1. In the fourth paragraph, the author states that "most governments in democratic nations throughout the world are filled with officials who act in ways that further the polarization of wealth," but also that few citizens of these nations "would vote explicitly for this program." How would the author most likely resolve this apparent paradox?

2. A 2014 study by NASA predicted catastrophic consequences for civilization due to irreconcilable differences between "Elites," who control access to increasingly scarce natural resources, and "Commoners," the mass of people who are resource-poor. If accurate, what impact does this have on the argument put forth in the passage?

3. How would the author most likely respond if told that inequality is actually decreasing in some parts of the developing world?

SOLUTIONS TO SIMILAR QUESTIONS

1. This lengthy question is actually a type of Other Reasoning Within the Text, the kind in which two seemingly conflicting statements are reconciled by finding a third statement that explains how they can both be true. For this paradox resolution, a helpful clue comes from P3's suggestion that neoliberalism is *embraced by leaders on both ends of the accepted political spectrum*. If the only options voters have to choose from are neoliberals, that is, politicians backed by capitalists who favor policies that increase inequality, then it explains how such people are in power despite what voters would want.

2. The key for this Strengthen–Weaken (Beyond Passage) question is to understand that this NASA study concerns the *effects* of inequality. Because the author is concerned with the *causes* of inequality, a study of its effects would have no significant impact.

3. For this Apply question, there are a few possibilities. The author could claim that this new data is outside the scope of the discussion, which primarily concerns developed democracies. Alternatively, the author might respond by asking to see how organized labor is in these parts of the world, to see if it carries support for the thesis that inequality will decrease when labor is politically ascendant.

This chapter continues on the next page ▶ ▶ ▶

16.3 CARS Practice Passage I

(QUESTIONS 1–6)

Hope and fear are the quintessential political emotions, for both take as their object an unknown future, rife with possibilities for cultural flourishing or social dissolution. The one always accompanies the other, for we inevitably dread that our aspirations might remain unrealized, and cannot but yearn for our anxieties to prove unwarranted. An era may come to be dominated by one or the other pole, but its opposite can only be repressed temporarily—witness the opportunistic ascendance of the theme of "Hope" in US politics subsequent to the unabashed fear-mongering of the "War on Terror."

Given the centrality of hope and fear in politics, there can thus be no question that the most authentically political of all works of fiction are novels of utopia and dystopia. The former term, a hybrid of "good place" (the ancient Greek *eutopos*) and "no place" (*outopos*), is a coinage of Sir Thomas More, whose 1516 *Utopia* is regarded as the urtext of both genres, notwithstanding that the literary construction of ideal societies is found as early as Plato's *Republic* nearly two millennia prior. Utopian fiction celebrates human potential, particularly the power of reason, which is supposedly capable of engineering a more perfect world than the one that the arbitrary forces of nature and tradition have yielded.

The first great dystopian novel was not published until 1921, more than four centuries after More's original *Utopia*. Yevgeny Zamyatin's *We* depicts the dark side of human reason, what has come to be known as "instrumental rationality," a robotic logic in which efficiency is valued for its own sake, and citizens are mere means for the advancement of political ends, which must remain unexamined. Zamyatin's literary personae are granted numbers rather than names and treated accordingly. Instrumental rationality is readily apparent in other icons of dystopia: Aldous Huxley's *Brave New World*, George Orwell's *Nineteen Eighty-Four*, Margaret Atwood's *The Handmaid's Tale*, and (more recently) Suzanne Collins's *The Hunger Games*. Though each novel uniquely paints a dire tomorrow, all portray humans as cogs in a vast social contraption, the overarching illogic of which belies the tidy sensibility of its everyday operations.

As with their emotional antecedents, utopia and dystopia are inextricably intertwined, evident in their deep structural commonalities. Each in its distinctive way emphasizes the fate of the transgressor, the individual who would privilege personal desires over the ironclad imperatives of state. Such free spirits cannot be tolerated within the body politic any more than a cancerous cell within the body physical. The analogy is imperfect, of course, since a tumor does not feel. From the transgressor's perspective, a vantage taken up far more commonly in novels of dystopia, the well-oiled social machine becomes a torture apparatus. Indeed, a tremendous amount of toil and violence are required for the proper maintenance of a device that runs so contrary to nature; the most effective social lubricants are blood, sweat, and tears.

Ironically, utopias and dystopias are intended to be immutable and self-perpetuating, which would preclude the very possibility of politics; a certain future will bring either despair or confidence, but not the restless blend of hope and fear that accompanies uncertainty. In other words, both genres represent human coexistence as a problem and the state as its solution. The utopian novel seeks to answer the political question, while its counterpart calls into question an emerging answer. The most profound works of speculative political fiction reject this dynamic entirely—which, in its crudest form, merely recapitulates instrumental rationality—suggesting perhaps the real problem is envisioning human life as a problem to be solved.

P1.

P2.

P3.

P4.

P5.

1. Which of the following statements, if true, would most strengthen the author's claim that "utopia and dystopia are inextricably intertwined" (paragraph 4)?

   A. A dystopian society always seems like an ideal political order to the members of its ruling class.
   B. Most utopian societies allow for the questioning of overarching political objectives.
   C. Dystopias do not actually require significant amounts of violent force to be maintained.
   D. Many works of speculative fiction can be classified as neither utopian nor dystopian.

2. Which of the following does the author consider to be a point of difference between utopian and dystopian literature?

   I. The depiction of violence as necessary for maintaining social order
   II. An emphasis on the role that reason plays in shaping society
   III. The likelihood of considering the point of view of a social deviant

   A. I only
   B. III only
   C. II and III only
   D. I, II, and III

3. By stating that "the analogy is imperfect" in the fourth paragraph, the author most likely intends to suggest that:

   A. people in a society should be regarded as more than just parts making up a whole.
   B. human societies are far more complex than the cells that constitute a single human body.
   C. comparisons between any two ideas can only ever be imprecise.
   D. transgressors are not treated identically under utopian and dystopian social orders.

4. The author refers to *The Handmaid's Tale* in paragraph 3 in order to:

   A. argue that women are just as talented as men at writing speculative fiction.
   B. challenge the idea that society should be organized rationally.
   C. give an example of utopian literature that explores the concept of instrumental rationality.
   D. offer an instance of a novel in which humans are treated as means rather than ends.

5. Based on the discussion in paragraph 4, which of the following would be LEAST likely to be regarded as a "transgressor"?

   A. A citizen of a dystopia who tries to lead a rebellion against the powers that be
   B. A citizen of a utopia who neglects political duties to spend more time with loved ones
   C. An official in a dystopian society who uses torture to reprogram disobedient citizens
   D. A criminal in a utopian society who is punished for questioning the state's legitimacy

6. The author's primary concern in the passage is to:

   A. advocate for the superiority of dystopian over utopian fiction.

   B. discuss the characteristics of utopian and dystopian literature.

   C. challenge the notion that human life is a problem to be solved.

   D. argue that the most politically relevant emotions are hope and fear.

This chapter continues on the next page ▶ ▶ ▶

16.4 Practice Passage II

(QUESTIONS 7–11)

In the late 18th century, citizens throughout rural Massachusetts shut down courthouses attempting to conduct debt collection hearings, farmers in western Pennsylvania and other parts of the western frontier refused to pay an excise on whiskey, and members of the Pennsylvania Dutch community in the east of the state harassed officials attempting to assess a direct tax on houses. In each case, the government's initial response to protests of "taxation without representation" led to an exacerbation of tensions: radicalized citizens banded together, creating armed militias in open rebellion against the ruling regime.

These popular uprisings against taxation and economic hardship were not—as many Americans would now assume upon hearing such descriptions—revolts against the British monarchy in prelude to the American Revolution (1775–83). Rather, Shays' Rebellion (1786–87), the Whiskey Rebellion (1791–94), and Fries's Rebellion (1798–1800) occurred after the British had been vanquished. Though each episode has distinctive historical significance, it is particularly instructive to examine the evolving reaction to popular protest by the incipient United States government.

In the case of the uprisings throughout western and central Massachusetts that would come collectively to be known as "Shays' Rebellion," the federal government existed in a much attenuated form, enfeebled due to the considerable amount of sovereignty ceded to the thirteen original states under the Articles of Confederation. After subsistence farmers, veterans of the Continental Army, and other rural citizens found themselves hard-pressed in 1786 by debts incurred during hard times and taxes newly levied by the Massachusetts government, they began to revolt, at first just closing down courts but soon organizing armed militias, culminating in an attempt led by veteran Daniel Shays to seize a federal armory in Springfield. The federal government lacked the funds to assemble its own militia and counter the uprising, so it was left to the governor of Massachusetts, James Bowdoin, to handle—and he had to turn to assistance from more than a hundred wealthy merchants to bankroll mercenaries, who quashed the rebels.

The moneyed and propertied interests—creditors to whom many debts were owed—had been unnerved by the events in Massachusetts, and were instrumental in the creation and ratification of the new Constitution, which greatly concentrated power in a more robust central government. When many western farmers refused to pay a 1791 excise tax on whiskey, the newly empowered federal government was able to muster a formidable response after resistance grew more organized. In 1794, President Washington himself led a massive federalized militia of nearly 13,000 troops that would effortlessly scatter the resistance forces. The reaction by President Adams to the smaller rebellion led by John Fries years later would be similarly heavy-handed.

This tendency toward increased centralization of power has only worsened since the 18th century. As the federal government has accumulated strength, state and municipal governments—and, ultimately, the people—have lost their sovereignty. And while the moneyed had to foot the bill directly to protect their property (and continue collecting their rents) in quelling Shays' Rebellion, since the adoption of the new Constitution in 1789, the federal government has been able to make the people pay directly for their own repression—a fact recently highlighted in the assault, covertly orchestrated across several cities by the Federal Bureau of Investigation and Department of Homeland Security, on the 2011 Occupy movement. In the end, the people have only traded one master for another: the feudal relic of British monarchy has been usurped by a modern bureaucratic behemoth, ultimately in thrall to the nouveau aristocracy of corporate "persons" and the rapacious class of executives that constitute the homunculi within.

P1.

P2.

P3.

P4.

P5.

7. The author writes in paragraph 5 that "the federal government has been able to make the people pay directly for their own repression." Judging based on the rest of the passage, this is most likely intended to signify that:

   A. popular uprisings no longer occur in the United States due to more successful control of citizens.

   B. imprisoned protestors are sent a bill for the expenses accrued while they are behind bars.

   C. protesting ultimately incurs worse consequences for individuals today than it did in the 18th century.

   D. the government requires citizens to pay taxes, which are partly used to fund police and military responses to protests.

8. The author's attitude toward "moneyed and propertied interests" (paragraph 4) can best be characterized as:

   A. indifferent.

   B. positive.

   C. negative.

   D. ambivalent.

9. The author most likely omits specific details of the events in the first paragraph in order to:

   A. set an expectation that is reversed in the following paragraph.

   B. express the primary thesis of the passage more concisely.

   C. downplay the significance of the events being addressed.

   D. conceal a general lack of knowledge on the subject matter.

10. Which of the following is an assumption made by the author in the second paragraph?

    A. The response to Fries's Rebellion was more heavy-handed than the response to Shays' Rebellion.

    B. The British monarchy is entirely unlike the US federal government that eventually replaced it.

    C. A significant number of Americans today are unfamiliar with the rebellions that occurred after the Revolution.

    D. The British played a covert role in the rebellions that took place after their defeat in the American Revolution.

11. Some scholars have argued that in response to the 2007–2008 financial crisis, the US federal government did less to protect citizens whose homes were taken away in fraudulent foreclosures than to defend the banks that engaged in this criminal behavior. If true, what impact does this have on the passage?

    A. It challenges the author's central argument.

    B. It supports the author's central argument.

    C. It weakens the assertion that the people have exchanged one master for another.

    D. It strengthens the claim that the wealthy shaped the creation of the US Constitution.

Practice Passage Explanations

PRACTICE PASSAGE I: A HUMANITIES PASSAGE
Sample Outline

P1. Hope and fear = political emotions, inseparable

P2. Utopian and dystopian novels are most political; utopian fiction celebrates reason (ex. More's *Utopia*)

P3. Zamyatin's *We* = 1st dystopia; dystopian fiction explores dark side of reason, "instrumental rationality" (list of examples)

P4. Commonalities between utopia and dystopia: focus on fate of transgressors, need for toil and violence

P5. More in common: no politics, view human life as problem (Author: profound fiction questions this)

Goal: to discuss the characteristics of utopian and dystopian fiction, emphasizing their similarities

1. (A)

Look at the line in context to get a better sense of what to expect: "As with their emotional antecedents, utopia and dystopia are inextricably intertwined, evident in their deep structural commonalities." The "emotional antecedents" line refers to the discussion of hope and fear in P1, which noted how "one always accompanies the other," even though one might come to dominate for a time. **Choice (A)**, which suggests that a dystopian society always looks like a utopian one from the perspective of the rulers, would definitely support this point, showing how utopia is inseparable from dystopia.

(B) Opposite. In P3, the author notes that "instrumental rationality," featured regularly in dystopian fiction, creates a society in which "citizens are mere means for the advancement of political ends, which must remain unexamined." If utopias allowed the examination of political ends, this would constitute a point of difference, rather than similarity.

(C) Opposite. Violence is addressed predominately in P4, where the author discusses commonalities between the two. Because utopias are suggested to be as violent, this choice would create another point of difference if true.

(D) Faulty Use of Detail. While this choice does not weaken the claim, as the other wrong answer choices do, it is largely irrelevant. Just because they are both absent sometimes does not mean they must always occur together, as "inextricably intertwined" suggests.

2. (B)

Roman numeral **(I)** appears twice, so begin with it. Violence is discussed in P4 as a commonality between utopian and dystopian literature, so this is not a point of difference. Since **(I)** is false, **choices (A)** and **(D)** can be eliminated. Numeral **(III)** must be true, since it appears in the two remaining options (confirmed by a line from P4: "From the transgressor's perspective, a vantage taken up far more commonly in novels of dystopia ..."), so only **(II)** needs to be evaluated. At the end of P2, the author asserts, "Utopian fiction celebrates human potential, particularly the power of reason ...," so utopian literature does emphasize reason. In P3, the author discusses the crucial role that "instrumental rationality" ("the dark side of human reason") plays in *We* and a number of other dystopian novels. As another point of similarity, **(II)** is thus false and **(C)** is wrong. Because only **(III)** is true, choice **(B)** is correct.

3. (A)

Return to the line in context: "Such free spirits cannot be tolerated within the body politic any more than a cancerous cell within the body physical. The analogy is imperfect, of course, since a tumor does not feel." The suggestion is that humans are different than cells, that they deserve to be considered as more than just expendable parts of a larger whole, because they (unlike tumors and other cells) *can* feel. **Choice (A)** matches most closely with this reasoning. **(B)** In the analogy, cells (parts of the larger whole that is the body) are being likened to people (parts of the larger whole that is society). This choice mischaracterizes the analogy because it compares the whole on one side (society) to the parts on the other (cells). **(C) Distortion.** The author is not suggesting that every analogy is imperfect, only that the particular analogy being discussed is. **(D)** While this might pose a different kind of problem for the analogy, it does not make sense in context. The author cites "a tumor does not feel" as a reason for the breakdown, which has nothing to do with the differences between utopia and dystopia.

4. (D)

In P3, the author lays out the various characteristics of dystopian fiction, emphasizing especially the idea of "instrumental rationality," which is described as "a robotic logic in which efficiency is valued for its own sake, and citizens are mere means for the advancement of political ends, which must remain unexamined." The author mentions "Margaret Atwood's *The Handmaid's Tale*" as part of a list of "icons of dystopia," and so is giving an example of a novel that explores the concept of instrumental rationality. Thus, **choice (D)** is correct. **(A) Out of Scope.** The author never discusses gender explicitly, nor compares authors of different genders. **(B)** While the author seems to be critical of instrumental reason in this paragraph, the idea is not significantly challenged until P5. **(C) Opposite.** *The Handmaid's Tale* is said to be one of the "icons of dystopia," so it would not be utopian fiction, as suggested in this choice.

5. (C)

To determine the *least* likely example, first clarify what the author means by a "transgressor" in P4: "the individual who would privilege personal desires over the ironclad imperatives of state." Someone would not be a transgressor if they were acting on behalf of the state, such as an official who was trying to reprogram actual transgressors in a dystopian society, as in **choice (C)**. **(A) Opposite.** This would be a textbook case of transgression, since the citizen is fighting against the state ("the powers that be"). **(B) Opposite.** Though this might not seem so bad, this would count as privileging some other value over the state, so the individual would be a transgressor. **(D) Opposite.** Questioning its legitimacy would clearly be acting against the imperatives of state, so this criminal would count as a transgressor.

6. (B)

Though the author begins with a discussion of hope and fear in P1, the primary focus of every other paragraph is on the qualities of utopian and dystopian fiction, as in **choice (B)**.

(A) Out of Scope. The author primarily emphasizes the similarities between the two genres, and never really suggests that one is better than the other.

(C) Faulty Use of Detail. This is only raised in the final paragraph, so it does not address the passage as a whole.

(D) Faulty Use of Detail. The argument concerning hope and fear is almost entirely limited to P1. It serves as an introduction to utopia (which represents hope) and dystopia (which represents fear), but is not the primary concern of the entire passage.

This chapter continues on the next page ▶ ▶ ▶

PRACTICE PASSAGE II: A HISTORY PASSAGE

Sample Outline

P1. Government responses to tax protests in 18th C. Massachusetts/Pennsylvania led to armed militias

P2. Shays', Whiskey, and Fries's Rebellions—against US authorities, not British

P3. Shays' Rebellion: federal government had little power; merchants had to pay for militia to stop rebels

P4. Whiskey Rebellion: after new Constitution, federal government had power to muster militia (Fries' too)

P5. Author: centralized power has only gotten worse; government now serves corporations and executives

Goal: to discuss the US federal government response to 18th Century tax protests and argue that power has become more centralized

7. (D)

Read the quote from the question stem in context to get a sense of what to look for: "And while the moneyed had to foot the bill directly…in quelling Shays' Rebellion, since the adoption of the new Constitution in 1789, the federal government has been able to make the people pay directly for their own repression." The contrast with Shays' Rebellion is instructive, since the author notes in P3 that "[t]he federal government lacked the funds to assemble its own militia and counter the uprising," while this is not a problem in P4 with the federal response to the Whiskey Rebellion. The inference to be drawn is that the new government can levy taxes, which it can then use to respond to a popular uprising—even if that uprising is itself a reaction to the taxes levied, as was the case with the Whiskey Rebellion. The only answer that reflects this line of thinking is **choice (D)**.

(A) Opposite. The author cites a recent example (the 2011 Occupy movement) of a kind of popular uprising immediately after raising this point, so this choice is contradicted by the passage.

(B) Out of Scope. While this offers a possible explanation, the passage never discusses anything of this sort.

(C) Out of Scope. No comparison is ever made between the kinds of consequences dissenters face today versus the 18th century, so this choice could not reflect the passage.

8. (C)

While the language used to describe the "moneyed and propertied interests" tends to be relatively neutral in P4, the author's negative attitude towards the wealthy comes through in P5, particularly in the closing sentence, with the mention of a "rapacious class of executives." Thus, **choice (C)** is correct.

(A) While the author is relatively neutral in P4, the language used in P5 suggests that the author is far from indifferent.

(B) Opposite. The author never says anything positive about the moneyed.

(D) Since the author says nothing to praise the wealthy but only uses negative language in describing them indicates that the author's attitude is not one of ambivalence (a mix of positive and negative feelings).

9. (A)

Though this is ostensibly a question about the first paragraph, properly answering it requires understanding how P1 connects to the rest of the passage. A key hint comes in the transition into P2: "These popular uprisings against taxation and economic hardship were not—as many Americans would now assume upon hearing such descriptions—revolts against the British monarchy ..." The author has made the descriptions in P1 deliberately ambiguous in order to create an expectation (these tax protests are against unfair British taxes) that is almost immediately overturned (the protests are actually against taxes imposed by American authorities), which serves to highlight the fact that the American officials were acting just as unfairly as the British. This corresponds most closely to **choice (A)**.

(B) Though concise expression would be a reason to omit details, the primary thesis does not really emerge until later in the passage, particularly in the final paragraph.

(C) Opposite. This choice is contradicted by the discussion in P2, where the author notes that "each episode has distinctive historical significance," going on to state how "particularly instructive" their contrast is.

(D) Opposite. Plenty of details are provided in P3 and P4, so it's clear that the author does not generally lack knowledge about the subject.

10. (C)

Be sure to stick to the discussion in P2, since the question stem specifically references it. There, the author suggests that "many Americans would now assume" that the rebellions described in P1 were against British authorities, when they were actually against American ones. In suggesting that many Americans will make that assumption, the author is actually assuming these individuals are unfamiliar with the events described, and would not be able to recognize them from the descriptions. This matches with **choice (C)**.

(A) Though there is the suggestion at the end of P4 that the reactions to the Whiskey Rebellion and Fries' Rebellion were both "heavy-handed," this is not an assumption made in P2.

(B) Opposite. The author deliberately compares the American Revolution against the British monarchy to these rebellions against American authorities in order to highlight similarities, not differences.

(D) Out of Scope. There is no suggestion in the passage that the British played any role in these Rebellions. The British are merely raised as a point of comparison.

11. (B)

The situation described in the question stem seems to echo the idea from the last sentence, that the US federal government is "ultimately in thrall to the nouveau aristocracy of corporate 'persons' and the rapacious class of executives that constitute the homunculi within." This is an aspect of the author's central argument, that the people have been disempowered as more power has been accumulated in the federal government, and that this government represents the interests of the wealthy first and foremost. Thus, **choice (B)** is right.

(A) Opposite. As explained above, the author's argument is actually bolstered by the new information.

(C) Opposite. If anything, this claim would be strengthened, since the evidence in the question stem makes it clear that the people are not in charge.

(D) While the new situation makes it clear that the wealthy have influence *in the 21st century*, this in itself proves nothing about what happened *in the 18th century*, when the new Constitution was created and ratified (explained in P4).